W9-AGI-139

UNFINISHED REVOLUTION

Daniel Ortega and
Nicaragua's Struggle for Liberation

Kenneth E. Morris

Lawrence Hill Books

Library of Congress Cataloging-in-Publication Data

Morris, Kenneth Earl, 1955-

  Unfinished revolution : Daniel Ortega and Nicaragua's struggle for liberation /
Kenneth Earl Morris.

     p. cm.

  Includes bibliographical references and index.

  ISBN 978-1-55652-808-8 (hardcover)

  1. Ortega, Daniel. 2. Frente Sandinista de Liberación Nacional 3. National
liberation movements—Nicaragua—History—20th century. 4. Nicaragua—Politics and
government—1979-1990. 5. Nicaragua—Politics and government—1990- I. Title.

  F1528.22.O78M67 2010

  972.8505'3—dc22

                                                                    2010006406

Interior design: Jonathan Hahn

Published by Lawrence Hill Books, an imprint of
Chicago Review Press, Incorporated
814 North Franklin Street
Chicago, Illinois 60610
ISBN 978-1-55652-808-8
Printed in the United States of America
5 4 3 2 1

For Dalia Castro

We press onward toward the sunrise of liberty.

—Augusto César Sandino

We were not born at the top, we were born at the bottom and we're used to fighting from below. . . . Brothers and sisters, let us continue the battle for democracy, let us continue the battle for national dignity, let us continue the battle for Nicaragua. . . . Together with Sandino . . . we will govern from below, we will govern from below, we will govern from below. We will defend from below, we will defend from below. For Nicaragua from below.

—Daniel Ortega

CONTENTS

ACKNOWLEDGMENTS

My thanks for helping me write this book go foremost to the Nicas who often in just befriending me ended up telling me a lot about their lives and their country. Among those whose names I know are Dalia Castro, Raquel Mendoza, Raquel Rosaldo, and Yorlennys Bermúdez. Foremost among those whose names I never caught are "El Toro" ("The Bull") and the guys who hang out with him on the street corner, although there are plenty of others.[1] Some people do good work on Nicaragua by flying into Managua with a press pass and staying at the Intercontinental Hotel for a week or so, but if it were not for my Nica friends and acquaintances I would have felt lost in my attempt to understand their culture and country. Insofar as I have been able to understand their world, it is because they have welcomed me into it.

To this list of Nicaraguan friends I will append Julián Guevara. He was my interpreter in Nicaragua and belongs in a more formal category of appreciation, though he never got around to interpreting anything. This was not because my Spanish is so great, though I muddled through a lot of conversations without him, but rather because by the time I started seriously asking for interviews Ortega had been president long enough to prevent anyone from talking. Those on his side would not talk without permission, which was never forthcoming, and those opposed to him seemed reluctant to talk for fear of reprisals. (Of course, there are exceptions among his opponents; some talk all the time. However, because they make their opinions so well known, there is little reason to interview them.) Julián and I sat around a lot, chewing the fat between phone calls, e-mails, and trips to Ortega's compound. Eventually I said, "Hey, Julián, why don't I just interview you?" He laughed, but it wasn't really that silly of an idea. Julián was in the Sandinista government in the 1980s and has been in politics ever since. He knows Ortega. Julián certainly knows a lot, and while I never did formally interview him, he was a great guy to talk with about his country.

More formally, I want to thank the courteous and helpful staffs of the Instituto de Historia de Nicaragua y Centroamérica at the Universidad Centroamericana in Managua and the Biblioteca Dr. Roberto Incer Barquero at Banco Central de Nicaragua, also in Managua. One institute archivist, whose name I unfortunately never caught, proved especially helpful early on when he performed an unauthorized search of the database thus saving me a lot of time searching for old newspaper articles. Another, María Auxiliadora Estrada Rivera, provided ongoing, expert assistance.

In Costa Rica, two stalwart friends, David Moreno and Olga Campos, offered their help whenever I needed it. Their contributions cannot be overestimated. I could always rely on them to clean up an e-mail I needed to write in Spanish, and both have pretty good detective skills. Together we found a woman rumored to have been one of Humberto Ortega's mistresses, for instance. Olga even took to calling herself "Agent oo-Olga." She had the good sense to route me to Carlos Porras, a mutual friend, who came through with Ortega's poetry in the usual way this happens in Latin America: he is friends with the editor of the volume of poetry in which it was published, who therefore had a copy. We had a good drinking session in conjunction with the poetry exchange.

Although I knew when I began this project that Nicaragua had commanded considerable interest in the United States during the

1980s, I was intimidated to discover how many experts on Nicaragua are still there. Fortunately, most are academics, and thus willing to help others undertaking research in their fields of expertise. Karen Kampwirth especially went well beyond kindness in the amount of help she provided me, and I really appreciate her fielding and responding to so many of my e-mails. Others, including Victoria Gonzalez, Abraham Lowenthal, Shelley McConnell, Jennifer McCoy, James Roberts, and Thomas Walker, provided thoughtful and helpful responses to my inquiries. So did Robert Pastor, a policymaker in the Carter administration and later with the Carter Center. Both Kathy Hoyt and Chuck Kauffman of the Nicaragua Network, the leading Washington-based advocacy and information group regarding Nicaragua, were helpful, as was Liz Light from the British equivalent, the Nicaragua Solidarity Campaign. Most if not all of these mentioned, I believe, are hoping that this book turns out OK, but it is tough to enter a field in which others have labored so long and meet their high standards. Insofar as this book does, credit goes to these colleagues.

I was pleased to stumble upon some as yet untapped sources housed at Stanford University's Hoover Institution for War and Peace, and to receive excellent assistance from several of the archivists there. William Ratliff was especially helpful, no doubt because he had acquired some of the information back when he was researching events in Nicaragua for the book he coauthored. As happens when a researcher doesn't have any formal institutional affiliation, I had to finesse access to some library collections. My daughter, Halie Morris, sent me a few sources from the library at Northwestern University (and also spent a couple of afternoons translating Ortega's poetry for me); my brother, Richard Morris, sent me another crucial article; and my librarian friend, Deb Sommer, performed a few database searches for me.

Meanwhile, my friend Chris Rehn was constantly supportive and even read and commented on a few draft chapters. Glenn Seavers—well, what can you say about him besides that God broke the mold after he was born? I am sure we disagree about many things regarding Nicaragua—he is definitely "Danielista" while I am more reserved in my judgments—but he is a blast to talk to, a great friend, and his story about the time he bought a Land Rover in Nicaragua is hilarious. Of course, I couldn't have started this book had my agent, Janet Rosen of Sheree Bykofsky and Associates, not thought to show my proposal to my editor, Yuval Taylor, who together with Michelle Schoob proceeded to demand revisions that eliminated its most egregious flaws. The flaws that remain are my own fault.

INTRODUCTION

THE FIFTH SUMMIT OF the Americas, held in Trinidad and Tobago in April 2009, was anticipated with more enthusiasm than usual for a meeting of the sixty-one-year-old Organization of American States (OAS). Like its parent organization, the United Nations, the thirty-four-country OAS is not usually a center of excitement. The more powerful members, principally the United States though occasionally others, often do whatever they want regardless of what the OAS or its charter stipulates. This leaves the OAS in the unenviable position of passing toothless resolutions, administering programs, and holding meetings. Even so, a meeting of the OAS can be interesting. It provides a forum for leaders from Latin America, the Caribbean, and North America to meet (and sometimes spar) with each other. The 2009 Summit stimulated special interest due to the presence of the newly elected President Barack Obama. Not since John Kennedy had the election of a U.S. president inspired more hope for improved relations among the countries of the Americas. Who was this new president, and what would his election mean for hemispheric relations, which had frankly been turning pretty chilly?

There were other new faces at the summit. One of these was Daniel Ortega Saavedra, the recently elected president of Nicaragua. To be sure, Ortega was already well known, perhaps even infamous. Next to Fidel Castro, he might have been the best-known political figure in Latin America and the Caribbean at the time—and for the same reason. Since the triumph of the Cuban revolution, the only other successful revolution in the Americas was Nicaragua's in 1979. That was led largely by Daniel Ortega, who assumed the role of coordinator of the governing junta and then became the first elected president of a free Nicaragua. During most of the 1980s he also waged, and ultimately won, a war against counterrevolutionaries supported by the United States. His political and revolutionary resume was as solid as they come, and he was hardly a stranger to the other American dignitaries. He was also something of a curiosity. He had been out of office since 1990, and during the intervening years he had been beset by scandals that ranged from sexual molestation to election tampering. During the 1980s, he had been a scruffy former guerrilla fighter. In 2009 he looked pudgier, balder, and more scarred from his sixty-three years. Now that this aging revolutionary and global rabble-rouser was back in power, how would he affect North-South relations in the Americas?

Meanwhile, contentious political issues festered beneath the surface. Among these was the perennial question of Cuba. Cuba was excluded from the OAS in 1962 on the grounds that it lacked the democratic prerequisites for membership. Some believed that the exclusion of the island state had more to do with the hemispheric hegemony of the United States than it did with Cuba's democratic deficiencies. But now Cuba was changing, and United States policy toward it appeared to be on the precipice of change too. An ailing Fidel Castro had turned the country's leadership over to his brother Raul. Barack Obama had implied that he would consider lifting the U.S. embargo against Cuba while working toward a thaw in their icy relations. Would Cuba become an issue at the summit?

The question of Cuba was really only the anchor for a larger and more diffuse set of issues. For about a generation, most of the countries in the Americas had steered a roughly rightward course, with global financial institutions like the World Bank and the International Monetary Fund guiding local leaders along a vaguely free-market path known as the "Washington consensus." The results seemed to include political and, to a lesser extent, economic stability. Doubters could point to heavy-handed military interventions, however, especially in the 1970s and '80s, which arguably only created the illusion of political stability by vanquishing opponents. The continent's economic stability could also be questioned. Although each country had its own particular economic story to tell, on the whole, prosperity in Latin America and the Caribbean had hardly brought affluence to all. Tens of millions of people remained poor—many of them desperately poor—while the bankers and politicians patted each other on the back for a job well done. Indeed, in some countries, like Nicaragua, most measures of economic and social well-being showed the population to be worse off than it had been during the years of leftist revolution and war. For instance, when Daniel Ortega was reelected president of Nicaragua in 2006, he inherited a country that was poorer, sicker, and less well educated than when he left office in 1990.

Meanwhile, left-wing sentiment had been fomenting in the Americas during the years leading up to the summit. Led for the most part by Venezuela's president, Hugo Chávez, who is well financed by his country's oil wealth, the cry began to be heard for something that Chávez likes to call "twenty-first-century socialism." He has never clearly articulated what exactly "twenty-first-century socialism" entails, however. Daniel Ortega, who juxtaposes "twenty-first-century socialism" with what he calls the "savage capitalism" of the United States, outlines the basic idea in his rhetoric: the capitalist agenda that has been foisted upon Latin America and the Caribbean by the United States and other wealthy countries has failed and must be replaced by a softer socialist alternative. And these leftists are not merely talking. Together with Castro, in 2004 Chávez formed an international organization, the Bolivarian Alliance for the Peoples of Our America (ALBA), to promote his agenda for twenty-first-century socialism, and by the time of the summit a half dozen countries had joined ALBA. On Daniel Ortega's first day as president of Nicaragua, he signed papers to make Nicaragua a full member of ALBA. Prior to the Summit of the Americas, the ALBA member countries had met privately to hammer out strategy for the summit.

It fell to Daniel Ortega to be the left's hatchet man at the summit. Chávez was cordial by comparison, especially to Obama, and beamed when the two shook hands. The only hint that Chávez gave of wanting to advance an agenda came in the form of a gift that he gave to the new U.S. president. The gift was a book, *The Open Veins of Latin America: Five Centuries of the Pillage of the Continent*, by Uruguayan author Eduardo Galeano. First published in 1971, the book is a semi-classic history of Latin America from a leftist perspective, stressing the role that imperialist powers (as well as local elites) played in shaping the continent. Although right-wing commentators in the United States pounced on Obama for accepting the book, he was for the most part able to sidestep their criticisms. The copy of the book that Chávez gave Obama was in Spanish, which allowed Obama to joke that he thought it was a book that Chávez had written, prompting Obama to consider giving the Venezuelan president a copy of one of his own books. It was not, in short, an international incident. If the right wing in the United States wanted to become upset about the "humiliation" involved in the president accepting a book offering a left-wing interpretation of Latin American history, that was their prerogative. All Chávez was doing was signaling his desire to have the new U.S. president understand his views in the context of a friendly first meeting.

Daniel Ortega was not as restrained. He was one of only five speakers to address the summit, and was allotted ten minutes for his speech, but Ortega droned on for almost an hour. His speech—really a lecture—purported to summarize the history of imperialist oppression in Latin America since the middle of the nineteenth century, a period during which the United States in particular was a culprit, and he paid special attention to the saga of United States–Cuba hostilities. Ortega said he was ashamed to attend the summit when Cuba was excluded from participation. In an attempt to be charitable, he did excuse President Obama from personal responsibility for the Cuban Missile Crisis, and in fact was on record as an enthusiastic Obama supporter. Ortega had enjoyed reasonably good relations with President Jimmy Carter as well as many other people from the United States, and was convinced that the problems caused by the superpower were systemic more than personal. Thus he persisted in his diatribe against, principally, U.S. imperialism. If there had been any questions about Ortega's views having mellowed over the years—or of the Latin American left remaining politely submissive—Daniel Ortega's speech answered them directly. He was every bit the anti-imperialist firebrand he had always been, and spoke as a member of a solidifying leftist base.

For many observers, of course, the Daniel Ortega who delivered this speech was an anachronism, a throwback to a time when repressive dictators ruled banana republics only to be met by romantic revolutionaries while plumes of smoke rolled into the skies. Barack Obama seemed to discount him as such when asked what he thought about Ortega's speech. Obama quipped that it was "long" and left it at that. In his own seventeen-minute speech, he wisecracked that he appreciated that the president of Nicaragua had at least not blamed him for events that happened when he was an infant. The line elicited muffled laughter from many attendees. When also asked (twice) what she thought about Ortega's speech, Secretary of State Hillary Clinton simply changed the subject. She pretended that she did not hear the question and commented on the fabulous entertainment at the summit. The consensus was that Ortega was better off ignored than engaged.

The attitude toward Ortega inside Nicaragua is similar, albeit angrier. His reelection to the presidency in 2006 was achieved with only 38 percent of the popular vote, and his ability to claim a victory with so small a plurality was a product of his backroom deal making. He is not a particularly popular president in Nicaragua, where well over half the population was not even alive the last time he served; even many of his former friends in the Sandinista National Liberation Front have turned against him. Majority opinion in Nicaragua sees him as another dictator, or at least one in the making, and many of his compatriots wince with embarrassment when their "president" (which many put in quotation marks when referring to him) delivers a harangue of the type that he gave at the Summit of the Americas.

Yet Ortega should not be dismissed this easily, either abroad or at home. Throughout his life his enemies and opponents have consistently underestimated him. Nobody would have thought that a poor kid growing up in a Managua barrio and struggling to finish high school would have overthrown a U.S.-backed dictatorial dynasty of almost a half-century's duration. Thousands of others tried; most died or gave up. Ortega succeeded. Neither would anyone have thought that the man Ronald Reagan called a "dictator in designer glasses" and worked to overthrow would outlast him. After Ortega was defeated for reelection in 1990, partly due to actions of President George H. W. Bush, no one expected him to claw his way back to the pinnacle of Nicaragua's government. However, here he was, thirty years after helping lead the Nicaraguan revolution, a head of state lecturing a U.S. president who was an infant when Ortega embarked upon his revolutionary activities. He is a man his opponents dismiss at their peril.

Less than two months after his strident speech at the Summit of the Americas, the OAS quietly lifted its forty-seven-year ban against Cuba. A few weeks after that, Ortega once again found himself at the center of an international stage. When the Honduran military ousted President Manuel Zelaya in late June, Ortega provided him with refuge and championed his cause. This time he was on the same side as the Obama administration and the OAS. All along, Ortega has quietly implemented a number of effective anti-poverty programs at home in Nicaragua, and has even rejuvenated the popular Nicaraguan baseball league. While his critics continue to accuse him of authoritarian aspirations and worse, the reality is that his polled support among the rural poor climbed to a majority for the first time during the summer of 2009. In fact, in October of that year, he was able to pressure Nicaragua's supreme court to change the legal restriction that would have prohibited him from running for reelection as an incumbent. Trend lines suggest that he may well win with majority support when he runs in 2011. It is simply a mistake to underestimate Daniel Ortega's political savvy.

It is also a mistake to misunderstand his moral passion. While he is given to making serious moral compromises in the pursuit of power and has made more than his share of personal moral mistakes, he is driven by profound moral ambition. The foundation of everything that Ortega has ever done is his uncompromising commitment to those who Frantz Fanon once called the "wretched of the earth." Unfortunately, given its long history of domination by foreign powers, Nicaragua has far too many of the earth's wretched. Ortega's lifelong struggle has been to bring liberation to these people. If it takes delivering a strident speech to further this goal, he will definitely do that. Indeed, he will do much more.

1

THE MAKING OF
A REVOLUTIONARY

NICARAGUA, MOST OF ITS population and many visitors believe, is the most beautiful country on earth. Volcanic mountains tower beside shimmering lakes before the landscape melts into jungle thickets in one direction and pristine seashores in the other. Exotic wildflowers sprout forth from the dense underbrush while plump water droplets glisten on fat banana leaves after the tropical rains. It lies between Honduras to the north and Costa Rica to the south. Its sunsets are especially spectacular. The sky will curl around a darkening land, hugging it in a blaze of colors, only slowly to fade into the encroaching nightfall. Then the glow from a hundred flickering lights comes slowly into view. These are not the stars, but the fires from the wood stoves on which many Nicaraguan families still cook—beans and rice, usually plantain, sometimes a little chicken or pork, often corn tortillas—and their faint lights punctuate the blackness.

Yet there is danger too. Almost every day nature issues a warning in the quiver of the earth, ever so slight, as the tectonic plates beneath the isthmus that links North and South America adjust their positions. About once a generation, at no predictable intervals, nature makes good on this daily warning. The land buckles with such ferocity that buildings fall to rubble in an instant, the dreams of yet another generation dashed as quickly. Meanwhile, for about half the year, when the rains come, torrents of water rush down village and city streets, temporarily turning them into raging rivers. Periodically nature unleashes its full aquatic fury by hurling hurricanes across the fragile land. The damages often total hundreds of millions of dollars, and death tolls can reach the thousands.

Nevertheless, nature is not the dominant force in Nicaragua, and has not been for nearly half a millennium. The fiercest destruction has always appeared in human form. The conquistadores who arrived in 1522 quickly reduced the native population from around a million to fewer than a hundred thousand. This 90-plus percent elimination of population was achieved in the usual ways—exposing some of the natives to European diseases, selling others into slavery, and slaughtering still more outright—and was far more catastrophic than any natural disaster.[1] Indeed, nature is not to blame for the fact that many twenty-first-century Nicaraguans still cook on wood-fired stoves—or often go hungry. As Daniel Ortega insists, Nicaragua not only has the potential to feed itself but also to become the "breadbasket of Central America." It is not the land but human beings who are to blame for Nicaragua's failure to realize its agricultural potential. Nor is the landscape to blame for the fact that although not much more than two hundred miles separate Nicaragua's Pacific and Caribbean coasts, the trip from one to the other is still better taken by plane. Nicaragua's mountainous interior is rugged, but that hardly excuses the country's continuing failure to build decent roads. And the absence of decent roads is one reason agriculture production lags. If farmers cannot get their crops to market before they spoil, they understandably do not bother to raise them in the first place.

Moreover, although there have been relatively tranquil interludes, the story of Nicaragua more often than not is a story of dominant foreign powers, usually allied with local elites, oppressing the population into subservience and savaging those who resist. Nicaragua's recent revolutionaries and present-day leaders were born into a world soaked in the blood of the violent past. This past shaped what their outlooks would be even before they were born, and understanding it is the first step in understanding the continuing struggle of Nicaraguans for the liberation of their bewitching land.

The Impress of the Past

THE FIRST MISTAKE MANY foreigners make about Nicaragua is to minimize the mark that Spanish domination left on the country. It was exactly three hundred years after the Spanish conquistador Gil González commanded the first expedition into Nicaragua in 1522 that Nicaragua finally gained independence from Spain. Nicaragua's more proximate history involves its domination by the United States, but the Spanish were fiercer and more brutal than their successors. Except for pockets along Nicaragua's Caribbean coast, separated by geography and British rule from the more populous and politically dominant Pacific coast, Nicaragua bears the marks of its Spanish legacy much more deeply than those of its more recent associations with other countries. It is a Spanish-speaking, predominately Roman Catholic country in which the bulk of the 5.5 million inhabitants are of mixed Spanish and indigenous ancestry.

Historical legacies are primarily relevant to the present only to the extent and manner that people remember them. It is with this in mind that a tale, often told by Nicaraguan men standing on street corners, about the founding of their country is worth repeating. As the story goes, when the Spanish conquistadores arrived they had spent three long months at sea in the company of only other men. Accordingly, as soon as they set foot on land they had one goal in their minds: sex. The easy acquisition of this goal, however, was thwarted by the presence of native men. The conquistadores handled this complication by killing or enslaving whatever native men they came across, and then raping the women.

This street-corner story stands in sharp contrast to the founding myth in the United States, namely the Thanksgiving story, according to which the United States was founded by God-fearing pilgrim families searching for religious freedom in a new world. Their tale is one of progress premised upon hard work, strong values, and social cooperation. As the Thanksgiving story has it, the pilgrims and the natives even sat down together as brothers and sisters, each sharing what they had, to enjoy the bountiful harvest feast that God had provided. The Thanksgiving story is no more accurate than the street-corner tale told by the Nicaraguan men. The mythical meanings of the two stories, however, are diametrically opposed. The American myth tells of a bountiful land where success lies within reach of anyone of strong character who is willing to work in harmony with others to achieve their common dreams. The American myth also places couple-centered families at center stage. The Nicaraguan myth has none of these components. The new world does not provide bounty enough for everyone, and in fact there is not enough to go around. The strong must take what they want from the weak. Moreover, this is why the strong arrived in the new world in the first place—not to create a God-fearing community but to plunder the land for profits. (The conquistadores were after gold, and they got a lot of it.) Nor did they arrive as families, but rather as single men who raped and murdered and enslaved. Superior moral values do not prevail in this Nicaraguan story, but rather raw power.

It goes without saying that Nicaragua celebrates no Thanksgiving holiday. For Nicaraguans recalling their founding, life is a zero-sum affair. A person is either a conqueror or among the conquered. And none of this is to say that Nicaraguans feel imprisoned by a myth of their founding any more than adults in the United States take the Thanksgiving story as historical fact. Nicaraguans can and do see life as other than zero-sum, and in particular as allowing for all parties to gain. They also understand the importance of hard work, strong values, nuclear families, and social cooperation. Even so, myths of foundings—like the foundings themselves—can have subliminal influences over the way people feel and act in the present. If you listen, for example, you will notice that Nicaraguans use the verb "to conquer" (*conquistar*) in everyday speech with greater frequency than it is normally used in English. In fact, it would appear that a Nicaraguan will sometimes use "to conquer" where an American would use "to succeed" (a verb that has no Spanish cognate). It is only a matter of connotations, but it is as if to this day, for Nicaraguans, "succeeding" involves "conquering."

Nicaraguans may see the world as divided between the conquered and the conquerors, but the Spaniards also provided them with an alternative to each extreme of this awful dialectic: the romantic figure of Don Quixote. Most literate Nicaraguans know this story as well as most people in the United States know *Huckleberry Finn*. *Don Quixote* tells us that winning or losing—conquering or being conquered—is not necessarily life's most important outcome. More important sometimes are the integrity of people's dreams and the nobility of the vision that animates their quests. Reality has no hold on Don Quixote, and his defiance of it, coupled with his insistence on superimposing a glorious frame onto it, comprises his inspiration. Many Nicaraguans are at least a little like Don Quixote in their elevation of passion and romance over practicality and reason.

The quixotic impulse was eventually institutionalized in Nicaragua. Romantic resistance fighters—or guerrillas—to this day camp out in clusters of a dozen or so like-minded comrades and dream of overthrowing whatever regime happens to be in place, though rarely do they have a clear idea of how their revolution will succeed or what they would do if it did. And the national sense of humor perpetually finds amusement in one's own and others' foibles—provided the foibles are the inversions of noble intentions. A T-shirt recently for sale in Managua's central shopping mall links these two forms of the quixotic impulse by depicting two armadillos, one labeled "ordinary" (*común*) and the other "Nicaraguan" (*Nicaragüense*). The difference is that the Nicaraguan armadillo is wrapped in ammunition belts full of grenades, and carries a rifle and a pistol.

The institutionalization of the quixotic impulse eventually took a literary form as Nicaraguan culture became infatuated with poetry. The catalyst was the great Nicaraguan poet Rubén Darío (1867–1916); since Darío, many literate Nicaraguans have tried a hand at poetry, and not a few have followed Darío in achieving world reputations for their art. As Daniel Ortega, a sometime poet himself, once quipped, "In Nicaragua, everybody is considered to be a poet until he proves to the contrary."[2] Through poetry, as through humor, Nicaraguans have found a means of imaginary escape from the awful alternative of conquering or being conquered—or becoming real guerrilla fighters. As such, poetry is their sublimated satisfaction, and it is so popular that when one filmmaker set out to make a movie about Nicaragua, he appropriately entitled it "Land of the Poets." Yet the filmmaker may have become more deeply immersed in Nicaraguan realities than he expected to be—in quixotic Nicaraguan fashion, he never actually got around to making the film.

Too much cannot be made of these kinds of subtler legacies, which continue to permeate the culture. To this day, the conqueror versus conquered dialectic is very much in evidence, and revolutionary movements tend especially to attract a lot of quixotic types. Meanwhile, other aspects of Nicaragua's Spanish heritage surface, such as the time Ortega tried to explain his political philosophy to an uncomprehending interviewer from the United States in terms of its anchorage in Spanish-Catholic traditions.[3] It was always easier for Americans to label him a Marxist, which he never really was, than to understand his Spanish-Catholic views. But not everyone draws the same things to the same degrees from their traditions. Ortega does tend to see the world in terms of conquerors versus the conquered (and frankly seems especially to see gender relations in this framework), but he is not very quixotic in disposition. Instead, he is incredibly practical in his objectives and methodical in pursuit of them. Of course, he embodies his cultural traditions in other ways. He believes that he has some powers of ESP, for example, and has written poetry.[4] He chooses the parts of his cultural heritage that suit him, rejects other parts, and is molded by the whole of it more than even he is aware.

HAD INDEPENDENCE FROM SPAIN brought true national sovereignty to Nicaragua, much of the Spanish legacy in the country might have evolved differently. As it was, the break from Spain really only provided Nicaragua with another dominating foreign power. As a result, independence reinforced rather than relaxed Nicaragua's self-conception as a conquered people. Nicaragua was a small, poor country, too weak to defend itself either militarily or economically against its aggressors, and was allied with other countries that were not much stronger. Though linked briefly with the Mexican Empire (which might have served it better in the long run), Nicaragua soon switched its loyalty to the fragile Central American Federation, which included Costa Rica, El Salvador, Guatemala, and Honduras. The federation proved advantageous to Nicaragua almost a quarter of a century later, when member countries lent military assistance to repel a would-be conqueror, but it was rarely that strongly united. It frequently fragmented into impotency, a political failure that has left historians to wonder why a strong Central American federation is so elusive a goal, especially when the United Fruit Company managed to unite several countries into banana republics.[5] In any event, the federation rarely provided Nicaragua with reliable political protection and was of no assistance in deflecting the interest that the United States soon took in the country. Having introduced the Monroe Doctrine in the year following Nicaragua's independence, the United States essentially claimed hegemony over all of Latin America. (The Monroe Doctrine, directed against Europe's further intervention in the Western Hemisphere, implied that the

United States could then do as it wished in Latin America.) It took a specific interest in Nicaragua, especially for the right to build a trans-isthmus canal through the country.

Obviously Panama was eventually chosen as the site for the canal. (Panama was part of Colombia at that time. The United States backed separatist groups in Panama to help it break away from Colombia in exchange for the right to build a canal there.) But Nicaragua was originally the preferred and probably superior site. Nicaragua boasts one of the largest lakes in the hemisphere, Lake Colcibolca (Lake Nicaragua), and using this ready-made body of water in canal construction would have been easier from an engineering standpoint than building the canal through Panama. In fact, it appears that the main reason Panama was chosen over Nicaragua was that a savvy French lobbyist, Philippe Bunau-Varilla, misled Congress into believing that a canal through Nicaragua would be vulnerable to volcanic eruptions. Bunau-Varilla was working on behalf of French investors who had forty million dollars to gain from a canal through Panama. Money and political cunning therefore determined the site of the canal, not engineering ease.[6] Nevertheless, after the Panama Canal was built, the United States retained an interest in Nicaragua, because it contemplated constructing a second canal. Even today, talk of a second canal through Nicaragua can be heard, with Russia a recently interested sponsor.

There was a pressing need for a canal through Central America. Until 1869, when the first transcontinental railroad was completed, overland travel across the United States was arduous. Depending upon the points of origin and destination, the journey could take months, and it was fraught with so many difficulties that death en route was a distinct possibility. The alternative, traveling by sea, required going all the way around the tip of South America. The incentive to construct a canal through Central America was therefore enormous, and it increased dramatically during the 1840s, when gold was discovered in California. With the gold rush, Americans had a new reason to want to cross the continent and to ship their gold back east. Accordingly, because Britain retained influence on Nicaragua's Caribbean coast (and the Monroe Doctrine allowed that existing European colonies could remain in place), the United States sat down with Britain to negotiate what became the Clayton-Bulwer Treaty, signed in 1850. According to the terms of the treaty, the United States and Britain would share rights to a future canal through Nicaragua. The only country that came away from the negotiations without any rights was Nicaragua.

There followed one of the most bizarre events in all of Central American history. A filibuster from the United States named William Walker took it upon himself to conquer Nicaragua. Walker's motives were mixed, but they included both avarice and hubris. To some extent, Walker and his band of mercenaries were simply putting a business scheme in motion. Nicaragua was contested territory for the moguls of the era, and as the prospect of the canal loomed, Walker wanted to claim the country in order to profit from it. The political situation in Nicaragua at the time made Walker's scheme viable. The country was divided into two opposing political parties, the Liberals and the Conservatives. The Liberals were largely supported by the United States while the Conservatives were backed by Britain. The tensions between the two factions were sufficiently grave to enable Walker to negotiate an agreement with the Liberals to lend them armed support in exchange for his election to the presidency in 1856. Beyond personal ambition, Walker had self-styled patriotic motives. A Southerner who believed in manifest destiny, Walker thought that Central America would ultimately be incorporated into the United States, and he wanted any new state to be a slave one. Accordingly, as president he legalized slavery and decreed that English would be the official language of Nicaragua. Thus in one fell swoop the country turned into an English-speaking, slave-owning state of the United States under a conquering dictator.

But though it was weak, the Central American Federation was not about to put up with Walker. Aided by Walker's business rivals in the United States, it resisted with military force. He was deposed as president after only a year, though it was not until 1860 that Walker was finally captured and executed in Honduras. The Central American countries have their own ways of commemorating the defeat of this Yankee imperialist. In Nicaragua, the commemorative date is September 14, in memory of the 1856 Battle of San Jacinto, which turned the tide against Walker. (In Costa Rica, which also celebrates on September 14 by singing the national anthem at 6:00 P.M., April 11 is a national holiday as well, commemorating the Battle of Rivas in Southern Nicaragua, won by the heroism of Costa Rican native son Juan Santamaría, who lost his life determining the outcome.) Falling as it does right next to the September 15 date of Nicaragua's independence from Spain, the country today splits the difference and celebrates for the entire September week in which both dates fall. Although Walker is largely forgotten in the United States, he is remembered in Nicaragua, his defeat a symbol of the country's continuing struggle for independence.

The United States did not leave Nicaragua alone. It did, for over a generation, more or less ignore it (minus reserving the rights to build a canal). However, this meant leaving the country in the hands of local oligarchs bent on profiting from the exploitation of the Nicaraguan peasantry, occasionally with U.S. accomplices. While Nicaraguans perpetrated the slaughter of thousands of indigenous people to make way for the coffee boom, by 1892 U.S. citizens were the registered owners of 12 to 13 percent of the lucrative coffee-growing soil made available by this subjugation of the peasant population.[7] The Boston Fruit Company, soon to be gobbled up by the United Fruit Company, operated in Nicaragua by the 1880s. Nicaragua emerged the quintessential banana republic, a society in which an impoverished peasantry labored for local elites who grew crops for export rather than developing industrial or viable local economies. The consequences were devastating. Poverty and internal inequality festered. After all, when raw materials are exported, finished goods have to be imported.

The exporter of raw materials loses a little more in e
The economic model is premised upon a conq
conquered mentality. The economy does not grow
ity, only for the few, and their profits come at the ᴄᴀᵽ
increasing subjugation of the majority. As long as the economic
elites hold the power, the system persists—especially when they
enjoy the protection of powerful foreign benefactors.

And Nicaragua's benefactor was a loyal one. The United
States withdrew its troops from Nicaragua in 1857, preferring
to exert its influence behind the scenes by working as much as
possible through local leaders. Between 1865 and 1877, however,
the U.S. Marines once again occupied parts of Nicaragua, chiefly
the major cities of Managua and León. After withdrawing forces
once again, the United States then sent troops back to the country in 1894, 1896, 1898, 1899, 1907, and 1910. Finally, by 1912,
the Marines once again occupied the country, and except for a
brief exit in 1925 they remained for over twenty years. The United
States argued that the reason for its presence was "to protect American life and property," but not far behind that justification was
the old one of "the white man's burden." Most of the elites in the
United States were after all white men, and most of them genuinely
believed that they were not merely a superior race but also that
they had created a superior civilization. At the time, racism was
legally institutionalized inside the United States, and it was the
rare member of the white, male, Protestant elite who doubted his
natural moral superiority over darker-skinned, poor Catholics in
a country perceived to be a jungle backwater. Accordingly, just as
the Spanish conquistadores before them had justified their plunder of Nicaragua and suppression of its people by introducing
the survivors to Christianity and the glories of Spain, the elites in
the United States easily adopted a patronizing attitude toward a
country they dominated, almost as an afterthought.

Understandably, Nicaraguans did not see the United States as
a kindly benefactor. As Tomás Borge, one of the founders of the
Sandinista National Liberation Front (FSLN), which ultimately

won the revolution in 1979, wryly observed about the Marine occupation, "What did they leave us? Chewing gum, the expression 'okay,' some kids with more or less pale blue eyes, and an irreversible national rage."[8] One Nicaraguan felt the pinch of oppression most keenly—Augusto César Sandino. A mechanic by trade and a seeker of spiritual enlightenment by disposition (a penchant for mysticism pretty much went with being a rebellious Nicaraguan, since rejection of early oppression often is accompanied by questioning the established religions that legitimize it), Sandino had an epiphany. "If in Nicaragua there were one hundred men who loved it as much as I did," he realized, "our nation would recover its absolute sovereignty, [which has been] endangered by the Yankee Empire."[9] Sandino proceeded to look for the hundred men he sought, and he inspired them with a political-mystical vision that motivated them to wage one of the earliest and most successful guerrilla war campaigns in history. Between 1927 and 1933, he and his band of freedom fighters battled the occupying Marines so ferociously that the United States agreed to withdraw. Although he ultimately failed to win liberation for his country, the revolutionary movement that did—the Sandinistas—took its name from him.

But as so often happens to the quixotic romantics—and Sandino was one—the gallant guerrilla commander was double-crossed by more practical men. In 1934 Sandino was gunned down on his way to signing what he thought would be the peace treaty. His assassination was then followed by the slaughter of hundreds of his supporters, including men, women, and children. Sandino's assassin is not known, nor the person who ordered it or the killings that followed. It is accepted as fact that Anastasio Somoza García was behind both. Educated in the United States and speaking flawless English, Somoza was the man the United States chose to control Nicaragua. The United States no longer had any interest in having a military presence in the country. It had strong-armed local elites into agreeing to the Bryan-Chamorro Treaty (ratified in 1916), which gave the United States exclusive rights to build a canal in Nicaragua. It preferred to turn over the management of Nicaragua to insiders. But it wanted a strongman in Nicaragua to guard U.S. interests. Somoza struck the United States as just the man. Accordingly, the United States helped to install him as the head of a new Nicaraguan militia, the National Guard, which would replace the Marines, and then helped to train this force.

It is said that Franklin Delano Roosevelt once quipped, "Somoza is a son of a bitch, but he is our son of a bitch." Robert Pastor, who served as the Latin American expert on President Carter's National Security Council when the Nicaraguan revolution erupted, and later worked with the Carter Center monitoring elections in Nicaragua, claims that Roosevelt never said this.[10] If not, he might as well have, for the remark surely captured his sentiments, as well as those of many subsequent U.S. presidents who served during the almost half a century that either Somoza or one of his sons ruled Nicaragua. Somoza quickly showed himself to be both more ambitious and more ruthless than the United States expected him to be. He was not content merely to command a National Guard, for example, but quickly muscled his way into the presidency of the country. In 1936, with three thousand Guardsmen, he ousted President Juan Bautista Sacasa and arranged to have himself "elected" president on the first of January 1937 by a vote of 107,201 to 108. Thus began a dictatorial dynasty that lasted until the revolution in 1979. During the interim, the Somozas turned the National Guard into one of the largest and most ruthless military-police forces in the world. The Guard may have murdered upward of twenty thousand innocent Nicaraguans during its reign of terror, often after torturing them, and arbitrarily imprisoned and tortured tens of thousands more. They also controlled much of the vice in the country. Tempting the Guardsmen with the proceeds from criminal activities while encouraging acts of ruthlessness was intentional Somoza management strategy. He wanted the National Guard alienated from the rest of the society so that they would be forced to be loyal only to him.[11] Meanwhile, the Somoza family amassed a personal fortune, often at the expense of the populace, that is estimated to have reached controlling interest in 60 percent of the entire economic activity of the country. Washington had not predicted that Somoza would enrich himself to this extent or wield power so ruthlessly. But every time the United States wanted something—military bases during World War II or during the Bay of Pigs invasion of Cuba, for example—the Somoza regime offered it. Indeed, the Somoza regime allegedly made campaign contributions to U.S. politicians, including a one-million-dollar cash contribution to Richard Nixon's reelection campaign.[12] The Somozas were sons of bitches, but they were the sons of bitches of the United States, and every U.S. president knew this.

THE WILLINGNESS OF PRESIDENT Dwight D. Eisenhower to send troops into Guatemala in 1954 in order to oust the left-leaning but democratically elected President Jacobo Arbenz Guzman, who had implemented land-reform policies that the United Fruit Company opposed, suggests that Washington's Latin American foreign policy veered toward actively supporting strongmen, like Somoza, who would do its bidding over elected leaders. But the Kennedy administration set a different tone in its Latin American policy, and that tone on the whole was both welcomed and helpful in Nicaragua. It sent then-ruling Luís Somoza strong messages that brutality and tyranny would not be tolerated. Nicaragua prospered during the Kennedy and Johnson administrations more than it ever had before. However, there are many variables, and it is difficult to tease out the most salient ones. During the Kennedy and Johnson administrations, for example, Nicaragua was governed by the most benevolent and democratic-minded of the Somoza dictators, Luís Somoza Debayle. Since Luís Somoza was more restrained in his repression than either his father had been or his brother would be, there was less of an incentive for the United States to interfere during his reign.

Why the United States failed to restrain the Somoza regime may be best answered by taking a quick glance into the Carter administration. Jimmy Carter was generally regarded as a "good gringo" in Nicaragua. When the Nicaraguan Revolution erupted during Carter's presidency, he did signal his reservations with the Somoza dictator Anastasio Somoza Debayle on human rights grounds, and in the end joined the chorus of countries calling for his abdication. Carter was late in recognizing that the regime's days were numbered and even wrote the dictator an embarrassing letter in 1978 congratulating him on an improving human rights record when it was already a foregone conclusion that he would, and should, be deposed. Then, when Carter recognized the inevitability of the revolution, his policy toward Nicaragua aimed to establish a post-revolution government that would essentially exclude the revolutionaries but would include the hated National Guard. The Nicaraguans did not see this policy as supportive of their national sovereignty. They saw it as "Somocismo without Somoza," a continuation of the repressive regime under a new figurehead, and resoundingly rejected it. Joining them in their rejection were at least a half dozen other countries that had allied themselves with the Nicaraguan revolutionaries and understood that the break from Somoza—and by extension, the United States—had to be a complete one. Basically, the Carter administration's policy toward Nicaragua, while better intentioned than those of many other presidential administrations in the United States, betrayed a disquieting ignorance of what was really happening in and morally necessary for the country.

Jimmy Carter's problem was that he was just too busy to attend to Nicaragua. At the time, after all, he had his hands full with the Iranian revolution and the Soviet invasion of Afghanistan. Moreover, just as when the United States initially underestimated Somoza's ruthlessness, it was perhaps easy, or at least convenient, for the United States to wink at the regime's continuing repression of the country. Indeed, the United States had not yet appreciably altered the condescending view it held of Nicaragua back when the Marines occupied the country. During the guerrilla war spearheaded by Sandino, a seemingly well-intentioned

Marine passed a Nicaraguan girl on the street, thought he recognized her, and asked, "Aren't you Bandit Pete's daughter?" The girl replied, "That's *General* Pedro Altimirano to you, mister son-of-a-bitch tough guy."[13] The United States had a pronounced tendency to see itself as Nicaragua's benefactor when in the eyes of many Nicaraguans it was a foreign oppressor. As a result, even a busy President Carter was able to imagine as late as 1979 that the largely criminal National Guard could be transformed into a law-abiding peacekeeping force. The explanation for the United States permitting its "son of a bitch" to continue to rule Nicaragua, in short, may lie in the attitude of smug superiority supported by profound indifference that often accompanies a superpower engaged in "imperial overreach"[14]—coupled with the pressures from economic interests in the country to maintain hegemony over a dependent and profitable neo-colonial outpost.

Daniel Ortega tended to embrace this kind of explanation for U.S. involvement in Nicaragua. Throughout his life he recognized that there were "good gringos" as well as bad ones, and he believed that much about the American political giant deserved admiration. He was also a product of U.S. as well as Spanish domination, an unrepentant New York Yankees fan who loved rock music, Hollywood movies, and Coca-Cola. He could discourse about the Protestant influence on the United States, the presidential administration of Franklin Roosevelt, and political arguments made by James Madison in the *Federalist Papers.* Meanwhile, during the 1980s his wife subscribed to *Time, Newsweek, Satellite Dish, Vogue, Glamour, Harper's Bazaar, Cosmopolitan,* and *Hair and Beauty Guide.*[15] Nevertheless, Ortega could never bring himself to trust the United States. When Barack Obama was elected president, Ortega told everyone who would listen that this would change little about the United States' actions in Latin America. Although he was personally enthusiastic about Obama's election and had publicly supported it, Ortega was convinced that the system of imperial domination in the United States was more powerful than the men and women elected to control it.[16]

Jimmy Carter was a still a student at the U.S. Naval Academy and a weekend Sunday school teacher when Daniel Ortega was born in the ironically named town of La Libertad in Nicaragua's mining and cattle-raising department of Chontales. (States or provinces are called "departments" in Nicaragua.) Carter's boyhood in the rural apartheid South was probably as similar to Ortega's boyhood as possible for an American at the time. In both regions, a darker-skinned majority toiled in near-medieval conditions for a lighter-skinned minority—in the case of the gold mines in Chontales, the controlling minority were Germans— while subsisting in primitive poverty. Indoor plumbing, running water, electricity, education beyond a few primary grades, health care, and other accoutrements of modern life were often lacking. When the mines hit hard times and the Ortega family was forced to cast around for work, they traveled by mule. In 1950, they finally made their way to Managua. They lived in a barrio named after Somoza, across from a park named after Somoza, near a statue of Somoza, and close to a stadium named after Somoza.[17] Ortega grew up in the shadow of Somoza's dictatorial control of his country, and he grew up poor. He therefore always knew who was to blame for his poverty: Somoza, and by extension the U.S. government that supported him. Shaping this understanding were his parents, in particular his father, who taught him to hate Somoza and distrust the United States, but who also inspired him with stories of how one man, Augusto César Sandino, had once found a hundred others who loved their country as much as he did, and sent the Yankees home.

Don Daniel's Son

JOSÉ DANIEL ORTEGA SAAVEDRA was born on November 11, 1945, to Daniel Ortega Cerda and Lydia Saavedra Rivas.[18] He was the eldest surviving child of the couple—two earlier children had died—and he enjoyed all the emotional privileges that a welcomed eldest son might be expected to have. Named after his father (and called "Danielito"), Ortega enjoyed a close relationship with him until his death in 1975. His mother was one of his staunchest supporters throughout her long life (she died in 2005). She boasted of his achievements in school, visited him regularly during his seven years in prison, helped to organize hunger strikes on behalf of him and the other political prisoners, vouched for his Catholic faith (which was very important to her), and was active in the group "Mothers of Heroes and Martyrs" after the revolution. As the eldest son, Daniel also had authority over his siblings. Humberto, born only fourteen months later and frankly regarded by many as the smarter brother, always deferred to Daniel's leadership, supporting his brother at all times. A third son, Camilo, born in 1950, likewise followed his elder brother's lead until his death in the 1978 insurrection in Masaya. A daughter, Germania, born in 1948, was much loved by Daniel. He wrote a poem for her and his mother from prison. But at the time, females in Nicaragua and the Ortega household were accorded different roles than males, and Germania was never included in the boys' activities. A photo of the children taken in the mid-1950s even excludes her.

Except for being somewhat slight of build and having poor eyesight, Daniel Ortega was a healthy, active, and much-loved brother and son, and enjoyed the good fortune to be born to a married couple who remained together for life. His parents had even married in a church ceremony.[19] This was and remains somewhat unusual in Nicaragua. A combination of poverty and machismo often prevents couples from forming stable marriages, resulting in upward of half the households in Nicaragua being headed by single women. Women seem to prefer this arrangement more than men do, presumably because they question the value of committing to a man who cannot support a family yet who may insist upon the prerogatives claimed by members of his gender anyway.[20] The marriages that are established and endure are frequently common-law unions. Neither of Ortega's parents was a child of married parents. Rather, both were born to lower-class women and higher-class married men. This is a familiar pattern in Nicaragua too. Both Sandino, the inspiration and namesake of the revolutionary movement, and Carlos Fonseca, the intellectual founder of the Sandinista Front, were the offspring of unions between philandering higher-status men and lower-status women. The circumstances of Daniel Ortega's parents' births were therefore not unusual; unusual rather was that they chose to marry in a church ceremony and to remain together.

This marriage endured in part because each was comparatively mature when they wed in 1941: Daniel Ortega Cerda celebrated his thirty-sixth birthday that year, Lydia Saavedra Rivas her thirty-third. They remained together for over thirty years, and appear to have been happy. Another factor in their enduring marriage, as well as the church wedding with which it began, is social class—or at least class aspirations. Though uneasily anchored into the social strata of their more elite fathers, both had connections to Nicaragua's higher classes. Lydia was raised in the household of her father and his wife. She was even sent to secretarial school in Managua, a mark of some class privilege, and later briefly taught elementary school, another mark of at least middle-class standing. Her family's status, however, was largely limited to the small town of La Libertad, which at the time had only a few thousand residents and remained isolated from the important centers of Nicaraguan life. Although her father briefly served as mayor, ran a general store, and dabbled in other business ventures, he was hardly among the landed gentry. He was merely more successful than most. Daniel Ortega Cerda's class background was less personally secure but higher overall. Raised in poverty by his mother, he nevertheless knew and at turns had the support of his father, Marco Antonio Ortega, who was the director of an elite private school in Nicaragua's colonial town of Granada, the Instituto Nacional de Oriente, where his students had even included Anastasio Somoza García (prior to his departure for college in the United States). In fact, Daniel Ortega Cerda's stepbrother, Alfonso

Ortega Urbina, rose to become the minister of foreign relations in the Somoza regime during the 1960s.[21]

Daniel Ortega's parents also displayed their class allegiances in their lifestyle. When he met his future wife, for example, Daniel Ortega Cerda worked as an accountant for La Esmeralda gold mine in La Libertad. This was not a high-status job, and Lydia even called him a cashier as well as an accountant.[22] However, according to Thomas Walker's notion of the Nicaraguan class structure—namely that it is divided between the approximately 20 percent who do not work with their hands and the 80 percent who do—Daniel was in the upper 20 percent of the class structure.[23] After the mine closed, forcing the family to relocate to Managua, the elder Ortega went into the import/export business. This too was white-collar work. In Managua, Daniel and Lydia's boys were not only all sent to school and expected to graduate from high school—an achievement that would place them in the educated upper crust of Nicaraguan society—but they were also sent to private, Catholic schools. This cost money that the family did not have, and the boys did periodically drop out after their parents fell too far in arrears of the tuition payments. Danielito not only made it through high school, however, but also spent a year as a law student at Managua's premier Catholic university, the University of Central America. For a Nicaraguan at the time, this was a sign of genuine achievement. Out of a population of around two million, there were no more than a couple thousand college students in the entire country. (The sons and daughters of Nicaragua's elite were typically sent to college and sometimes even high school abroad, usually in the United States.) Meanwhile, although the Managua barrio in which they settled was humble by global standards, by Nicaraguan standards it was distinctly middle class. Moreover, although Daniel Ortega's claim to having mixed Spanish and indigenous ancestry is probably true, neither his features nor his skin tone reveal a lot of indigenous blood. Racially, in the way these things were assessed in Nicaragua at the time, his parents were comparatively privileged too.

By marrying and remaining married—and perhaps even by postponing marriage and children until they were old enough to manage the responsibilities of family life with the appropriate maturity—Daniel and Lydia displayed attitudes consistent with their class backgrounds and aspirations. But except for their marriage, their experiences failed to validate their class strivings. They were regularly frustrated in pursuing their dreams.

THE FIRST TWO CHILDREN born to Daniel Ortega Cerda and Lydia Saavedra Rivas were named Sigfrido and Germania. Sigfrido made it three years, Germania two, but both eventually died. The causes of their deaths are unknown, perhaps because childhood deaths were common in those days.[24] In 1928, fully 40 percent of Nicaraguan children had died before their third birthdays and 60 percent before reaching adulthood.[25] Statistics from the United Nations for 1950 put overall life expectancy in Nicaragua at forty-one years for men and forty-four years for women, averages that indicate high death rates among children and young adults. The earliest year for which the United Nations reports infant mortality statistics in Nicaragua is 1960, and in that year 13 percent of babies died during their first year of life. (For comparison purposes, the infant mortality rate in the United States in the same year was 2.6 percent.) Sigfrido and Germania seem to have died of poverty—or, more accurately, of an economic and political system in which resources were so unequally distributed that even the children of the fledgling middle class were at high risk of preventable childhood death.

That system of economic inequality prevented the senior Ortega from succeeding in his career. Daniel Ortega Cerda admired the Germans who owned and managed the gold mines in Chontales. He revealed his affection for them in the names that he bestowed on his first two children. However, he was at that time perhaps a little naïve. He gave no evidence of realizing that, as the revolutionary leader Dora María Téllez later put it, "the companies would take the gold and the Nicaraguan miners kept the tuberculosis."[26] Later, when the mines closed and he was scrounging for work, he named his next child after himself. When he brought his family to Managua to try to make a fresh start at forty-five years old, the family moved around quite a bit, the result of being evicted for nonpayment of rent.[27] Meanwhile, after struggling to build an import/export business in Managua and securing rights to import wire fencing from a Hungarian company, Daniel lost the account to a group of German nationals. Reports are sketchy and unreliable, but there is some suggestion that the elder Ortega's career suffered a specific, major setback tantamount to bankruptcy.[28] Perhaps the loss of the Hungarian account was this event. In any case, the Ortega family never truly prospered. They were perpetually late in paying school tuition, forcing the boys to leave school until money could be found for them to return. They periodically lived off the meager proceeds that the family earned by running a small neighborhood grocery store (*pulpería*) out of their home. When Daniel Ortega Cerda later arranged to import gold for dental fillings and built a customer base among dentists, he likely realized that the gold originated in Nicaragua, but crossed the Atlantic twice so that foreigners could profit from it.

The hardships and setbacks of the Ortega family were neither unique to them nor their fault. They were hardworking, enterprising, and ambitious for themselves as well as their children, yet they consistently failed to rise above the edge of poverty, and they periodically slipped below it. Their problems were rooted in a system of economic and political domination that prevented almost everyone in Nicaragua unattached to the Somoza regime from succeeding at anything. In 1953, Anastasio Somoza García even rigged the outcome of the Miss Nicaragua beauty pageant.[29] The dictatorship knew few limits. Meanwhile, as late as 1970, the earliest year for which the United Nations has statistics and a year that followed a decade of unprecedented economic growth, almost a quarter of Nicaraguans were still undernourished. The poverty the Ortega family experienced was common throughout

Nicaragua, and they actually did better than most. They were in the upper quintile of the class structure.

HUMBERTO ORTEGA, WHO AFFECTIONATELY refers to his father as Don Daniel (in part to distinguish his father from his brother, who had outgrown the diminutive "Danielito"), may capture some of his father's inner life when he describes him as a lifelong rebel.[30] Humberto emphasizes his father's political rebelliousness in order to link the sons' political activities to their father's influence, and the political link between father and sons is strong and direct. This emphasis, however, may amount to putting a post hoc political spin on a trait that was diffusely personal as well. It would appear that Don Daniel resented the prominent father who treated him like the bastard son he was. This resentment intensified with the frustrations that life hurled at him, and increasingly he channeled it into politics. The personal foundation for Don Daniel's rebelliousness is suggested by political activities that were on the whole uncoordinated and unsystematic, more suggestive of insolence than insurrection. "Rebel" may be the appropriate word to describe him.

Don Daniel's first recorded act of political rebellion was to switch his loyalty from the Conservative to the Liberal party. In the context of the times, this was virtually pointless. The opposition between conservatives and liberals in Nicaragua had by then become essentially a regional rather than an ideological dispute. The two sides (and there were sometimes more than one party in each camp) basically reflected the historical tensions between the colonial cities of León and Granada. Liberals were based in León, conservatives in Granada, and the liberal/conservative divide rarely amounted to more than a question of which urban oligarchs would rule. Moreover, most successful political operators in Nicaragua tended to maneuver between the two sets of political parties, playing one against the other or brokering agreements between them. (The United States did this, shifting its support from one party to the other when it suited its strategic interests.) Since Don Daniel came from Granada, site of the conservatives, changing his party allegiance to the liberals was the rough political equivalent of running away from home, having little political, but seemingly ample psychological, significance. Later, when Somoza's rise came nominally through the liberal political faction, Don Daniel found himself in the embarrassing position of having to leave liberalism too.

Of course, by switching his political allegiances Don Daniel was guided by some political principle. At the time that he identified himself as a liberal, the United States was backing a conservative political regime in Nicaragua. Perhaps Don Daniel was already energized by opposition to the United States. If he was, though, he took his time showing it. It wasn't until March 19, 1933, when Sandino's guerrilla warfare against the Yankees had already met with victory, that Don Daniel contacted the rebel general. He sent Sandino a letter that said, in part, "Count me as among your unconditional and loyal soldiers," from his hometown of Granada.[31] Don Daniel was by then twenty-seven or twenty-eight years old, and thus rather mature to be finally finding the time to express his support for a guerrilla campaign that had been waged for six years and had already reached its culmination.

The next year, after Sandino's assassination, Don Daniel took a riskier step by writing a public letter accusing Somoza of the murder. This resulted in a brief imprisonment by the National Guard. Somoza gave him the chance to take a test on a biography of Sandino that Somoza had commissioned. The biography, it goes without saying, purposely painted the guerrilla commander as a lunatic rather than a champion of Nicaraguan sovereignty, and as such was part of Somoza's attempt to control information in Nicaragua. (Years later, the Sandinistas would have to use the archives in Cuba to research Sandino's life, as Somoza had successfully rid Nicaragua of most relevant sources.) After Don Daniel read the biography and passed the test, he was promptly released. Somoza even gave him some money to help him get situated afterward. Reading between the lines, Somoza was basically treating Don Daniel as the wayward son of a prominent father, and frankly Don Daniel probably expected this treatment. Don Daniel knew that Somoza had attended his father's school, after all. Don Daniel risked little with his tepid political acts. Indeed, his final act of defiance was to send back the money Somoza had given him. Somoza responded by sending a telegram that read, in part, "then eat shit" (*entonces comé mierda*). The telegram became part of Ortega family lore, and Don Daniel proudly showed it to visitors. But with it his political activities basically ended.

There is a certain pathos to the story of a man who was proud of an insulting telegram. It is as if, by his early thirties, Don Daniel was already defeated. To name his firstborn son after a German tells of his admiration for the man, but it also hints of a little defeatism, as if Don Daniel was not proud enough of himself to bestow his own name on his son. Then, as the years wore on, Don Daniel took a typical turn of defeated Nicaraguans, power-less to redirect their fates. He looked to the mystical. In his case, it was theosophy, a kind of pantheism that blends Hinduism with Christianity and sees God revealed in nature.[32] It does suggest that his rebelliousness was diffuse and unsystematic. He never pub-lished his thoughts about theosophy—or anything else for that matter—although his father had published. Don Daniel seemed disgruntled, and justifiably so, but was never able to channel his frustration into much that mattered.

Yet it may be more from a father's failures than his successes that sons draw their inspiration. Don Daniel's sons had to under-stand, at least subconsciously, that their father was a defeated man. Living with that humiliation surely fueled their rage. And Don Daniel and Lydia Saavedra did not leave the boys any doubt about where their rage should be focused. In the aftermath of the Cuban Revolution, Don Daniel listened defiantly to loud radio broadcasts from Cuba, just to let all his neighbors and any passing National Guardsmen know where his sympathies lie. Then, when the revolutionary Sandinista movement began to take shape during the early 1960s, Don Daniel welcomed more than a few of its adherents into his home for spirited conversations. He even lent his car, an old Buick station wagon, to the Sandinistas on occasion.[33] Lydia Saavedra Rivas had long lent her support too, since she had quietly supplied goods to Sandino's militia—including General Pedro Altimirano—when they stopped in her father's store in Chontales.[34] Meanwhile, both parents proudly supported their sons when, barely into their teenage years, they became involved in the insurrectional activities that would ultimately bring a revolution to Nicaragua.

Becoming a Sandinista

MANY IN NICARAGUA FELT the way the Ortega family did about the Somoza dictatorship, and when the revolution finally came in 1979 it was one of the most popular in human history. But longing for liberation and achieving it are two very different things. Unless the longing is channeled into a coordinated project consistent with the history and aspirations of the people, it is bound to be limited to only isolated and ineffectual acts of defiance. This was the problem that Nicaragua confronted during the bulk of the Somoza years: opposition to the dictatorship was not coordinated into a coherent national revolutionary project. The achievement of the Sandinistas—the Frente Sandinista de Liberación Nacional, or FSLN—was to create just such a coherent project, and therefore finally succeeded where others had failed. Its success, however, did not come quickly. The FSLN spent nearly two decades gestating, and even after spearheading the revolution it only partially reflected the values and ideals of the wider political culture. Nevertheless, the story of the Nicaraguan Revolution is in large part the story of the FSLN, which Daniel Ortega joined while they were both in their formative stages.

Prior to the rise of the FSLN, the absence of a coherent and popular revolutionary project was apparent everywhere in Nicaragua, but perhaps nowhere more so than in the city of León on September 21, 1956, when Rigoberto López Pérez assassinated Anastasio Somoza García. There is some evidence that others were aware of and tangentially involved in the plot. Tomás Borge writes that he and fellow future founder of the FSLN Carlos Fonseca met Rigoberto López Pérez shortly before the assassination at a print shop in León, where owner Edwin Castro printed the three issues they managed to publish of the radical student newspaper, *El Universitario*.[35] The two were students at the National University in León at the time, and they were already committed to revolutionary action, but it appears that neither had more than a general idea of the plot to assassinate Somoza.[36] This did not stop the National Guard from arresting Borge along with hundreds of others on suspicion of conspiracy. He was imprisoned for two long years after the crackdown. However, there was no coherent plan for action following the assassination. President Eisenhower immediately had the wounded dictator airlifted to Panama for medical treatment (although he died anyway). Somoza's son Luís Somoza Debayle quickly assumed the office of the presidency, and Somoza's other son, Anastasio Somoza Debayle, already headed the National Guard. The twenty-seven-year-old assassin (whose occupation was—predictably—said to be "poet") was himself instantly gunned down by Somoza's bodyguards. Many in Nicaragua quietly cheered the assassination of the hated dictator, but it changed nothing of political importance inside the country.

The situation was similar in 1958 and 1959, when news of Fidel Castro's victories in Cuba arrived in Nicaragua. On January 1, 1959, when Cuban dictator Fulgencio Batista was finally overthrown, fireworks decorated the Managua skyline; Nicaragua's leading newspaper, *La Prensa*, reported celebrations spontaneously erupting in multiple locations; and shouts of "Viva Cuba Libre" and "Viva Fidel" rang throughout the country.[37] The excitement had less to do with any special fellow feeling on the part of Nicaraguans for Cubans or any specific ideological support for

Castro, but more to do with what the Cuban revolution sym-
bolized for Nicaraguans yearning for their own liberation. Thus,
perhaps predictably, Nicaraguans immediately threw themselves
into a rash of revolutionary action. As early as 1958, ragtag guerrilla forces formed in Nicaragua, mostly in the northern high-
lands, intent upon liberating their country by force. Invariably,
the revolutionary zeal of these forces was matched only by their
utter lack of preparation, and they were quickly quashed. Fonseca
and Borge themselves went to Cuba for revolutionary training
in 1959 in order to prepare to launch an attack from Honduras.
Despite having received strategic advice from Che Guevara, the
band of guerrilla fighters was ambushed by the National Guard at
El Chaparral, Honduras. Nine were killed and fifteen wounded,
including Fonseca.

Much of the disgruntlement with the Somoza regime during
the late 1950s and 1960s was centered at the universities. Students
protesting at the National University in León annoyed Somoza
so much that in 1960 he arranged to establish the University of
Central America in Managua under the auspices of the Jesuits in
the hopes that it would be more supportive of his status quo. As
fate had it, the University of Central America quickly became an
even more radical campus than the National University, which
may have been inevitable in the atmosphere of those years. The
protesting university students were not much more focused than
their guerrilla brethren in the mountains. On July 23, 1959, the
National Guard attacked a student demonstration at the National
University, wounding almost a hundred and killing six. This
enraged the students and prompted them to adopt the label
"Generation of '59," but it did little more than temporarily fuel
their fury. They still lacked coherent revolutionary ideology and
an organizational apparatus. Thus, while the students were not
as a rule complacent, and mounted periodic protests, the campus mood was generally more cautious, even introspective. Much
discussion at the universities throughout the 1960s centered on
the relationship between the students' Catholic faith and their

desire for political change, and therefore what moral limits their faith placed on their political actions. This kind of discussion tempered revolutionary zeal. The faculty and other intellectuals were also more moderate. On the tenth anniversary of the July 23, 1959, massacre, a manifesto was issued by dozens of Nicaraguan intellectuals (among them Sergio Ramírez, who would later join the Sandinistas), which called for significant reforms in Nicaragua's government and economy.[38] However, it did not call for revolution.

This was the state of affairs when the Sandinista National Liberation Front was supposedly founded in the summer of 1961 by three young men: Carlos Fonseca, Silvio Mayorga, and Tomás Borge. This founding at a meeting in Tegucigalpa, Honduras, may be invested with more historical importance than it deserves. Matilde Zimmermann, Fonseca's biographer, rejects it altogether. She quotes an early Sandinista, Rodolfo Romero, who told her, "There was never any congress, any convention, any founding assembly. . . . The FSLN was created in the heat of battle."[39] Since neither Fonseca nor Mayorga survived the revolution, the only participant in the alleged founding meeting left to ask was Borge. He did not seriously dispute Romero's or Zimmermann's contention. "In reality," said Borge, "I do not think it is right for one to say that only we three founded the Frente. . . . . Behind us were others." Although Borge did recall the meeting—thus verifying that one took place—he was quick to insist that many who were not present at the meeting "are also founders." Then he proceeded to list nine other "founders," all of whom were also then dead.[40] In fact, in early 1961 the three FSLN founders were calling themselves the Movement for a New Nicaragua (MNN), and it does not appear that the FSLN began to incorporate "Sandinista" into its name until 1963. Prior to then it was generally called the Frente de Liberación Nacional (FLN). More to the point, it was not until 1969 that the FSLN developed a formal written platform. To be sure, the Front (often called the Frente) had not only adherents before then but also a literature. It seems to have consisted mostly of documents authored by Fonseca, which were circulated and discussed among members. Additional literature appears to have been appropriated from abroad, the bulk of it focusing on strategies for successful insurrections and guerrilla war campaigns. Certainly the Front's platform was part of this literature, circulated in drafts and parts over months or even years before being formally adopted. Even so, the Front existed and functioned before it had a platform or official name.

In many ways, then, the FSLN followed the quixotic trail blazed by other revolutionary initiatives in Nicaragua at the time. It tried—twice—to liberate the country by force during the mid-1960s, for example, and failed spectacularly both times. The first attempt was in the summer of 1963 when a band of no more than a few dozen guerrillas sought to engage the National Guard near the Coco and Bocay rivers, just below Honduras on the Caribbean side of the country. Although they managed to spark a few skirmishes with the Guard, their more serious enemies proved to be hunger, disease, and accident. As Tomás Borge later recalled, we "had no base of support inside the country, except in our imagination and desire, nor even a minimal infrastructure in the zone to be invaded. . . . There was, on the other hand, an excessive emotional identification . . . with the armed experience of Cuba."[41] The second military campaign began in May 1967 and lasted through August of that year. Centered in the Pancasán region near Matagalpa (and known as the "Fila Grande" or simply the "montaña" among FSLN members), this campaign was at least regarded as a political success by many in the FSLN for bringing public attention to the resolve of the revolutionary movement. It was a disastrous military failure, however. Not only did it fail to spark the wider revolution that would presumably liberate the country, but it also ended in an August 27 massacre in which approximately a third of the forty or so guerrillas, including one of the three official founders of the FSLN, Silvio Mayorga, were killed.

Meanwhile, the internal organization of the FSLN developed along lines suited to the clandestine revolutionary movement it was. A hierarchy was established in which subordinates were recruited by superiors and then provided with no more information than they absolutely needed in order to accomplish their assigned missions. They often did not even know the names of their superiors, who always used aliases (Ortega's was Enrique); neither were they informed about the structure of the overall organization or its broader objectives. As a practical matter, members moved among a series of safe houses, sometimes wearing disguises, and often communicated with one another through written code. Since FSLN members were hunted down and killed by the National Guard, the less a member knew, the less information could be extracted from him or her through torture. Even so, it was an extremely militaristic and hierarchical organization. The only ideological commitment that was an absolute requirement for membership was to revolutionary violence. Beyond this, members were permitted to hold different opinions on almost any subject.

As such, the FSLN resembled many other revolutionary movements in Nicaragua at the time, albeit with a tighter organizational structure. Its difference from them is probably traceable to the singular talent and moral character of its chief founder, Carlos Fonseca. The brilliant bastard child of a wealthy businessman and a servant woman, raised in a one-room shack in Matagalpa, Fonseca was the kind of special leader that every political movement needs but few find. His intellectual abilities were enormous—he taught himself French in high school, for example, in order to be able to read the only copy of the *Communist Manifesto* he could find—but they were matched and arguably even exceeded by his moral character. The most striking aspect was his genuine respect for women and corresponding rejection of machismo. Fonseca and the Sandinista Front that developed under his leadership were realistic about gender relations. There were no puritanical rules, and Fonseca's personal celibacy followed by a monogamous marriage was not a standard that others were forced to follow. It was simply expected that everyone would treat each other with dignity and respect, regardless of gender, and behave responsibly in their personal lives. The Front welcomed women, even in combat and leadership positions. These expectations were eventually incorporated into its written rules—and infringement of these rules was grounds for disciplinary action—but Fonseca led more by example than by decree. No one ever seriously challenged his leadership of the Front, even Borge, who was Fonseca's senior in years and experience. Indeed, second only to Sandino, the Sandinista Front was Carlos Fonseca.

Fonseca's intellectual journey reveals much about the ideology of the Sandinistas. Fonseca began with Marxism, which he originally saw as the ideological antidote to Nicaragua's oppression.[42] He wrote his senior thesis (required for high school graduation) on the topic of "Capital and Labor,"[43] was active in the Communist Party at the National University of Nicaragua, and was selected by it to attend the Sixth World Congress of Students and Youth for Peace and Freedom in Moscow in 1957. Based upon that visit, he published his first book, *Un Nicaragüense en Moscú*, in 1958. However, Fonseca soon realized that his attachment to communism was a mistake. His reservations naturally included specific criticisms of both communism and the Communist Party in Nicaragua. At issue most narrowly was the party's doctrinaire adherence to the supposed law of communism, which assumed that a revolution would not be possible until after Nicaragua industrialized. Fonseca wanted to liberate his native Nicaragua immediately. Fonseca's ultimate rejection of communism, however, was due to something more fundamental. By the early 1960s, Fonseca switched from what he considered the "false Marxism" of the Communist Party to a form of revolutionary nationalism anchored in Nicaragua's own traditions under the Sandinista banner. Indeed, the more he considered the problem of his own country's oppression, the more he realized that a crucial aspect of that oppression involved Nicaraguans having been kept ignorant of their own history of rebellion and revolt. A political culture based on an opposition between regionally based liberal and conservative oligarchs, who typically hammered out compromises with the approval of their American sponsors, prevented Nicaraguans from understanding that viable indigenous political alternatives even existed. In fact, one of the most enduring consequences of Fonseca's visit to Havana in 1959 was the serendipitous discovery that the leaders of the Cuban revolution were better acquainted with Nicaragua's own Augusto César Sandino than he was. Fidel Castro and Che Guevara had studied Sandino's military strategy in Mexico three years earlier, and both were admirers of the rebel general.[44] This discovery, along with Fonseca's own persistent questioning, helped him point the FSLN toward the development of its own distinctly Nicaraguan revolutionary ideology, which he himself spent years in the Cuban archives developing.

It would be a mistake, though, to conclude that Fonseca provided the FSLN with a pristine revolutionary ideology, or even the ideology it required. In reality, the meaning of Sandinismo remained vague.[45] Although it was stripped of its Marxism—for example, religious faith was welcomed into the movement, and Fonseca's wife was a devout Catholic even as he remained an atheist—quasi-Marxist themes predominated. Moreover, whether in the study of Sandino or others, attention tended to be directed more to matters of military strategy than to justifications for revolution in the first place, or even to the necessary components for a good society to presumably follow a successful revolution. The Sandinistas began with the commitment to revolution and did not need to persuade themselves of its correctness. Even so, Fonseca set a tone for the Sandinista movement that was searching and thoughtful, in which ideas were believed to matter, and in which reading and study were perfectly legitimate—even required—revolutionary activities. Meanwhile, in part because Fonseca's ideas themselves constantly evolved, the FSLN quickly began to operate almost like a graduate school seminar as leaders discussed ideas in an atmosphere of collegiality. Paradoxically, at the leadership level this hierarchical, clandestine revolutionary movement operated democratically. The leaders discussed virtually everything among themselves, seeking consensus rather than taking orders or counting votes. Then, as the procedural rules for the FSLN developed, they permitted any member to challenge any other one as long as the challenge was not personally disparaging but intended to improve the person and thus the movement as a whole.[46] In this way, though the ideology of the Front remained in some flux, Fonseca created an atmosphere of inclusiveness and inquisitiveness for the Sandinista movement that enabled its members to believe that ideas mattered.

In these and other ways, the FSLN developed an internal culture that distinguished it from other revolutionary movements in Nicaragua. The essence of this culture—and its advantage—was not found in its formal ideology or even its organizational structure. It was rather in the FSLN's continuing efforts to learn from its mistakes and to improve itself (morally as well as militarily) in an atmosphere of democratic collegiality. Were it not for this, the Front surely would have failed. There were plenty of times since its official founding in 1961 that the Front existed more in spirit than it did in reality. In 1964, for instance, the Front had only one safe house and two pistols, a little cloth, and some crayons, according to member Jacinto Suárez.[47] It was not much to launch a revolution with. Moreover, the Front lost most of its membership, including most of its leaders, along the way. Fonseca himself was killed by the National Guard in 1976. However, he left the FSLN with a moral inspiration that lived on.

DANIEL ORTEGA MET CARLOS Fonseca and the other founders of the Front early. Humberto Ortega writes that Fonseca was instrumental in forming the youth movement that the Ortega brothers joined in 1960, when Daniel Ortega was only fourteen years old, and that by 1962 Fonseca had visited the Ortega family home.[48] As fate would have it, the Ortega family lived in the same Managua neighborhood where the FSLN, then fewer than a dozen or two adherents, was forming during the early 1960s.[49] Why that neighborhood was a site of foment is unknown, but being a lower-middle-class Managua barrio was not irrelevant. Managua was then emerging as Nicaragua's premier city, and the old rivalries between León and Granada were giving way to the larger and growing capital city. Also, contrary to Marx, it would seem that the lower middle class is more prone to revolutionary enthusiasm than the working class, because it has a stake in the system yet feels vulnerable. But other, more specific factors made the barrio a suitable site for the FSLN. One was the presence of a Masonic lodge—Sandino had been a Mason. By 1958 or 1959, Ortega would visit the lodge after school to hear stories about Sandino's achievements from men who had been members of his guerrilla forces. There also appears to have been a priest or two at the local church who was an early devotee of the theology of liberation. This blending of Marxism and Christianity would not be institutionally expressed by the Church until the 1968 Latin American Episcopal Conference held in Medellín, Colombia, announced that the Church would henceforth adopt a "preferential option for the poor," or find cogent theological expression prior to the publication of Gustavo Gutierrez's *Theology of Liberation* in 1971, but it was foreshadowed by a 1967 encyclical published by Pope Paul VI. More to the point, the theology of liberation arose from the base of the Church, not from its leaders. Ortega's neighborhood parish appears to have been such a base.

So it happened that Daniel Ortega was drawn into revolutionary politics at a time when most boys are still playing sandlot baseball. He still loved baseball, and he and his father regularly attended the games of the Nicaraguan league. He discovered his failing eyesight on one of these outings: his father asked him the score, and Danielito could not read the scoreboard. By the summer of 1960 he was already involved in a demonstration in favor of changing the name of Roosevelt Avenue in Managua to Sandino Avenue, and he participated in a protest commemorating the first anniversary of the July 23, 1959, murder and wounding of students at the National University.[50] The events were part of a concert of activities under the auspices of the youth movement that had formed earlier in the year, activities that led to his first arrests and imprisonments. Called the Patriotic Nicaraguan Youth (Juventud Patriótica Nicaraguense, or JNP), the organization tellingly adopted "neither left nor right" but "for the salvation of the homeland" as its statement of principles, while actually being composed of many children of conservatives.[51] Following the summer demonstrations, the young people became involved in a November plot orchestrated by conservative opponents of Somoza to overthrow the regime by force. The plot was discovered by the National Guard, which not only quashed it but also obliterated the JNP. (It never reconstituted itself, but sank into the alphabet soup of oppositional movements.) Near his fifteenth birthday, Ortega found himself in prison. It was not his first time, either. The previous January he had been briefly jailed for agitating against the government.[52] The November incarceration only lasted a few days, but he was back the next year for a third brief imprisonment. This time Ortega was caught participating in a demonstration outside the U.S. embassy in Managua that got out of hand—the protesters set fire to some vehicles.[53] It is not clear which, if any, of the organizations that sponsored the event Ortega was affiliated with, but by that time it may not have mattered. Ortega was already an insurrectionist and beginning to pay the price for that via periodic imprisonments.

Jacinto Suárez, who grew up less than a block away from Ortega and was his peer in both age and politics, recalled one of his own first political acts.[54] In 1963, the local Catholic Church planned a ceremony to commemorate the students killed by the Guard at the National University. From Suárez's account, it appears that very little happened. He and Ortega were simply goofing around in a cemetery after the ceremony, angry at the political situation of their country, and acting out. Evidently some words were exchanged with some Guardsmen, and perhaps a little vandalism occurred, although Suárez did not say. That night, though, clearly registered with Suárez and seemingly changed his life. From then on he was a committed revolutionary. Suárez is one of the few survivors from those days. He is still active in the FSLN. But by 1963 Ortega was a veteran agitator, committed to the revolution and seemingly already affiliated with the newly named FSLN.

Early the following year Ortega finally made the papers.[55] He was convicted in January 1964 of assaulting a National Guard barracks in the city of Rivas, an act the court correctly considered "attempting rebellion." The newspaper got his name wrong— identifying him by his mother's rather than his father's surname— and misspelled the name of at least one of his accomplices, Selim Shible. Actually, it is possible that the newspaper intentionally misidentified the defendants out of sympathy for their cause and was hoping to protect them. The newspaper, though, as well as the court, might have taken more notice of these "alleged revolutionaries." Rivas is not terribly far from Managua, less than a hundred miles south, but for high school students to travel that far in order to target a National Guard barracks suggests that they had gone beyond the sporadic antics of disaffected teenagers and were instead caught up in a more serious revolutionary organization. The court did not fully appreciate this, and it did not keep the teenagers incarcerated very long. As a result, later in 1964 Ortega was arrested again on his way back from Guatemala, where he had gone for additional training, presumably in the tactics of guerrilla warfare, under the auspices of the FSLN.[56]

Meanwhile, Ortega was also trying to finish high school. He was a good student, and while studying at the Colegio Pedagógica, a private Catholic high school in Managua operated by the Christian Brothers, he even received a letter inviting him to join the order and enter the priesthood.[57] Tomás Borge received such an invitation too.[58] The intelligence, discipline, and moral commitment that make for good priests also make for good revolutionaries. Although he considered the priesthood, Ortega was already too deep into politics. He never abandoned the Church, but his passion for politics was stronger. Reciprocally, the order either rescinded its offer, expelled him from school, or both. Ortega's political activities became too much for most high schools to tolerate, so he kept having to find a new school to take him. In 1962 his parents briefly sent him to high school at Colegio Santa Cecilia in Guatemala, in part to protect him from the trouble his political involvements created for him in Managua, although he soon returned to a tiny Managua school, Instituto El Maestro. By that time, though, he was already beginning to live underground, as all serious FSLN members were soon forced to do. Ortega's vulnerability was prominently displayed February 12, 1966, when he showed up to sit for his high school graduation exams. The National Guard arrived at the testing site with orders for his arrest. The Guard did admit that they had located him earlier in his barrio but had waited to arrest him, suggesting that Ortega was not yet completely underground. Ortega explained that he only wanted to realize his goal of graduating from high school.[59]

The school gave Ortega temporary asylum while his parents filed a petition with the court on his behalf. The specific outcomes of that day's events are lost to history. Ortega did eventually manage to graduate from high school as well as briefly enroll in the University of Central America, but his educational ambitions were hardly paramount. In fact, within two years of his graduation he would be serving a fourteen-year sentence in a Somoza prison, convicted on charges of bank robbery but known to have committed murder as well. By then he was also a veteran of guerrilla warfare and a leader of the FSLN. He also counted himself fortunate to be alive. The Sandinista slogan was "A free homeland or death!" and Daniel Ortega always assumed that his reward would be death.[60] It had been the fate of many of his comrades already. Only two weeks before he was captured in the autumn of 1967, for example, Ortega had by chance left the safe house where he was staying only the day before the Guard arrived, guns blazing, killing everyone.

2

A FEW MORE MURDERERS AMONG MURDERERS

ON THE NIGHT OF October 23, 1967, Daniel Ortega killed for the first time. It may be the only time he ever killed anyone, though he assumes that he later killed others in guerrilla combat, but he does not know for sure. He recalls having fired indiscriminately at the enemy while the enemy returned fire. People died, but whether the bullets from his gun were the fatal ones or not, he does not know. He does know, however, that he killed Sergeant Gonzalo Lacayo of the National Guard in cold blood under a streetlight on a Managua sidewalk that October evening. He and three accomplices went to Lacayo's neighborhood armed with submachine guns for the express purpose of killing him. In fact, when they first spotted their victim, they passed by without incident since he was talking with a neighbor. The assassins did not want to kill an innocent bystander or leave any witnesses. When they circled back and found Lacayo alone under the streetlight, the target was perfect. Ortega let loose a volley from his submachine gun before Lacayo could draw his weapon.[1]

The Sandinistas called executions like these *ajusticiamientos*, which translates to "bringing to justice," and Ortega never felt guilty about his involvement in this assassination. It obviously affected him, though. Only twenty-one years old, he was now convinced of his own personal commitment to revolution. Youthful rebelliousness was behind him; he was deadly serious now, and from that point forward there would be no turning back. As he later explained, if killing Lacayo had been motivated by personal hatred, his Catholic faith would have caused him to feel guilty. Under the circumstances, though, Ortega considered the execution to be a necessary part of the Sandinista revolutionary project. "Did the members of the French Resistance feel guilty about killing Gestapo officers?" he asked rhetorically. Of course they did not. In like manner, after the slaying, Ortega shouted, "Long live the Sandinista Front!" and never allowed the incident to trouble him.[2]

It may trouble some that a small group of self-appointed revolutionaries—most of them young men barely out of their teens—felt secure enough in their moral judgments to mete out "justice" like this. Yet it was not as if Nicaragua operated under the rule of law during the Somoza regime. The law was whatever the dictator decided it would be, and in circumstances like this it may be hard to fault dissidents for determining justice in their own way. Moreover, Lacayo was notorious for his cruelty, and both Ortega and one of his accomplices that night, Edmundo Pérez, had personally experienced it.[3] Lacayo was the head of the National Guard unit that had brought Ortega and Pérez back from Guatemala under arrest in 1964, and he made a point of making that trip a living hell for his prisoners. He removed their shoes and belts, even tore out the zippers of their pants—to prevent them from being able to run away should they find the chance—and then tied their hands behind their backs and their feet together. He forced them to squat in the back of a Land Rover and placed large rocks on top of their thighs. Then, in this helpless position, he beat their heads and faces with a club. Lacayo was not content merely to beat his prisoners, though. He had the Land Rover stop along the way so that he could pick up debris from the road, which he forced his prisoners to eat. Ortega and Pérez ate chicken feathers, cigarette butts, leaves—whatever Lacayo placed on the rocks and ordered them to eat—because when they had refused Lacayo smashed their faces into the rock. Ortega quickly realized that it was preferable to eat the garbage than to lose his teeth. At one juncture, Pérez vomited. Lacayo forced him to eat his own vomit. Since Lacayo had tortured other members of the FSLN with equally creative cruelty, he was easily placed toward the top of the list of the Guardsmen that the Sandinistas sought to "bring to justice."

The FSLN had also developed a policy of *recuperaciones* ("recoveries"), the term they used for their robberies of banks and other businesses. Their justification for these thefts was that the money was only there because the ruling elite had stolen it from the people, thus a "recovery" by a people's revolution was warranted. As a practical matter, the FSLN also needed funds to operate, and they got those funds mainly from theft. In a September 1968 article on the "history of subversion," Nicaragua's leading daily newspaper, *La Prensa*, was already able to attribute ten separate robberies to the FSLN.[4] The Sandinistas were proud of these activities. As late as 1970, Carlos Fonseca was publicly listing *recuperaciones* as among the revolution's key successes.[5] Moreover, they had a genuine Robin Hood aspect. Borge writes that, according to witnesses to one bank robbery, the intruders announced: "This is a hold-up by the FSLN. We aren't going to hurt you. We want the money to overthrow the Somozas."[6] And there is little evidence that anyone in the FSLN personally benefited from them in any appreciable way. The funds were always channeled into the movement, and while full-time revolutionary operatives were supported from the proceeds, they lived humbly in shared safe houses in poor barrios or in wilderness guerrilla camps.

Ortega participated in *recuperaciones,* but it is not clear how many—or exactly what his duties with the Front were during those early years. Borge writes that Ortega only began his "active participation" (meaning full-time work) in the FSLN in late 1966, yet he was obviously involved much sooner.[7] This fits Ortega's biography, since in February 1966 he was still trying to graduate from high school. It appears that he enrolled in the University of Central America immediately afterward in the spring of 1966 (the academic year in Nicaraguan universities runs from March through December, with the winter months being their vacation), since in June of that year he traveled to Cuba under the auspices of a student conference, although in reality his objective was to smuggle arms back to Nicaragua.[8] He was not very diligent about his studies; July found him in León trying to attack a Somoza caravan.[9] His main role at the university was to assist his friend and fellow student Casimiro Sotelo develop a student chapter of the FSLN. Thus, Ortega likely became involved full-time in the FSLN around late 1966. In that capacity he returned to Cuba to obtain more weapons in January 1967, and by February he was appointed head of the "urban resistance" for the Front. At that point he became one of the FSLN members expected to live completely underground—that is, in safe houses, under assumed names, and often wearing disguises when venturing out.[10] Then, during the summer of 1967 he joined the guerrilla warfare in Pancasán, where he distinguished himself as a combatant by taking quick command of a dangerous situation and engineering the escape of all involved.[11] Fonseca, however, believed that Ortega's talents were better used in Managua, or at least as a liaison between the guerrillas in the mountains and the urban resistance, so he ordered him to return to Managua even though Ortega asked to remain in Pancasán.[12] The order was fortuitous, though, as Ortega left before the August 27 massacre in Pancasán in which most of the guerrillas were killed. Back in Managua, one of Ortega's tasks was to rob La Perfecta, a milk company, which he did on August 6. It was not a task without danger; his childhood friend Selim Shible was killed during that robbery.[13]

Together with Axel Somarriba, Ortega robbed the Bank of London and Montreal in the Kennedy Boulevard district of Managua on June 22, 1967. According to *La Prensa*, the robbers got away with 150,000 córdobas.[14] Tomás Borge writes that the amount was 225,000 córdobas.[15] Whatever the exact amount, it was an impressive sum, about one hundred thousand dollars in today's currency. Ortega and his codefendant were convicted of it in court. The evidence against them was so overwhelming that, although the headline for the story about the trial in *La Prensa* exaggerated when it blared that the two were convicted "in twenty minutes," the clock-watching reporter did note that the judicial tribunal only deliberated for twenty-eight minutes before returning the guilty verdict.[16] It was an open and shut case, and Ortega went to prison for over seven years. Later, though not confessing to this robbery specifically, Ortega freely admitted that he had robbed banks.[17] Robbing the Bank of London and Montreal was only one of the acts of "urban resistance" that Ortega undertook during his pre-prison year as a full-time revolutionary.

But Ortega believes that he was only apprehended, imprisoned, and convicted for the robbery because of the murder of Gonzalo Lacayo. The assassination of one of their own unleashed the National Guard's full fury. It retaliated with such ferocity that it made a public relations blunder. After raiding the safe house that Ortega had just left on November 4, 1967, and killing four FSLN members, the Guard justified its murders by announcing that the slain had been Lacayo's assassins. In reality, only one of those killed, Edmundo Pérez, had been involved in the assassination.[18] But with this claim the Guard boxed itself into a public relations quagmire. It could not very well hunt down others, like Ortega, and claim that they too were responsible for the assassination. Instead, the Guard hunted Ortega down and ultimately captured him on November 18 on the grounds that he was wanted for bank robbery. They brutally beat him after his capture—Ortega still bears a scar on his temple—and then allowed him to languish in prison for sixteen months before his trial even came up on the docket.

The trial was noteworthy, as was the way the press covered it. As usual, Carlos Fonseca had set the standard for Sandinistas on trial during his own July 9, 1964, trial (on charges of conspiring to assassinate the dictator). Instead of defending himself, Fonseca's eloquent *Declaración* accused the regime of being guilty of far more heinous crimes. Reprinted in full the next day by *La Prensa*, Fonseca's *Declaración* showed the fledgling movement the propaganda value of turning a trial into political theater.[19] Ortega was never as eloquent as Fonseca, but he was at least as shrewd and committed. Since he knew that he would be found guilty anyway, he was not about to miss the opportunity to use his trial for the cause.[20] Defense attorney Humberto Obregón Aquire did not bother to argue the facts of the case. Instead he submitted that the case had more to do with the "criminal facts in our society." The defense further argued that the case was not even about the two defendants but rather about "the youth of Nicaragua," who were compelled to live in an "imperial regime." As might be expected, this line of argument annoyed the judges. The president of the judicial tribunal, Rudolfo Morales Orozco, pleaded with the defense to focus on the facts of the case, and at one point Judge Vargas Sandino screamed in exasperation, "We are judging the defendants for robbery!" Nevertheless, the defense did not relent. Though irrelevant to the issue of guilt or innocence, the defense proceeded to present evidence that Ortega had been tortured by a guard, Lieutenant Agustín Torres Lopéz, during the sixteen months he had awaited trial in prison. The aim, of course, was to win public sympathy for the defendants and their cause rather than a verdict of innocence. Ortega was not trying to defend himself, but rather to fuel the fires of insurrection.

The press played along. *La Prensa*'s coverage of the trial did not necessarily side with the defendants, but neither did it overlook the fact that the trial served fundamentally as political theater. Indeed, the newspaper took pains to describe aspects that could have been left unmentioned. It observed that the National Guard "practically took possession" of the courthouse, stationing at least fifty soldiers there, as if braced for an attack by guerrilla forces to liberate the accused. It also noted that the trial took place at night. The clock-watching reporter pointed out that the trial did not begin until 7:05 P.M. and that the verdict was rendered at 1:48 A.M. the next morning. The story ran on page one of the

Sunday paper (above the fold), and continued on page ten, where it was illustrated by two large photographs. Nicaragua's literate middle class could not overlook the story or fail to be intrigued by its political dimensions. No one believed that Daniel Ortega was convicted of bank robbery. Everyone knew that he was convicted of being a revolutionary.

Of course, a sign of the times may be that there was no byline to identify the reporter who wrote the story. *La Prensa* was then headed by Pedro Joaquín Chamorro. He had made no secret of his opposition to the Somoza regime a few years earlier, and he had even been involved in a 1959 action that sought to overturn it by force. His later assassination by Somoza's henchmen on January 10, 1978, was the event that many believe finally brought Nicaragua's middle class into the revolutionary fold. Chamorro was never himself Sandinista, however, and he often editorialized against what he perceived to be the excesses of the movement. His own lineage extended back to the pro–United States Nicaraguan presidents who preceded the Somoza dictatorship. On the balance, both Chamorro and *La Prensa* were moderates in the context of the times. Yet even moderates dared not have their names attached to the stories they wrote, especially when they obviously sympathized with the accused revolutionaries.

Ortega's brazen acts of 1967—bank robberies, guerrilla fighting, and a cold-blooded assassination—should probably be placed in the political context of the times. That context was one of brutal political repression. On January 22, 1967, for example, when conservatives staged a demonstration against the Somoza regime in Managua, the demonstrators remained peaceful, but the National Guard did not. The Guard slaughtered forty demonstrators that day, while it did not itself suffer one casualty. It was not a battle but the repression of democratically minded conservative citizens by a brutal dictatorship. If young men and women resorted to revolutionary violence, who could blame them? They were putting their bodies on the line for the liberation of their homeland. In Ortega's case, that body would rot in jail for a good long time.

Prison

"You lose your shyness a bit," quipped Ortega about the experience of having to wait in line to use a single prison toilet so filthy that no one dared sit down on it, and then to have those waiting for their turn cheer you on if your business was accomplished quickly. It was the same with the single shower. Showers were allowed on Tuesdays, Thursdays, and Fridays in La Modelo prison in Tipitapa on the outskirts of Managua where Ortega was held. After the initial torture—which in addition to the usual kicks and beatings, sometimes while hooded, included electric shocks directly to the testicles—prison life mostly settled down into a blur of animalistic monotony. The prisoners awoke at six or seven in the morning, waited in line to use the toilet, were usually allowed some sunlight at 9:00 A.M., and spent the afternoons reading or writing in their crowded cells. The worst part of the imprisonment was actually not what the prisoners themselves had to endure, but witnessing the suffering of others and being helpless to intervene. When the screams of a fellow prisoner being tortured echoed through the ancient stone building, there was nothing a prisoner could do but endure them. Prisoners felt a similar helplessness when family members visited, their eyes uncontrollably moistening. Prisoners learned how to survive—or learned not to care if they did not—but they could never learn to bear the suffering of others, or to accept their own helplessness.[21]

There were high points, if there can be any such thing in prison life. Ortega and the other political prisoners quickly learned that some of the prison guards privately sympathized with the FSLN. They were simply doing their job to support their families. In prison Ortega learned that it was difficult, almost impossible, to draw a sharp line between the Nicaraguans who supported the revolution and those who did not. Later in life, he would show that he had learned this lesson well by extending merciful amnesty to those who became caught up in the counterrevolution. At the time, though, sympathetic guards managed to see that the Sandinistas usually had access to a hidden radio, so they could listen to news of events happening outside the prison walls. This news was especially important to Ortega after the leftist Salvador Allende was elected president of Chile in 1970 only to have his government toppled by a coup orchestrated by the United States in September 1973. Ortega was a student of politics, and he took the Chilean example to heart. If he ever got out of prison and managed to win the revolution, he vowed that he would not repeat Allende's mistakes. Those mistakes, Ortega concluded, amounted to Allende being too lax in defending his left-wing government. Secretly supportive guards helped Ortega stay abreast of these and other events, and helped him obtain the reading material he desired. Ortega became something of an amateur expert on the French Revolution. He liked to read history, which he scoured for lessons applicable to the present, although he also read classics, such as Proust's *Remembrance of Things Past.*

A prison culture developed that helped to turn Ortega and his fellow political prisoners into national heroes. Both the prisoners and those outside periodically launched hunger strikes in attempts to improve the conditions for the political prisoners, and their continuing incarceration made the political prisoners a constant issue in various political demonstrations.[22] However, this celebrity did not help them much. For the most part, they were housed with the regular prisoners and intentionally kept separate from each other lest their "prison culture" become too organized. Even when let out of their cells, to wait in line for the toilet, for example, the prisoners were often made to sit on the floor. The guards did not want them to stand and mingle with one another. Of course, over the years, the separation was only partly successful. Indeed, it is telling that the only political prisoners serving with Ortega who survived the revolution, Jacinto Suárez and Lenín Cerna, both remained personally loyal to him for life. Almost all of the other surviving Sandinistas split with Ortega during the 1990s—but not Suárez or Cerna. The men seem to have forged a bond in prison that no later differences among them could break. In fact, it appears that simply having served time was the crucial component of this bond. Tomás Borge, who had also served long sentences in Somoza prisons, similarly remained loyal to Ortega and the FSLN for life. Those who defected from the Front, usually in ideological huffs, tended to not have endured long-term incarcerations.

Meanwhile, there were messages from the outside. The National Guard never managed to break the code that the Sandinistas developed for communicating with one another, including prisoners. Ortega generally knew what the FSLN was planning, and to some extent he contributed to those plans as well as to the development of the Front in general. A document he wrote and had smuggled out from prison in 1968, for instance, became part of the Front's discussion literature, and he himself was "promoted" to the National Directorate of the FSLN while in prison (though pending his release).[23] No doubt Humberto Ortega's lobbying on his brother's behalf played a role in his "promotion," although Daniel had already distinguished himself as a loyal Sandinista and talented revolutionary. At the same time, Rosario Murillo, a young woman who Ortega remembered casually from his childhood, began sending him copies of her poems. Murillo came from more affluence than Ortega—she had been sent abroad to study in Europe, for example—but in Managua she secretly allied herself with the FSLN while working as a secretary for La Prensa's literary supplement and developing her own skills as a poet.[24] Murillo never visited, as that would have identified her to the authorities and been too dangerous. She was also married during most of the years that Ortega was imprisoned. Years later, the two would marry.

UNDERSTANDABLY, ORTEGA DOES NOT like to talk about his prison years. They were too painful, and insofar as he does talk about them he sometimes admits that they left him psychologically as well as physically scarred. Neither does he share the poetry he

A FEW MORE MURDERERS AMONG MURDERERS

wrote during those years. His brother, Humberto, claims that Daniel wrote more than ten poems while he was imprisoned, trying his hand at Nicaragua's national art form.[25] Those poems are for the most part kept under lock and key, perhaps because Ortega believes that they are too revealing of his inner life at a vulnerable time. It may be that the poems are just not very good. Poetry can translate poorly, so rendering his words into English may make his poetry appear worse than it is. But Francisco de Asís Fernández, a Granada poet, found four of Ortega's prison poems and published them in an anthology of Nicaraguan political poetry.[26]

The poem that may be most revealing of his prison experiences is one entitled simply "In the Prison." One suspects that it was written early during his incarceration, because its theme is torture and the utter depravity of prison existence. It tells how one street-smart revolutionary experienced prison life:

In the Prison

Kick him like that, like that
in his balls, in his face,
in his ribs.
        Pass the stick, the billy club,
talk, talk son of a bitch,
let's see, get the salt water,
taaaalk, we don't want to fuck you . . .
—Most Honorable and Reverend
        Archbishop,
Most Excellent and Illustrious
        Ambassador.
Peace, respect for others,
wealth, democracy.
    Handcuff him
    put him in Tiny
    you're going to eat your own

shit bastard,
—*La cucaracha, la cucaracha*
no longer can he travel
since he's missing, since he's missing
a leg to walk on.
  The shit and the piss,
damn, so many people.
The deputy cell leader
don't anybody listen to that guy,
let him suckle, let him sleep on the floor
and if he makes a move, beat him
—The work camps, Auschwitz, Buchenwald,
Nicaragua.
Then, today the 4th of July
the veteran (he got rid of a mountain of blacks)
Military Attaché (Black Flag kills them in flight
  and finishes them off on the ground)
will honor
the heroic and gallant
        soldiers.
  Big Lips, John the Writer, Sleepy,
  Little House, —you went away and left me
  in the prison
  when you judged me for nothing
  but a thief—.

New Bull, Little Donkey, the Vulture,
the Black Ace,
        Lollipop,
here comes Lollipop
        Row Boat, judged by his fuck
this kid is the cat's meow.
        If you give me food you can screw me,
for three cigarettes I'll suck you.
The moon, the irises, god,

the apolitical poet.
—Just through here passed
a tiny flying dove,
in its beak it carried flowers
and in its wings its love.
      — Yesterday I gobbled up an arm bone.
      Yes, I've been in the office
      for ten years,
      I'm from the outside.
Hurry up I have to win,
listen to the guys
      how they cry,
they haven't eaten,
tomorrow they're coming
to claim their prize,
finish quickly.
—Watch those men
careful they're taking out a little piece of paper.
They already know
      eyes and ears.
—Yesterday there was a big fight
up on the mountain,
—talk more quietly,
it's all coming together.
Some really pretty little
girls came by to visit,
we don't recognize
Managua in a
      miniskirt.

IT IS OFTEN REPORTED that one of the poems Ortega wrote while in prison is entitled "I Never Saw Managua in Miniskirts." It is possible that the poem does not exist and the reference is to the last line of "In the Prison." Torture is interspersed with desperate prison sex, and both are juxtaposed against the alluring sexual innocence of girls (*pijuditas*) in miniskirts.

Ortega dedicated another poem, "That There Be Fruits," to his mother and sister, although interestingly he makes a boy the protagonist. It is as if women, in this case mothers and sisters, exist for the men in their lives, and care most about what their men achieve. Since this is probably only an unintended aspect of the poem, it suggests that Ortega held fairly traditional views about gender roles, despite Fonseca's more forward-thinking urgings. The poem has another, more overt theme of the costs of reaping the revolutionary harvest being high (and involving taking care of "maggots" like Lacayo), but necessary:

That There Be Fruits

to Lydia and Germania

When the farmers decided
to cultivate the land
they foresaw that they would need to take away
the stones
the thorns
the weeds.
That their hands would be bloodied
and that their feet would be cut
That they would have to take care of
the maggots
and the locusts
and the rats.

That the cleaning would be hard
but that when all was said and done
in spite of fire and wire
the harvest would come

and that in it
the boy
would tiptoe smilingly to find his place
for always

and for the centuries of the centuries.

Another poem repeats the same theme, and once again infuses it (perhaps subconsciously) with gendered allusions. Even so, the political point is clear, and the poem reveals something of Ortega's classical education. (It was always too easy for his enemies, especially in the United States, to portray him as little more than an uncultured street thug. President George H. W. Bush, for example, dismissed him as an "animal at a garden party."[27] Though neither an intellectual nor pretending to be, Ortega was comparatively well educated.) The Greek (and before then, Libyan) myth to which he alludes is interestingly a gendered one. Medusa essentially symbolizes the evil mother, sirens are temptresses, and amazons are fierce female warriors. While making his political point, the enemy is feminized:

The Ships

We know where
the Golden Fleece is.
They use it
to construct
buildings and mansions,
to open foreign
bank accounts,
to take their little
airplane trips, and
to bathe their dogs

in lotion.
We know that it's OURS
and we're readying the ships.
You say Medusa
has an armored vest
and sharp claws.
We know.
    Perseus is with us,
    and there won't be siren songs
    or amazons.
        NO!

Finally, there is Ortega's most complex and disjointed available poem. It is difficult to discern any one theme in it. Once again, it assumes traditional gender roles. It is a poem about his mother's hardships, though it shifts to a justification of his own revolutionary actions—including the guilt that he claims not to feel for being a murderer. Perhaps the most tantalizing lines in the poem refer to the "illusion" of children. Ortega could be referring to himself and his brothers, then all caught up in revolutionary activities and unable to be good children, but it appears that he is referring to Sigfrido and Germania, the children who died. The poem is too cryptic to tell, and its attempt to end on an optimistic note is strained. However, it is another political poem, couched in the personal:

Mama: What It Cost Her to Throw Her Sorrows to the Fire

At this age
to wash, to cook, to iron,
to run after medicine
three times
to keep the landlord's ire at bay

cutting off the electricity
cutting off the water
to get eggs from where there are no chickens
. . . is not easy.

2

When she carried the illusion
of children
that told us
—even if it had been only in that last moment—
the tranquility that we only can hear.
It's not easy to find yourself
when all you have is what never had been
when you finish the same as you began
—hurrying—
when you have no grown children
just secret dead captives
when there is no Happy Birthday
no Mother's Day
no Merry Christmas
no New Year.

3

And the truth is that all this
if it were as we wished it to be
would be disgusting
would be unchristian—if it is christian—
criminal is the *mot juste.*
And we're just
a few more murderers
among murderers
who see with eyes
hearts that don't feel.
A few more among the murderers
—and really it's true

it wouldn't be easy at all—
from this million of mothers and children
that in only these four
inches of earth
—if they were lucky—
breakfasted
lunched
and dined
... on one mango.

4
The good thing is that we go on learning
and being that way
if it really is true that we're still running
it's not like the beginning
for there's more optimism
than regrets.

On the whole, Ortega's prison poetry shows a political mind that is experimenting with poetic expression but may be too rooted in practical politics to allow the reach for artistic expression to become fully unleashed. Ortega's writing suggests openness to the arts that many would welcome in a political leader. If there is a more serious criticism, it might be that the author seems strangely unaware of the degree to which themes of gender encroach into each poem, sometimes, it seems, subconsciously. There is nothing of course unusual about a man imprisoned during his twenties having his thoughts turn to issues of sex. Even so, Ortega's subconscious preoccupation with gender roles coupled with an incarceration that prevents him from socializing with women hints at troubles to come.

ORTEGA'S PRISON YEARS WERE, as the court intended, not good ones. At an age when free men learn a lot about themselves, the world, and sex, Ortega learned how to defecate in front of a cheering crowd. He did read seriously, educating himself for the challenges that would come, and his skills at handling people underwent refinement—as they must when survival requires getting along with the worst of humanity in awful conditions. Besides this, prison may have kept him alive. The course he was on prior to his capture was bound to lead to violent death; that was the fate of most of his comrades. By being caged, Ortega may have been protected. Though his prison experience left him psychologically damaged, he also discovered that the survival skills he mastered helped him to become a better revolutionary. He was tougher, more ruthless and calculating, when he left prison than he was when he entered it. Ironically, Anastasio Somoza Debayle may not only have saved the life of one of the leaders of the revolution that would topple his regime, but also instilled in him the psychological skills required to do so.

But first Ortega had to get out. For that, he needed help from the outside. For over seven years the FSLN remained neither powerful enough to stage a prison break nor popular enough to win the release of its prisoners by political means. In fact, during the 1960s and into the 1970s, Nicaragua was a revolutionary's worst nightmare. The Somoza regime's repression prevented the Sandinistas from developing into an effective insurrectional force. It took a literal earthquake to change this state of affairs. In the meantime, both the Front and the political prisoners languished.

The FSLN Languishes

REVOLUTIONARIES DREAD IMPROVING SOCIAL conditions as much as they hate repression, since either one extinguishes the fires of revolutionary enthusiasm rapidly. When a regime successfully represses would-be revolutionaries, it obviously thwarts the revolution they hope to spark. Yet repression can be turned into a public relations campaign by revolutionaries, who can use it to illustrate the brutality of a regime and thus to advance their cause. It is different when a regime manages to improve life for the majority of those it governs, or at least provides them with a realistic hope of improvements. This derails a revolution—without providing any public relations leverage. A population optimistic about improving conditions tends to support an existing regime. It is, of course, all slightly more complicated than this.[28] It is less about how much conditions are improving (or even deteriorating) under a regime, and more how conditions compare to the expectations the people have for them. It basically boils down to regimes successfully using a combination of the carrot and the stick. The carrot is offered to the people at large, coaxing them into loyalty by improving their lives, while the stick is used to beat back the remaining malcontents.

During the 1960s, the Sandinistas watched the Somoza regime use the carrot-and-stick approach—and in particular the carrot—with enormous effectiveness. In fact, for over a decade after the 1956 assassination of Anastasio Somoza García, the two instruments of power were wielded by two different Somoza brothers. One brother, Anastasio Somoza Debayle, headed the National Guard; he wielded the stick. He had been trained for this job at West Point. It is said that the elder Somoza did not believe that his namesake was well suited to a political career, because he was by temperament too selfish and ill-equipped with negotiating skills. Anastasio Somoza Debayle more or less admitted as much himself. Tachito, as he was called, considered himself more of a businessman than a politician. He confessed that he felt more at home in the United States than in Nicaragua and seemed to prefer gallivanting around the globe with his mistress to sitting in Nicaragua watching the pornography films he collected. In fact, by the early 1970s his wife and children had already settled in Miami, and he jokingly referred to himself as a "Latin from Manhattan."[29] He displayed his ruthlessness by keeping a tiger caged in a cell adjacent to his particularly prized political prisoners, just so he could threaten them with a good mauling.

His other son, Luís Somoza Debayle, was of different temperament. The elder Somoza felt that Luís possessed the skills of a
politician. Accordingly, he was sent to Louisiana State University
for his education, not West Point, and otherwise groomed for
a political future. As was planned, Luís assumed the presidency
after his father was assassinated. In that office he dangled the carrot before Nicaragua with considerable skill.

The unique aspect of Luís Somoza's presidency is that he gave
it up. Luís was the only Somoza ever to allow another to occupy
the presidency of Nicaragua, which he did between 1963 and 1967
when René Schick and then briefly Lorenzo Guerrero served. Luís
Somoza retained the power behind the scenes, however, and everyone knew this. Nicaraguans at the time distinguished between
what they called the "big president" and the "little president," or
Luís Somoza versus his stand-ins. Yet they persuaded themselves
of a thaw in the Somoza dictatorship during those years. Indeed,
under Luís Somoza a number of Nicaragua's long-dormant political parties were reenergized. In the 1967 presidential election,
a Conservative Party candidate opposed to the Somoza regime,
Fernando Agüero, even launched a serious campaign for the
office. Agüero and his supporters deluded themselves—a rally on
behalf of Agüero's candidacy was the one that drew the National
Guard's literal fire on and resulted in the deaths of forty demonstrators—but the fact that Nicaraguans could believe that a real
presidential election was possible reveals Luís Somoza's success:
he allowed Nicaraguans to hope for significant political reforms.
In fact, had Luís Somoza not suffered a fatal heart attack on April
13, 1967, it is possible that Nicaragua might have groped its way
toward liberation without a revolution.

Nicaragua even prospered economically under Luís. Between
1960 and 1971, the country's GDP increased at an inflation-adjusted
average of over 7 percent annually, which after subtracting population growth represented about a 4 percent real improvement every
year. This growth rate allowed Nicaragua to rank third highest in
all of Latin America in speed of development.[30] There are numer-

ous reasons to have reservations about the economic growth during this period, though. Among them is that corruption remained rife, with a Somoza or one of his cronies usually taking a payoff from any lucrative business venture. Nicaragua developed a technocratic class charged with managing the country's development aid, but many suspected this class was unnecessary and wasteful. Even when corruption and bureaucratic inefficiencies were not problems, the development model was not an ideal one from the standpoint of the population as a whole. Much economic attention was put into growing and exporting coffee and cotton. This was a boon to agribusiness—some 50 percent of the farmland was owned by only 2 percent of the farms—but not as advantageous for Nicaragua's small farmers, many of whom were displaced by the mechanized agribusinesses.[31] Developing an export-oriented agriculture caused Nicaragua to lose its capacity to feed itself from its own farms, and though exports increased dramatically, imports increased faster.[32] This was not a sustainable model of economic development over the long run. Borge summarizes some of these criticisms of the economy during this period by writing that economic growth was "a game of mirrors" premised upon "fictitious businesses and outright thievery" that allowed the wealthy to drink Scotch with slices of salted mango while the real economy "grew a scant few inches."[33] Nevertheless, it was economic development, and for the first time in their remembered history Nicaraguans had a reason to feel optimistic about their future. In fact, the growing affluence did trickle down somewhat to the population at large. The percentage of children enrolled in primary school increased from 66 percent in 1960 to 92 percent in 1977, while high school enrollments increased from 7 to 29 percent. At the same time, infant mortality rates declined, life expectancy rose, and the number of physicians per capita increased.[34]

Luís Somoza was not the only one behind these improvements in Nicaragua's politics and economy. Some of them may be attributed to the creation of a Central American Common Market, which encouraged trade among several Central American countries. A much larger player was the United States, which during the presidential administration of John Kennedy took a serious and initially enlightened interest in Latin America. John Kennedy, as well as his brother Robert Kennedy, believed as early as the 1950s—that is, even before the Cuban revolution—that Latin America was on a dangerous course. The principal problem, in their opinion, was economic. Secretary of State Dean Rusk summarized this problem a few years later by observing that "the defense budget of the United States . . . is roughly equal to the gross national product of all of Latin America."[35] Robert Kennedy extracted the challenge posed by this impoverishment when he concluded, "So a revolution is coming—a revolution which will be peaceful if we are wise enough; compassionate if we care enough; successful if we are fortunate enough—but a revolution which is coming whether we will it or not."[36] John Kennedy chose to act. In March 1961 he announced a program called the "Alliance for Progress" that asked for the direct and indirect investment of one hundred billion dollars into Latin America to promote its economic development.[37] Nicaragua received its share of these development dollars, and correspondingly, private U.S. investments in Nicaragua rose from eighteen million dollars in 1960 to seventy-five million in 1970. In fact, private U.S. investments rose faster in Nicaragua than in any other Latin American country during the 1960s.[38] Although the merits of the so-called modernization theory promoted by Kennedy administration aide Walter Rostow that justified these kinds of investments into poor countries as a means of sparking their economic development remains debated, these investments did assist Nicaragua. Moreover, with the checks came leverage. For example, Luís Somoza was induced to temper his authoritarianism lest he incur the wrath of the United States.

The enlightened assistance that the United States provided to Nicaragua, however, came coupled with darker assistance, with the result that the United States strengthened the Somoza stick at the same time that it sweetened the regime's carrot. The Cold War became a justification for increasing military assistance.

While President Kennedy believed in promoting economic development in Latin America, he also believed that restricting Soviet influence in the region should be a primary objective of U.S. policy. The bloody revolutions the Alliance for Progress was intended to prevent were after all assumed to be communist revolutions of the Cuban variety, and Cuba had turned into Kennedy's Achilles' heel. Moreover, Kennedy was not above patronizing political ethnocentrism. He believed, for example, that "governments of the civil-military type . . . are the most effective in containing communist penetration in Latin America."[39] Thus, while U.S. development dollars flowed into Latin America, so did U.S. military aid. By 1963 U.S. military aid to Latin America had increased 150 percent since 1960. Nicaragua received its share of this aid.[40] At the same time, the United States encouraged its Latin American allies to send their military police to the School of the Americas, where they received training in advanced military techniques by world-class experts. Somoza accepted this offer and sent all of his National Guard officers for a year of training. In fact, more Nicaraguan National Guardsmen were trained at the U.S. School of the Americas than were soldiers from any other Latin American country.[41] In other words, the United States both bankrolled and trained Nicaragua's repressive National Guard. Meanwhile, lest any doubt develop about the United States' willingness to use its own stick when it chose to, President Lyndon Johnson sent twenty-two thousand troops into the Dominican Republic in April and May 1965 to quash a revolt there. The invasion violated the nonintervention pledge to which the United States had agreed when it signed the charter of the Organization of American States in 1948, but the United States was not about to allow a legalistic technicality like this to prevent it from invading any country it chose to when it wanted to.

AFTER HE BECAME PRESIDENT in 1967, Anastasio Somoza's indifference to politics generally convinced him of the wisdom of keeping the effective policies of his brother and the United States in place, while he retained a firm grip on the National Guard. Late in that year, a "Special National Intelligence Estimate" produced by the Central Intelligence Agency (there were twenty-five U.S. "military advisors" in Nicaragua[42]) on "The Political Prospects in Nicaragua over the Next Year or So" prudently withheld judgment, pending the behavior of the newly elected Anastasio Somoza. The report was generally optimistic about the country's continuing "political stability." The CIA was aware of the FSLN, but curiously called it Cuban-sponsored while also acknowledging that there was no evidence of direct ties to the communist island—a kind of conflation of the Nicaraguan Revolution with the Cuban Revolution that would continue to influence U.S. policy toward Nicaragua for many years to come.[43] The CIA nevertheless regarded the FSLN as feeble. Noting that the Sandinistas probably had fewer than a hundred adherents at the time, the intelligence report judged that the "FSLN's present capabilities for conducting armed insurrection appear to be small."[44] The report was correct. Moreover, since Anastasio Somoza did not make any serious governing misstep for over five years, the general conclusions of the CIA report held true well into the 1970s.

Everyone in the FSLN believed that the economic advances and political reforms of the 1960s were a sham, and they fumed. They did not believe that the course of economic development that Nicaragua was on was sustainable, much less for the people, but they understood that it suppressed dissatisfaction with the Somoza regime. Neither did they believe that the political reforms of Luís Somoza would endure or would be sufficient if they did, but they realized that they gave the people hope. Indeed, they watched in 1965 as radicals lost the student elections at the National University, then the next year as they lost the elections at the University of Central America.[45] The mood of the country was turning reformist, and when the manifesto issued by intellectuals on the tenth anniversary of the July 23, 1959, massacre that had given the "Generation of '59" its name called only for reforms, that mood was underscored.[46] Meanwhile, the FSLN knew that the Guardsmen who hunted them were among the best-financed and best-trained repressive military police in the world, thanks to the United States. And few of their fellow Nicaraguans cared that the Somoza regime remained an exploitative and repressive one—or cared enough to support a revolution. The typical Nicaraguan read news accounts like those covering Ortega's trial in 1969 with keen interest, but their zeal tended to be reformist, not revolutionary.

As the 1960s melted into the 1970s, the FSLN languished. Many of its members were killed by the Guard; others were imprisoned. The most notorious who had avoided capture went into exile, mostly to Costa Rica, which in effect became the FSLN's headquarters. Humberto Ortega essentially settled there and emerged as one of the Front's key leaders (although his leadership did not meet with unanimous approval, as Fonseca's did). Humberto Ortega devoted most of his energies to plotting insurrectionist strategy, although he also participated in a bank robbery in Costa Rica. He was captured and briefly imprisoned, as was Carlos Fonseca in September 1969, an event that made the headlines in Nicaragua. The two then made a daring escape, during which Humberto was wounded so seriously that he permanently lost the use of his right arm. Fonseca also spent considerable time in Cuba, researching the life of Sandino and otherwise working on the ideological aspects of the Sandinista movement. Inside Nicaragua, other FSLN workers attempted to organize the rural peasantry.[47] These efforts required living with the peasants and were generally successful. Later, the FSLN could count on some support from them, a support they had sorely lacked in the early 1960s. However, these efforts would only bear fruit in the future. At the moment, the main problem the Front faced was the conditions inside Nicaragua. Until they deteriorated to the point at which the public would welcome a revolutionary agenda, the FLSN was for most practical purposes powerless.

As it happened, nature came to their aid.

Two Seismic Events

THE EARTHQUAKE THAT SAVAGED Nicaragua two days before Christmas 1972 was no ordinary tremor. It had been forty-one years since an earthquake of this magnitude rocked Nicaragua's Pacific lowlands. The results were disastrous. Managua, the country's capital and most populous city, was leveled. Residents could no longer find their way around the city, as most of the familiar landmarks were destroyed. The human toll was catastrophic. Ten thousand people died, twenty thousand more were injured, and fully three-quarters of the remaining 325,000 residents were left homeless.[48] Unfortunately for Ortega, the fortress of La Modelo prison withstood the earthquake. It was the exception. Ortega's childhood home was demolished, though his parents and siblings survived.

Instead of assisting the suffering people, though, Somoza, his cronies, and the National Guard used the disaster to enrich themselves even further, and their callous greed was apparent to all. The United States, for example, immediately sent thirty-two million dollars for disaster relief to the crippled country, but only about half of the money ever made its way to the victims of the earthquake.[49] The other half disappeared into the pockets of Nicaragua's government elites. Accounting for all of the sixteen million may be impossible, but most of it appears to have been siphoned off through bogus real estate deals. A person would purchase a piece of property (most of them on the outskirts of Managua) at obvious fire sale prices and then flip it to a buyer who used U.S. aid dollars to buy it. In one case, probably the most egregious one, a government official paid seventy thousand dollars for a piece of property that he conveniently sold to the government for three million a few months later.[50] As a result of this kind of misuse of aid dollars, Managua was not rebuilt after the earthquake. In fact, it has never been rebuilt. To this day, earthquake rubble remains in Managua, and instead of a downtown Managua has a new central shopping mall. The city itself has burgeoned into a hodgepodge of disconnected barrios sprawling uncontrollably for miles. As late as the 1980s, Ortega was repeating the familiar joke to visitors: "How are you finding Managua? If you find it, let me know where it is."[51]

But the corrupt mismanagement of foreign aid dollars was only one of the problems that beset Nicaragua in the aftermath of the 1972 earthquake. Another problem was that the National Guard itself looted Managua. No doubt some of the Guardsmen did not, and probably many of them switched back and forth between greed and helpfulness depending upon how they felt about a given situation, but after the earthquake there were next to no Nicaraguans left with any trust in their National Guard. Meanwhile, the United States dispatched six hundred troops to help maintain order. However, when the soldiers pitched their tents in the gardens of Somoza's residence, their physical proximity to the dictator declared exactly whose order they intended to maintain. There is no evidence that the soldiers from the United States participated in any of the lootings or otherwise took personal advantage of the catastrophe, but they were ordered to sit idly by while the local militia did.

Even Nicaraguans, accustomed as they were to living under a dictator, were aghast at the callousness the Somoza regime displayed in the aftermath of the earthquake, and the tide of public sentiment began to turn more solidly against it. Helping to turn the tide was Somoza's insistence upon running for reelection in 1974, a violation of a constitutional provision that his brother, Luís, had approved. It would obviously be another sham election. The shift against Somoza was most evident (and perhaps most important) in the business community, which had hitherto tolerated the Somoza dynasty in exchange for the economic opportunities it had managed to provide, but which became increasingly incensed by the regime's blatant and callous corruption following the earthquake. The tide also turned in the Roman Catholic Church, which refused to allow its relief efforts to be politicized, and thus corrupted, by the regime. As the 1974 election approached, the Nicaraguan bishops even issued a pastoral letter denouncing it.[52] Meanwhile, Monsignor Miguel Obando y Bravo sold a car that Somoza had given to him as a gift, using the proceeds for the work of the Church. Pedro Chamorro saw to it that the corruption of the Somoza regime was well covered in the pages of *La Prensa*, and university students began to replace their reformist sentiments with more radical ones. Recruitment into the FSLN, though still low in absolute numbers, began to increase. It might be an exaggeration, but Clifford Krauss writes that the only support Somoza had left came from the National Guard and Washington.[53]

The time was therefore ripe for the FSLN to act. To be sure, neither the country nor the Sandinistas was ready for revolution. The country might have been tilting solidly against Somoza, but it was not yet prepared for blood in the streets. The Sandinistas were not prepared for revolution either. Even if they, and in particular Humberto Ortega, were fairly far along in teaching themselves the strategies and tactics required for a successful revolution in Nicaragua, they lacked manpower, weapons, and the tools that a successful revolution would require. It was a sign of how much they had developed as a revolutionary organization that the events of 1972–1974 did not lure them into engaging in the kinds of quixotic and futile insurrectionist campaigns that they had launched in the past. This time they would proceed with more calculated coolness—they would proceed with the objective of actually winning the revolution.

The plan they settled upon was to raid a Christmas party those in the Somoza circle would be attending, take the revelers hostage, and demand as ransom both a good deal of money and the release of their political prisoners. In this way, they reasoned, they could simultaneously capture the public limelight for their cause and augment their funds and personnel. The plot was touch-and-go the whole way. Although they were well trained and prepared, the FSLN operatives who were to carry it out did not even know until the morning of the siege that it would take place that day or what the target would be. FSLN members had been sent out to various locations where Christmas parties might be held, including foreign embassies, under false pretenses in order to sketch the floor plans of the locations.[54] As it happened, the Sandinista leadership heard that a Christmas party would be hosted on December 27, 1974, at the home of José Maria (Chema) Castillo, president of Nicaragua's Central Bank, and in attendance would be various dignitaries, including U.S. Ambassador Turner Shelton, two relatives of Somoza, and the manager of the Esso Oil Company. An FSLN operative posing as an air-conditioner repairman managed to gain access to the house that morning to sketch the floor plan, so the raid was on.[55]

Thirteen FSLN guerrillas, five women and eight men, stormed the party, and with only a couple of exceptions the raid went flawlessly. One exception was that Castillo himself was killed. The FSLN had not wanted casualties, but Castillo went for a weapon and the guerrillas had no choice. (His daughter would later join the FSLN.) The other exception was that the U.S. ambassador, Turner Shelton, had left the party early, preventing the Sandinistas from holding him hostage. (Shelton could not speak Spanish, hardly a requirement for an ambassador to Nicaragua in Washington's eyes, so had probably left early out of boredom.) The basic objectives of the raid, however, were met. After allowing the staff to go, the guerrillas held fourteen prominent hostages. Somoza, then in Miami, quickly returned to Nicaragua to negotiate with the captors. With Monsignor Obando y Bravo acting as the intermediary, Somoza eventually agreed to pay a one-million-dollar ransom, allow the publication of uncensored FSLN propaganda, release the requested political prisoners, and provide a plane on which the guerrillas and released prisoners would fly to Cuba. Better, when the guerrillas and the political prisoners left for the airport, they were cheered by crowds of ordinary Nicaraguans along the way.[56] This would not be an unpopular or unwanted revolution when it occurred. On the flight to Cuba, Monsignor Obando y Bravo worried that a bomb may have been planted on the plane. He was assured that the FSLN had checked over the plane thoroughly and in fact forced the hostages to fly with them. They were no longer quixotic amateurs, but seasoned revolutionaries. They amused themselves during the trip by counting the million dollars in ransom money.[57] It was not a lot of money for Somoza, who was then worth around five hundred million, but it was a pretty decent nest egg for the revolutionaries.

Among the political prisoners released in those final December days was Daniel Ortega. His parents and his sister greeted his release with cake and Coca-Colas. It had been a long separation, and the Ortega family was never so anti-Yankee as to refrain from Coca-Colas when a celebratory occasion called for them. Yet he couldn't stay long—he had to join his brothers in leading the revolution that everyone hoped would liberate Nicaragua. It was the last time he ever saw his father, and he always regretted that Don Daniel did not live to see the revolution triumph. At the time, though, that triumph lay five years in the future, and the repression by the National Guard that followed this FSLN action caused many to doubt that liberation would ever come. However, these doubters underestimated Daniel and Humberto Ortega, as well as the spirit of the Nicaraguans who eventually welcomed the revolution the way they had cheered the guerrillas.

3

THE BATTLE WITHIN
AND WITHOUT

"I FELT TENSE IN freedom, claustrophobic," Ortega recalled about his release after seven years in the Somoza prison. "I just had a hard time. . . . If I entered a room, I would want to get out quickly. If I got into a car, I would start feeling desperate. It was as if the cell were always with me."[1] Although Ortega went on to say that he "overcame this" after a few months, the truth appears to be more complicated. Sergio Ramírez, who later served as Ortega's vice president, for example, believes that Ortega still retains a "prison personality"—"lonely, solitary, mistrustful, hard."[2] Ortega also continued to display eccentric characteristics consistent with long-term incarceration. When he became head of state and hosted dinner parties in his home—which is a private compound rather than a state structure, guarded by private security forces— he did not dine with his guests. Instead, he would slip into the kitchen and eat with the staff.[3] It is as if, after so many years of being treated like a caged animal, he continued to prefer to live like one.

In fact, the claustrophobia that Ortega experienced during his first few months of freedom only lifted when he returned to a prison-like lifestyle. This occurred in mid-1975, when he returned from Cuba to work in the Managua underground. He was at that point one of the Front's two on-site coordinators in Managua, sharing responsibilities with Eduardo Contreras, the commander of the Christmas party raid that had freed him from prison. By 1976, Contreras had been killed in a shootout with the Guard at a Managua safe house, and Ortega had assumed full responsibilities for the city. Contreras's death underscored the perilous conditions endured by the Sandinistas living underground. Ortega lived in a series of safe houses. His days were typically spent cooped up in small rooms in small houses, where the sweltering heat made dressing in more than underwear or shorts uncomfortable, and where speech louder than a whisper was too risky. He usually only went out at night—stealthily and often in disguise—and always used his alias, Enrique. Leticia Herrera, who worked with him in the underground, recalled the fear under which they lived in those days. Remembering one narrow escape in particular, she said that had Ortega waited only a few minutes more for a night meeting with a contact he would have been killed.[4] Amazingly, Ortega thrived in that environment. "I felt fine—I felt great!" he exclaimed. "All the defense mechanisms I had developed . . . became activated again. . . . The claustrophobia went away; everything went away."[5]

One of the ironies of Ortega's prison years was that they helped equip him with the psychological traits necessary for successful clandestine action, and provided him time to mature as a revolutionary strategist. As a result, although he entered and exited Nicaragua regularly during the middle and late 1970s, he was never again captured by the Guard. This required some skills in stealth, such as the time he snuck back into Nicaragua aboard a boat transporting livestock, but he enjoyed that lifestyle and was good at it.[6] However, while Ortega's psychological traits helped him succeed as a revolutionary, they had a darker manifestation as well. "I have a macho formation," he admitted to no one's surprise.[7] More unusual, though in keeping with the ideals of the Sandinista revolution, which from its inception included women as equals, was Ortega's addition that, "Consciously, I oppose machismo."[8] The problem, though, he went on to say, was that his macho point of view was largely subconscious. As events would soon reveal, this unconscious macho formation coupled with his emotionally stilting prison experiences catapulted him down a path of sexual oppression. His time in Somoza's cell made him that kind of man too.

Ortega soon became synonymous with the Nicaraguan Revolution. One of the reasons for this is frankly that many other Sandinista leaders were killed. Carlos Fonseca was killed in the mountains of northeastern Nicaragua on November 7, 1976. Daniel Ortega, supported by his brother Humberto, filled the FSLN's leadership vacuum. Some resented his rise, arguing that he manipulated his way into it through cunning or worse. To one degree or another, however, almost everyone in the FSLN suppressed their doubts and supported his leadership. They did so because Daniel Ortega, together with his brother Humberto, finally created a revolution that had remained only a dream for the others.

Making the Revolution

THE 1974 CHRISTMAS PARTY raid catapulted the FSLN into the revolutionary limelight at the same time that it provided a welcome influx of funds. The Front was nevertheless hardly ready to lead a revolution. While their daring defiance of the Somoza regime inspired many, the Sandinistas had only a fledgling political organization inside the country. Ortega's main responsibility between 1975 and early 1977 was to build a political organization in the nation's capital. It is unlikely that the FSLN had more than a couple hundred members in 1975, probably fewer. The Front also had virtually no support abroad. Although Castro graciously hosted the Sandinistas in Cuba, even he did not provide the FSLN with significant support until 1978. "The best help I can give you," Castro reportedly told Edén Pastora of the Sandinistas when he asked for help, "is not to help you at all."[9]

Worse, the Sandinistas were beginning to squabble among themselves. Humberto Ortega writes that the first hints of internal disagreements surfaced during a meeting of FSLN leaders held at a farm in Panama in late June and early July 1974.[10] Shirley Christian reported that the first signs of a serious rupture within the Sandinista ranks appeared in the aftermath of the Christmas party raid. Jaime Wheelock, a Nicaraguan who had studied in Europe and Chile, had returned to Nicaragua with solid credentials as an academic Marxist. He joined the FSLN and was promptly named to the Directorate, its inner circle. Wheelock did not support the Christmas party raid, calling it a "petit bourgeois diversion." In Wheelock's opinion, a successful Nicaraguan revolution would have to follow the more arduous Marxist path of organizing the proletariat into a revolutionary class, and a showy spectacle like a terrorist raid on a party of elites was just a detour. Evidently Wheelock argued his case abrasively, because tempers flared. Before long he was expelled from the FSLN and even briefly hunted by a Sandinista execution squad.[11] Meanwhile, Wheelock's forcefully argued opinions fueled other internal disagreements, with the result that by 1976 the FSLN had splintered into three factions. The animosity among the factions was so intense that Castro advised Colombian writer Gabriel García Márquez not to become too close to the Sandinistas because he could never know when one of its leaders would knife another in the back.[12]

The three factions within the FSLN became known as "tendencies" and eventually were given names. The faction that followed Wheelock was called the Proletarian Tendency (TP), and it was characterized by the insistence upon organizing the rural and urban working classes to mount a class-based revolution. The TP was the smallest and most intellectual of the tendencies and probably the least influential in the long run. Against it was a tendency known as the Prolonged People's War (GPP). Favored by Tomás Borge, soon to be the only surviving founder of the FSLN (as well as for a while by Castro, whose advice was regularly sought by the

Sandinistas), the GPP called for continued guerrilla warfare based in the mountains in fidelity with Sandino's original campaign. It was to some extent the strategy that had won the Cuban Revolution. The hope was that these attacks would eventually spark a national revolution. Finally, a third tendency, usually simply called the Terceristas, or sometimes the Insurrectional Tendency (TI), formed around the Ortega brothers, although Eduardo Contreras helped develop it before his death and Victor Tirado soon joined them in promoting it.[13] The Terceristas believed that it would be wisest to bring the battles to the cities and enlist the support of all groups opposed to Somoza, from whatever region or class they came, including the Church and the business sector.

Since there were three tendencies, the criticisms of each involved the other two teaming up against it. This made all the debates two against one and prevented a majority from forming in support of any one plan. In fact, the Sandinistas did not even like majorities, preferring to discuss matters until they could reach a consensus. In this case, however, even a majority was impossible. The Prolonged People's War tendency and the Terceristas argued that the Proletarian Tendency was imprisoned by an impractical Marxist-Leninist orthodoxy. The Proletarian Tendency and the Terceristas argued that the advocates of the Prolonged People's War were reveling in a romantic fantasy of rural guerrilla warfare that was no longer relevant. The Prolonged People's War and the Proletarian Tendency argued that the Terceristas were bereft of any guiding principles at all. They were accused of being opportunists who sought victory by any means possible, regardless of the compromises they had to make to achieve it. The disagreements among the tendencies were thoroughly debated and mutually understood, but they remained unresolved. The division of the FSLN was not all bad for the Sandinistas, though, since each tendency continued to work in the areas that it had staked out for itself under the broad rubric of Sandinismo. The tacit agreement among the factions in 1976 and 1977 was that they would all work toward the same general goal, known as the "accumulation of forces." This involved each tendency organizing the constituencies that it believed paramount—the TP among the workers, the GPP in the mountains, and the TI in the cities—with the hope of resolving their differences with one another later, after the FSLN was stronger. In hindsight, the strategy of "accumulating forces" was helpful. When it came time to launch the revolution, the Sandinistas enjoyed considerable good will among the people both in the mountains and in the cities—the GPP and Terceristas had made solid organizational inroads—and had managed to raise small armies of recruits. It is less clear that Wheelock's class-based organizational efforts were successful, since when the revolution came the bourgeoisie was at its helm. However, there was a Marxist cast to the revolution, and workers seemed to feel entitled to more authority than in fact they received, so the TP had obviously made inroads.

For Ortega, the period of accumulating forces involved identifying and recruiting members into the FSLN in Managua. The Front was actually quite selective in its search for members, carefully assessing potential recruits' abilities before inviting them to join. Mere hotheads and rabble-rousers were passed over in favor of a number with university backgrounds and other evidence of intelligence and responsibility. The recruitment was undertaken through personal contacts followed by personal invitations. A person could not simply join—membership came at the cost of being hunted by the National Guard—so new members had to be personally and carefully recruited. The procedure involved an existing member, operating under an alias, befriending a potential recruit long enough to be certain he or she was appropriate for the FSLN, and then extending an invitation to join. If the recruit agreed, the person who had recruited him or her became his or her contact person, known as the "responsible." Periodically a responsible would contact a member and assign a task, at first usually something innocuous like delivering an envelope somewhere, although as new members proved themselves they were drawn up into greater responsibilities. Members were never told more than they needed to know to complete a given task, and they were initially unaware of the true identities of their responsibles. Ortega's role was essentially that of responsible for the responsibles in Managua. Gioconda Belli, a prominent writer who rose toward the top of the FSLN, had as a responsible first Contreras and then Camilo Ortega, Daniel's younger brother. Only later did she learn either's real names or that Daniel Ortega had taken charge of the entire operation.[14]

In his capacity as head of the Managua underground, Ortega acted as the link between it and the FSLN as a whole. As such, he did not remain in Managua consistently, but traveled quite a bit to meetings elsewhere. For the most part, he traveled to Costa Rica, where the FSLN increasingly headquartered itself. Though officially pacifist and therefore neutral, Costa Rica's leaders, in particular its former president and strongman José Figueres, were not unaware of or unsympathetic to the revolutionary ferment in Nicaragua. More practically, they realized that like it or not they would eventually be drawn up into Nicaragua's troubles, whatever shape they took. While in the middle and late 1970s Costa Rica had not yet taken sides, the authorities made no concerted effort to locate or banish the Sandinistas who were increasingly living there. As Sandinista sympathizers in Nicaragua were found by the National Guard and forced to flee the country, a network of Sandinista safe houses developed in Costa Rica, mainly in the eastern San José suburbs of San Pedro and Sabanilla. Public opinion in Costa Rica was also anti-Somoza, although it was not necessarily pro-Sandinista before the revolution.

One Sandinista living in the southern San José suburb of Desamperados was Humberto Ortega. Although he was wanted for a bank robbery and for a jailbreak that had left one guard dead, Costa Rica made no serious attempt to find him. Edén Pastora, no doubt expressing sentiments shared by others, later faulted Humberto for essentially sitting out the revolution in Costa Rica instead of joining the fight in Nicaragua.[15] Humberto, however, had lost the use of his arm from wounds incurred during his jailbreak, which limited his abilities as a combatant. He was by disposition more of a thinker and a strategist than a man of action. And he was not especially personable. Belli, for example, writes that he had nervous ticks that made others uncomfortable, and that his fast-talking manner made him appear silly, like the Peter Sellers character in *The Pink Panther*. She also regarded him as duplicitous, quick to spin his own failures into successes, "like a Houdini."[16]

What he did contribute while in Costa Rica were several long strategy documents, and in 1979 he became one of the first Sandinistas (after Fonseca) to publish a book on the history of Nicaragua's revolutionary struggle.[17] Though still only representing the Tercerista tendency, Humberto's house in Costa Rica gradually became the headquarters of the revolution. During the period of the accumulation of forces, his brothers Daniel and Camilo frequently visited. By 1978 their mother also lived in Costa Rica, and it would appear that by 1977 Daniel also had a house there.

Years later, Humberto recalled the conversations the brothers had in those times. In essence, they were becoming frustrated with the strategy of accumulating forces. Although all three tendencies recruited new members, the National Guard was capturing or killing members faster. Fonseca's head—or maybe his hands, stories vary—had been delivered to Somoza in late 1976. Tomás Borge was once again in prison. By late summer 1977, Somoza's intelligence informed him that the Sandinistas had been reduced to fewer than fifty members, a number that Humberto Ortega writes was not far off.[18] The FSLN was simply losing ground.

Worse, the Ortega brothers worried that it was losing its public standing as the vanguard of the revolution at the very time that conditions for a revolution were ripening. Domestic opposition to the Somoza regime was growing, but it was mainly channeled into a reform-minded group, the Democratic Union of Liberation (UDEL), founded in 1974 and headed by the popular but comparatively moderate editor of *La Prensa*, Pedro Joaquín Chamorro. Unless the Sandinistas did something to reclaim their leadership of the revolution, a regime change could occur that would leave the FSLN behind. The Ortega brothers feared that a regime change spearheaded by moderates would not be radical enough. It might well amount only to "Somocismo without Somoza," or a similar regime under a different dictator. At the same time, while foreign support for a regime change in Nicaragua grew, the FSLN was not always thought to be the organization that would, or should, bring it about. José Figueres in Costa Rica hedged his bets, doing no more than supporting them indirectly. Meanwhile, the president of Venezuela, Carlos Andrés Pérez, and Panamanian leader Omar Torrijos were both persuaded that change in Nicaragua was necessary, but neither backed the FSLN. Pérez actively supported Chamorro and UDEL, even promoting him and his organization as an alternative to Somoza in discussions with the United States.[19] The FSLN was simply not at the forefront.

The brothers therefore decided to act, independently of the other tendencies. They would lead the revolution in their own way with their own plan. The other tendencies, they reasoned, would rejoin them once they tasted Tercerista success. Indeed, the brothers reasoned that their fellow Nicaraguans and the international community would also join them once they saw the plan succeeding. It was a brazen move, not without duplicity and risks, and principally put into motion by three brothers no older than thirty. However, they were a resolved team. The eldest had endured seven years in a Somoza jail cell, the middle brother was crippled from a gunshot wound, and the youngest was willing to die for their plan.

THE FIRST STEP INVOLVED recruiting a group of distinguished Nicaraguans who could speak for the goals of the FSLN while quietly being controlled by it. The FSLN would gain respectability by having distinguished figureheads at the forefront, and thus reassure both Nicaraguans and the international community that any revolution spearheaded by the FSLN would result in an orderly transfer of power to a recognized elite. Humberto personally recruited the original member of this figurehead group, Sergio Ramírez, in Costa Rica in 1976, although Ramírez's commitment was reinforced when he met Daniel privately in April 1977.[20] Born in 1942, Ramírez had published his first book in 1963 and was already a prominent Nicaraguan academic and writer who had recently returned from a two-year fellowship in Germany. Ramírez did not publicly admit to being affiliated with the FSLN for several years and appears to have believed that he was acting independently, though he held regular discussions with the Ortega brothers. In any event, Ramírez then played a leading role in recruiting other members to the group, which for most practical purposes he headed, albeit in consultation with the Ortega brothers. There followed meetings in San José, Costa Rica, and Cuernavaca, Mexico, in May and July 1977.[21] In the end, the group numbered twelve distinguished Nicaraguans, and became known as the Group of Twelve (or "Los Doce").[22]

The group functioned exactly as the Ortega brothers planned. It was perceived as an autonomous group, not connected to the FSLN, and more moderate in its agenda. Initial statements issued by the Group of Twelve were generally reformist rather than revolutionary. They did not, for instance, call for armed insurrection but rather the voluntary abdication of Somoza coupled with a serious national dialogue about a post-Somoza government.[23] The Ortega brothers, however, not only established and continued to influence the group but also supplied it with the military muscle to follow through on its demands. The Ortegas reasoned that the Group of Twelve would eventually turn to them to win the revolution by force, and in this way they would remain in control.

Forming the Group of Twelve turned out to be a masterpiece of political organization, as well as political propaganda, because it did capture the public spotlight both inside and outside Nicaragua. Statements issued by the Group of Twelve commanded attention in a way that statements issued by the FSLN never could. It also allowed the Ortega-led faction of the FSLN to forge links with more moderate reform-minded groups in Nicaragua, even conservative business groups. The principal linkage was made in the fall of 1977, when Pedro Joaquín Chamorro's UDEL was persuaded by the Group of Twelve to join forces with it, and Chamorro was named the group's thirteenth member. Eventually his membership led to an alliance with a group formed in 1978 by businessman Alfonso Robelo, the Broad Opposition Front (FAO), which in turn even included affiliation with the Superior Council of Private Enterprise (COSEP).[24] Although the comparison is inexact, owing to the different cultures and circumstances, COSEP occupied a position similar to but more powerful than the Nicaraguan chamber of commerce. This alliance was quite the opposite of the Marxist revolutionary strategy advocated by Wheelock.

But the alliances were indirect and tenuous. To some extent the Group of Twelve acted independently, and not a few members of COSEP would have shuddered if they had known that they were linked to the FSLN. The Ortega brothers had no philosophical reservations about this linkage and had a strategic reason to believe that they would end up not merely heading the coalition but even being welcomed by them. While they were left-leaning, socialist in sympathies, and informed by Marxist-Leninism, the Ortega brothers were not communists. They preferred a mixed economy in which a responsible private sector would play a significant role. They therefore did not perceive themselves as anti-bourgeoisie, or at least narrowly so, and wanted a revolution that would be nationalist, not Marxist. Strategically, they bargained that the bourgeoisie would ultimately need them. The bourgeoisie had not developed insurrectional capabilities necessary to win a revolution, nor even recognized that a violent revolution would be necessary. The Ortega brothers, together with all Sandinistas, believed that they knew better. Change would not come to Nicaragua without a bloody revolution, and, when the revolution came, the moderate reformists would realize that they needed the

FSLN. It did not matter if the coalition groups felt themselves to be autonomous at the moment.

THE NEXT STEP THE Ortega brothers took was on the military front. "We had to regain the military initiative," explained Humberto Ortega about the Front's brazen military offensives beginning in October 1977.[25] Admitting that failure was a distinct possibility and "would be a terrible blow for Sandinismo," Humberto nevertheless explained how, in the judgment of the Terceristas, failure to launch a military offensive posed greater risks.[26] The risks might not necessarily have included a continuation of the Somoza dictatorship, but they did include "Somocismo without Somoza." There was also a chance of the FSLN slipping into oblivion. The Ortega brothers believed that they needed to show their mettle as insurrectionists in order to claim their place as the vanguard of the revolution. Moreover, they considered themselves ready. The October strategy had been drawn up the previous May, based on an earlier strategy that Fonseca had helped to devise in 1975, which was in turn based upon a strategy that had been roughed out in 1973 based upon an analysis of the Chilean coup.[27] It was tight military strategy. The plan called for coordinating simultaneous guerrilla attacks against the National Guard and its installations on three fronts throughout the populous western regions of Nicaragua.[28] The idea was to spread the Guard thin and keep it on the defensive despite its superior military capability. Indirectly, the aim was to inspire the people to insurrection. And it was largely led by the Ortega brothers: Humberto remained in Costa Rica heading up the command headquarters, Daniel commanded the Northern Front, and Camilo headed the Central Front. Although others were involved—Daniel was assisted by Leticia Herrera, Victor Tirado, and almost forty insurgents—only the Southern Front was headed by someone other than an Ortega brother—Plutarco Hernández.

The October 1977 offensive, launched by a hundred or so FSLN members, will forever be dogged by the accusation that it was a failure of the first order. It was a military disaster from the start, immediately disintegrating into one debacle after another. "The supposedly synchronized military operations didn't even come close to being simultaneous," writes Gioconda Belli, who was part of the command center in Costa Rica at the time. A mechanical failure prevented one vehicle from making it into Nicaragua, a cache of rifles was ruined when someone tried to try to hide it in a river, other weapons shipments never made their way to their destinations, and so on. Only three of a dozen or more planned attacks were actually executed. The rest "got tangled up in a web of commands that were issued too late . . . general miscommunication . . . chaos."[29] Many Sandinista combatants were killed. The offensive did not spark the widespread popular insurrection that the participants hoped it would, either. Although the fighting continued sporadically well into 1978—Daniel himself took only infrequent breaks from his Northern command over a period of five months—a revolutionary victory appeared no closer at hand in March than it had the previous September.

Daniel and Humberto Ortega, however, were ecstatic about the offensive and continued to defend it throughout their lives. It was not easy, because it had ultimately cost them the life of Camilo in February 1978, as well as many loyal comrades. However, they never doubted its wisdom or success. About a year after it was launched (and before the revolution was won), Daniel Ortega insisted that the strategy had been "correct" because it put the FSLN "on the threshold of a decisive phase of the struggle." He said, "Without October there could have been no January, no February, nor . . . September," essentially arguing that the offensive set the stage for everything that followed. He further explained that it encouraged Nicaraguans to "identify with our program and our platform" and allowed the people to "recognize the FSLN as their political-military vanguard."[30] This had of course been its principal objective.

Humberto Ortega went on to explain how the offensive augmented the Front's standing abroad. He recounts how, in immediate response to the October offensive, a Guatemalan business-man was inspired to donate ten thousand dollars to the FSLN. A little later, President Pérez of Venezuela decided to publicly recognize the Group of Twelve and secretly shifted his support from the UDEL to the FSLN. The October offensive was therefore indirectly one of the reasons Pedro Joaquín Chamorro shifted his allegiance to the Group of Twelve, thus to the FSLN, and which started the process that eventually brought the FAO and even COSEP into the fold. More practically, Pérez's support soon opened up a spigot of money that he funneled to the FSLN. Omar Torrijos of Panama was impressed enough with the FSLN to con-tribute an average of a hundred thousand dollars a month to the Front throughout 1978. Earlier, when fighting in the Southern Front spilled over into Costa Rica, José Figueres was less will-ing to remain neutral. He was persuaded to send the Front three hundred rifles, fifty machine guns, rockets, bazookas, and ammu-nition.[31] Later, Costa Rica would wink at the arms that were run through it for the FSLN, and it helped to lead the diplomatic charge against the Somoza regime on behalf of the Sandinistas. Thus, while a military failure, the offensive was a political success. The revolution was not yet won, but the FSLN was leading one, not playing catch-up, and the Ortega brothers were leading the FSLN.

MEANWHILE, DANIEL ORTEGA WAS finding his revolutionary call-ing, and excelling at it. He became the Front's principal personal negotiator. He was initially reluctant to accept this role. Just as he had objected when Fonseca ordered him back from Pancasán to Managua in 1967 to head the urban resistance when Ortega wanted to remain and fight, so also he spent as much time as he could during the late 1970s in guerrilla combat. Not only did he command the Northern Front from 1977 to 1978, but later in 1978 he shared command of the Southern Front with Edén Pastora. Although he was regarded as a good commander, quick to make lifesaving tactical decisions, he was not physically well suited to it. His eyesight was so poor that he required a guide to walk through unfamiliar territory at night. But he excelled in matters of diplomacy. He had a knack for pleasing all parties, yet standing his ground, while getting others to like and to trust him. He of course displayed this talent in his ongoing relationship with Ramírez, which allowed him to influence the Group of Twelve, but nowhere was this talent more vividly displayed than during a meeting he had with Fidel Castro in Cuba on April 7, 1978. Until that day, Castro had not merely been reluctant to support the FSLN, he had also favored the Prolonged People's War. Daniel Ortega personally changed Castro's mind in one meeting. From that point on, Castro not only supported the FSLN but also the Tercerista strategy.[32] Since Cuba proceeded to send over forty shipments of arms to the Sandinistas, as well as to supply technical advisors, the outcome of that meeting was a clear victory for the revolution. Indeed, when Belli later railed against Castro for supporting the Ortega faction, neither her arguments nor Castro's hopes of being able to seduce her could alter his opinion. Ortega had convinced him, and he railed right back at Belli—moving ashtrays around the table to illustrate the wisdom of the Ortega brothers' strategy.[33]

While Daniel's contribution to the revolution was only beginning to take shape during 1977 and 1978—no one then knew the degree to which Nicaragua's fate would hinge on his personal persuasiveness—Humberto's role had long been fixed. He was the master strategist, the intellectual, the one who would remain behind the scenes to draft and administer the brothers' plans. Camilo had contributed in a different way, and his death left more than grief for the Ortega brothers. Camilo had been the nice brother, the peacemaker, the one everybody liked. Belli, who did not care for Daniel or Humberto, was enamored enough with Camilo to name her next son after him.[34] He was even nicknamed the "Apostle of Unity."[35] No one knows what might have happened had Camilo survived, but his temperament would have been an asset to the Ortega team. Humberto was usually respected, but he was not well liked. Daniel was personable and able to earn others' respect, but he was a difficult person to feel truly close to. One never felt that he was completely forthcoming, but always holding something in reserve. His "prison personality" could be sensed, and it left others suspicious. Little did they know that his psychological problems went deeper, or that they were being expressed and exploited in a sordid private life.

Private Demons

No sooner had Daniel Ortega been freed from prison and safely in Cuba than he found a girlfriend, Leticia Herrera. She was one of the guerrillas who had raided the Christmas party that secured his release. A Nicaraguan who grew up in a communist household in Costa Rica, Herrera was such a good high school student that she was offered scholarships for advanced study in the United States, France, Costa Rica, and the Soviet Union. Since the United States represented capitalist imperialism to her, she turned that offer down. She chose the Soviet Union, where she studied from 1968 to 1969. While there she joined a Sandinista cell, met her first husband, also Nicaraguan, and conceived her first child. The couple decided to move to Nicaragua to participate in the revolutionary struggle there, and they gave the baby to her husband's mother to raise. Herrera and her husband drifted apart, owing in part to their different roles in the FSLN and perhaps their quick romance at young ages. By the time her husband was killed by the National Guard in January 1975, the marriage was for most practical purposes already over. When Herrera learned that she was a widow, she was with Ortega in Cuba, and a romance was blossoming.[36]

It is not clear how Ortega felt about Herrera. He does not appear to ever have spoken about her publicly, and the usually gossipy Nicaraguans tend not to be aware of her. However, the two struck up a close working and romantic relationship, with the working relationship enduring for life. (During Ortega's presidential term that began in 2007, for instance, Herrera was named ambassador to Costa Rica, an important position given the hundreds of thousands of Nicaraguans who live and work in Costa Rica, often illegally and without rights.) They were in Cuba together during the first half of 1975, proceeded to live together in the Managua underground later that year, were together on the Northern Front during 1977 and 1978, and then together on the Southern Front later in 1978. There was likely more to it, but Herrera described her role in terms of being Ortega's guide, especially at night, given his poor eyesight. She more generally served as his assistant, companion, and lover. The two were sufficiently close to be regarded as married by at least a few, in accordance with the common law customs of the time and place.[37] In June 1978, Herrera gave birth to Ortega's first child in Costa Rica. They named their son Camilo, and Ortega's mother, who was living in Costa Rica, helped out when the baby was born. By all outward indications, Daniel Ortega, then in his early thirties, was en route to establishing himself as a husband and father with a capable woman of similar values.

The relationship, however, abruptly ended in September 1978, two months after Camilo was born, when Herrera left Ortega.[38] It is not difficult to guess her reasons. In early 1978, while Herrera was pregnant, Ortega had taken up with another woman, Rosario Murillo, and he did so with sufficient openness for those two to be regarded as a couple.[39] Since Herrera was the one who ultimately ended the relationship, the inference could be drawn that Ortega was interested in maintaining both relationships. When Herrera gave him an ultimatum, he chose Murillo. Herrera said that her father, who viewed women as naturally "submissive," told her that she was "insensitive" and did not "understand men" when she complained to him about the situation. He made the usual *machista* allowances for Ortega's philandering, although Herrera would not do the same. Soon after the baby was born, Herrera and Ortega served together on the Southern Front, but by September 1978 Herrera had moved to Honduras, where she continued her work with the Front away from Ortega. Her decision was final.[40]

Ortega, who admittedly had a revolution to run, reacted by moving in with Murillo and establishing a family with her. Herrera said she ended the relationship and moved to Honduras in September. Ortega was still (or again) on the Southern Front for at least a few days during that month, but Murillo's daughter remembered that Ortega and her mother began living together shortly after events that occurred in late August. Murillo, who had three children from two previous relationships, agreed to raise Camilo as her own. The immediate family instantly numbered six. Although their relationship was not solemnized in a Catholic Church ceremony for almost three more decades, Ortega and Murillo would remain together for life.

It is possible that Ortega and Murillo simply fell in love during 1978, and with a little modification this is the story that is usually disseminated about their romance. According to this story, Murillo and Ortega struck up a relationship while he was in prison, when the two exchanged poetry. They did not dare visit personally then, since that would have identified Murillo as a Sandinista and placed her in danger. Nevertheless, their love grew during those years, so when Ortega was released from prison the couple came together. The only small embellishment to this story is Ortega and Murillo had known each other casually during childhood, since they grew up near each other. This embellishment invested Murillo with "girl-next-door" qualities.

The fairy tale quality of this story strains credulity. For starters, neither one waited for the other. Upon his release from prison, Ortega took up with Herrera, while Murillo had a number of other relationships. When she arrived in Costa Rica in the fall of 1977, Murillo had a boyfriend, Quincho Ibarra, and three children.[41] As for Ortega, he not only started his relationship with Murillo while he was married to another woman soon to bear his son, but he also waited for Herrera to end their relationship. He seemed content to continue with two women, and would have done so if Herrera had not forced him to choose. Then, once he chose Murillo, he gave little evidence of intending to be faithful to her. His eldest stepdaughter remembers seeing him having sex with a maid immediately after he moved in with her mother.[42] A year later, Belli says, he openly flirted with her right in front of Murillo. She felt it strange that Ortega would show his interest so openly with Murillo present.[43] And there are other, later accounts of Ortega's philandering.[44]

There are other reasons to be suspicious of the "just so" story disseminated about the Ortega-Murillo relationship. For one, it is a serious commitment for a bachelor to assume instant responsibility for someone else's children. For another, Murillo and Ortega did not seem to have similar tastes or share lifestyle preferences. Murillo was a poet, attuned to cultural matters, and of a higher class background than Ortega. She was a hippie who wore lots of jewelry, hung posters of rock bands on the walls and beaded curtains in doorways, and drank herb tea with honey.[45] Later she became notorious for her interest in New Age religions and for relying upon astrological forecasts before making decisions, including political ones. Except for his attempts at writing poetry while in prison and passing openness to spirituality, Ortega had none of these tastes. He was a practical man—a revolutionary strategist, a hard-nosed negotiator, and a guerrilla fighter—not the kind of man who would mesh well with Murillo. For example, the FSLN colors were bold red and black. Later Murillo changed them to pastels on the theory that these colors are more spiritually calming.

She did help to run Radio Sandino during the revolution and later headed the Sandinista Association of Cultural Workers, but others believed that Ortega created these positions for her simply to keep her happy. "What damn use is there having that woman direct cultural activities from that outfit when there is already a ministry of culture?" complained Humberto Ortega, who hated Murillo so intensely that he avoided family gatherings where she would be present. He privately complained, "That woman is disgracing Daniel."[46] Poet and priest Ernesto Cardenal, who was the minister of culture, called her a "bitch" and repeatedly threatened to resign if Daniel Ortega would not stop her from meddling in the affairs for which he was responsible.[47] The first time that the FSLN allowed members to vote on their leadership, Murillo was voted out.[48] Love may be blind, but whatever Daniel Ortega saw in Rosario Murillo went unseen by others.

It is likely, of course, that some knew the truth. Humberto Ortega, for example, appears to have known something. His dislike of Murillo was simply too strong to be explained by personal animosity, and in fact he sometimes expressed it by objecting to Murillo's power, not to her person or abilities. At issue, he seemed to know, was a power-sharing pact that Daniel had negotiated with Murillo. Others noticed the power that Murillo wielded too, and suspected an arrangement. She could call and requisition military trucks that were desperately needed for the national defense in order to transport a group of artists somewhere, for instance, and Daniel would see that she got the trucks.[49] Everyone therefore suspected some kind of a power-sharing pact, but few understood what Daniel received for holding up his end of the agreement. Humberto seemed to know: Daniel Ortega got sexual power over Murillo's stepdaughter.

ZOILAMÉRICA NARVÁEZ, MURILLO'S ELDEST daughter, created a firestorm of controversy in 1998 when she publicly accused Daniel Ortega of sexually molesting her since childhood. Some refused to believe her. They argued that Ortega's opponents simply persuaded her to make the accusations in an effort to ruin him politically. Some thought that Narváez was psychologically troubled and imagining things. A few also suspected that Narváez had leveled the accusations with the intention of extorting money from her stepfather. On the other side, however, some instantly believed the accusations. Ortega, they reasoned, had character traits consistent with male sexual aggression, traits that are unfortunately condoned by Nicaragua's tradition of machismo. Indeed, although there are no reliable official statistics, it is widely believed (by men as well as women) that the kind of predatory sexual aggression that Narváez accused Ortega of displaying is reasonably common in Nicaragua. Evidently it is not especially unusual for a man to establish a relationship with a woman with the objective of claiming sexual rights over her daughter as well.

Unfortunately, the courts have never determined the truth of the matter. Ortega has craftily managed to keep the case out of court. At first he claimed immunity from prosecution owing to his position in the Nicaraguan government, a legal protection that in fact he enjoyed. (He could have voluntarily relinquished his immunity, and might have done so to clear his name if he were innocent.) Then he allowed only a perfunctory court hearing after the statute of limitations had elapsed, and the case was dismissed without Narváez being permitted to present evidence. By then Ortega's power in Nicaragua was great enough for him to be able to control the courts anyway. "Nicaraguan judges depend upon Daniel Ortega's will," explained Sergio Ramírez about the judicial system in Nicaragua by that time.[50] Not to be defeated so easily, Narváez then took the case to the Inter-American Commission on Human Rights. She won the first round. The commission agreed that she was denied justice in Nicaragua and put her case on their docket.[51] Before the case could come up, however, Ortega was reelected president of Nicaragua. He then threatened to withdraw Nicaragua from the Organization of American States, the institutional structure in which the Inter-American Commission on Human Rights is housed. Because withdrawing Nicaragua from the Organization of American States was within Ortega's power, and the withdrawal would have canceled Narváez's case, she had little choice but to give up. The case has never been heard by a court, and presumably never will be.

Behaving guiltily by avoiding a trial does not make Ortega guilty. He could be innocent of the charges and still have wanted to avoid standing trial. However, the evidence suggests that

Narváez is telling the truth. No one has ever linked Narváez's accusation to any of Ortega's political opponents at home or abroad, and Narváez herself was a militant Sandinista at the time she leveled the charge. She had nothing material or political to gain by accusing Ortega of sexually abusing her, and in fact had much to lose. She insists that she only filed the charge to rid herself of the Ortega name (Ortega legally adopted her in 1986, thus she bears his name) as a way of reclaiming her dignity as a person separate from her abuser. Meanwhile, witnesses corroborate her account.[52] Others knew what was happening in the Ortega-Murillo household, and some evidently were willing to testify on Narváez's behalf. In fact, the evidence against Ortega persuaded government officials in Honduras and Paraguay to issue public pronouncements against him. In the case of Paraguay, it was the leftist government of Fernando Lugo that denounced him.[53] Not least, there is the credibility of Narváez's forty-eight-page testimony.[54] This document contains none of the kinds of discrepancies that one would expect to discover in a fabricated testimony. The dates and places are all consistent with what is otherwise known about Ortega's whereabouts, an accuracy that would be unexpected if Narváez had imagined or fabricated her story. At the same time, there is what is known about Ortega, who admitted to battling a "macho formation," revealed that attitude in his promiscuous adult sexual behavior, and also admitted to suffering psychologically after his incarceration. Narváez's testimony has a ring of credibility when it speaks of a private confrontation between her and Ortega about the abuse in which he admitted to it and explained it as having been a result of the emotional problems born of his prison experience.

In any event, Narváez describes an almost twenty-year-long ordeal of sexual molestation and oppression by her stepfather. According to her, the incestuous assaults began more or less immediately after her mother and Ortega moved in together in 1978. She remembers that it began before her eleventh birthday, which was November 13, 1978. Initially, she says, the molestation began almost casually, with Ortega making immature sexual comments or crude jokes at her expense. Since she remembers these comments often being made in front of others, she recalls that her humiliation was intense. Ortega's inappropriate behavior, however, quickly escalated. He started entering the bathroom while she was showering, and continued to make suggestive sexual comments while ogling her naked body. He then began to masturbate while joining her in the bathroom, forcing her to watch while he viewed her. From there he proceeded to fondle her while masturbating, and then the bathroom was not enough. Ortega started slipping into her bedroom at night to fondle her and masturbate, which eventually led to forced fellatio and intercourse. The abuse was never merely sexual for Ortega. It was about domination. After the revolution triumphed and the family moved to Nicaragua, Ortega compelled Narváez to watch pornographic movies with him, jealously accused her of having sex with her classmates at school, and so on. Indeed, even into her adulthood and after she married, Ortega regularly placed obscene phone calls to her. It was as if in Narváez Ortega believed that he had found a personal sex slave he could control as completely as he was controlled in the Somoza prison.

This scenario can be interpreted in only one way, the predictable way: an adult male predator and a young female victim. However, Narváez's testimony reveals that there was an accomplice to the crime: her mother, Rosario Murillo. That Narváez does not think to accuse her mother while nevertheless providing ample reasons for doing so makes this reading of her testimony all the more damning. She provides the facts, just not the interpretation.

Murillo, Narváez's testimony makes clear, was a willing if silent accomplice in Ortega's molestation of her. Murillo's sister and Narváez's aunt, Violeta Murrillo, is among those who agreed to testify on Narváez's behalf. Violeta knew that the sexual abuse was occurring from the time she moved in with the family in Costa Rica during 1978 or early 1979. She claims that she confronted Murillo about it then, but Murillo dismissed her concerns. However, surely Murillo knew that her husband was raping her daughter. Narváez says that the initial sexual innuendos were often public. Murillo was certainly occasionally part of this public. Worse, time and again Narváez reports having turned to her mother for protection only to have Murillo reject her. "I resented my mother, whose loyalty was to my aggressor," recounts Narváez. "I didn't know if she would believe me." Or again, after begging her mother not to have to sleep alone and suffer Ortega's assaults, she remembers that "my mother insisted that I must accustom myself to sleeping alone." Although "to sleep alone" was a "torment" of fear, "my mother never permitted me to sleep accompanied." Indeed, Murillo "criticized" Narváez for complaining and accused her of "contaminating the whole family."[55] When Narváez made her accusations public in 1998, Murillo staunchly defended Ortega.

There are any number of ways to explain Murillo's complicity with Ortega's sexual aggression against her daughter,[56] but assuming that she was badgered into submission by an overbearing husband is not well supported by the available evidence. The problems with this explanation are that the molestation began before the relationship between Ortega and Murillo had time to develop repressive patterns, that there is no evidence of Ortega bullying Murillo in Narváez's testimony or elsewhere, and that Murillo appears to have known what she was doing. Ortega's molestation of Narváez started more or less immediately after Ortega and Murillo moved in together. Murillo knew she began her relationship with Ortega as the "other woman," and may have felt that she had to give Ortega something more than other women could. Murillo may have seen a way to gain power when Ortega made his lascivious interest in Narváez known. Instead of helping the man she claimed to love overcome an obvious emotional problem, or the daughter who depended upon her for protection, she exploited the man's weaknesses by offering him her daughter. In exchange, Murillo extracted real political power.

Managing the Popular Insurrection

COLLECTIVE MEMORY OF THE Nicaraguan revolution dates its popular onset some eighteen months prior to its July 19, 1979, triumph. The catalyst is thought to have occurred the morning of January 10, 1978, when *La Prensa* editor Pedro Joaquín Chamorro was gunned down on his way to work. Nobody could prove it—these things rarely can be proven—but Nicaraguans believed that Somoza ordered the assassination. He, or perhaps one of his business associates, probably did.[57] It was the last straw for the bulk of the population. Chamorro did oppose the regime and had recently joined the Group of Twelve while heading UDEL, but almost everybody opposed the regime. After some youthful forays in armed rebellion (for which he served prison time), Chamorro became a voice of moderation in immoderate times. The "crime" for which he was thought to have been killed involved publishing a series of articles during the fall of 1977 about a blood plasma center jointly owned by Somoza and a Cuban businessman. The center paid Nicaraguans for their blood plasma and then exported it to the United States for a healthy profit. Poor people in the United States of course also sell their blood plasma to make ends meet and not many people complain about that, but the symbolism of the stories in *La Prensa* did not sit well with an increasingly agitated Nicaraguan public. It appeared that Somoza was literally sucking the blood out of the people he governed and selling it to the imperialist power to the north. For Somoza to retaliate against this series of articles by having Chamorro gunned down in cold blood was too much for Nicaraguans to take. The stories were, after all, factually accurate. The assassination of Chamorro therefore set the country ablaze with rage against their dictator.

That rage was evident at Chamorro's January 1978 funeral procession, which drew tens of thousands of protesting Nicaraguans into the streets of Managua. The street demonstrations, however, were only the beginning. The construction workers' union called a strike to protest the Somoza regime, which drew the participation of some four thousand. The next day the strike was joined by COSEP, under the leadership of Robelo, although as a business rather than a labor initiative it was technically a lockout rather than a strike. A committee of business leaders who had been associated with Chamorro but who were led by Archbishop Obando y Bravo canceled talks with Somoza planned for February.[58] The usual interpretation, which there is no reason to doubt, is that the assassination of Chamorro persuaded members of the working and business classes that they were more vulnerable to Somoza's tyranny than they had imagined, and they no longer believed that dialogue with Somoza would be productive. They simply wanted him out. Then, in February, a spontaneous uprising erupted in Monimbó, an indigenous neighborhood in Masaya, which required six hundred National Guardsmen, two tanks, three armored cars, two helicopters, and two planes to suppress.[59] The uprising in turn prompted the archbishop to give armed insurrection his cautious approval in a February 9, 1978, pronouncement.[60] This too was a watershed. Throughout the 1960s and 1970s, liberation theology was in the air, and the democratization of the Church after Vatican II had allowed for a parallel "people's church" to arise alongside the formal Church in Latin America. The "people's church" took the form of "Christian Base Communities" (CEB), which were small, neighborhood gatherings in which a dozen or two Catholics would meet about once a week to discuss how Church teachings applied to their daily lives. On the eve of the revolution there were thousands of CEBs, and many were veering insurrectionist. The CEBs existed in some tension with the formal Church hierarchy, which in general resisted extending legitimacy to the "popular church" and cautioned against liberation theology.[61] To have the Church condone even the "defensive" violence of the insurrectionists, a distinction the archbishop's statement did attempt to make, came perilously close to endorsing the theology of liberation and all-out revolution.

It is therefore with good reason that most histories of the Nicaraguan Revolution date the beginning of the popular insurrection that eventually led to victory in the events of January 1978. Nevertheless, the trajectory was considerably more fitful than this, and from the vantage point of early 1978 a triumphant revolution was by no means inevitable. In fact, during the spring and early summer of 1978, insurrectionist sentiment subsided, largely because Somoza cleverly maneuvered to defuse it. With one hand, he launched a massive increase in the National Guard, with an eye toward augmenting his capabilities to suppress any future insurrections.[62] With the other, he politicked agilely with the United States. Although he traveled to the United States that summer in part to receive treatments for a heart condition, while there he lobbied his friends in Congress to support him in a battle that he insisted was against "communism." On September 22, seventy-eight members of Congress signed a letter sent to President Carter urging him to support Somoza.[63] Meanwhile, he acquiesced to pressure from the Carter administration to relax his repression, and took symbolic steps to display his commitment. Among these was to allow the Group of Twelve to enter Nicaragua, from which they had been previously banished. These initiatives prompted President Carter to send Somoza a letter congratulating him on his improving record of human rights. Although Carter had not intended the letter to serve as more than encouragement for Somoza's continuing improvement, it gave the dictator a document that appeared to show him enjoying the full support of the president of United States. When the time was right, Somoza did pull the letter out and wave it in front of the press.[64] Moreover, the letter showed that Washington assumed that Somoza would remain in power. Since the United States had always supported the Somoza governments, by military means when necessary, smart money in the summer of 1978 would have been bet on a better-behaving Somoza remaining at the helm of Nicaragua for a long time.

THERE WAS ALSO THE question of the nature of any regime that might replace Somoza if he were deposed, and specifically whether it would result in more than a continuation of "Somocismo without Somoza." The most credible groups calling for Somoza's removal that summer were the institutional Catholic Church, the Group of Twelve, and Robelo's FAO—which combined the groups that had comprised UDEL with others that until then had not taken a coordinated stand against the regime. While the Church's stand against the regime was noteworthy, it was by its very nature restricted. The Church hierarchy was not about to involve itself in politics in any but the most general ways, and it limited itself to calling for Somoza's abdication and a reorganization of the National Guard.[65] While the Group of Twelve was secretly allied with the FSLN, it too was reformist rather than revolutionary in tone. The FAO's political agenda was more ambitious, but still moderate. Overwhelmingly a coalition of moderate and even conservative groups—the furthest left that the FAO coalition veered was to include two trade unions among its member groups—the odds of an FAO-led replacement government being other than right-leaning were slim. Robelo himself was a millionaire businessman in a land of poverty, served as the head of COSEP, and had been educated at Rensselaer Polytechnic Institute in Troy, New York. Indeed, although it was not drafted until October 1978, the plan for a post-Somoza government proposed by the FAO included representatives from numerous business and conservative groups, but no representation from either the left or the bulk of the Nicaraguan population.

Meanwhile, the FAO's plan called for a "reorganization" of the National Guard, as did the Church's plan, but many (including the Sandinistas) believed that the National Guard was too systemically corrupt to be capable of reform. In mid-1978 it was simply no sure thing that the removal of Somoza would result in significant political change in Nicaragua, and it was also obvious that Somoza was not going to abdicate.

Thus, the situation was not as favorable for revolutionary victory as it appears in hindsight to have been, and the two remaining Ortega brothers knew this. Fortunately, they were in a pretty good position. Although they had obviously not predicted that Chamorro would be assassinated, they had already forged alliances with him and UDEL via the Group of Twelve, which led to alliances with Robelo's FAO. The brothers were of course not members of these groups—the FSLN was far too radical to be welcomed by them—but they were not without contacts within them. They also had connections within the Church. The Sandinistas had made a point of being involved in the CEBs, and in fact some Sandinistas were priests, while others (like Ortega) retained their Catholic faith. At the same time, they tried to cultivate good relationships with the Church hierarchy, calling for instance upon the archbishop to arbitrate acts like the Christmas party raid. Daniel Ortega and Archbishop Miguel Obando y Bravo were personally acquainted. Both were born in La Libertad, and Ortega briefly attended a Catholic high school where Obando y Bravo taught as a young priest.[66] Also the FSLN was capable of military action while the moderate groups were not, and the Ortega brothers could use that as a bargaining chip in their negotiations.

The Ortega brothers were nevertheless not in the center of the political opposition, and even their leadership of the insurrection was tenuous. The uprising in Monimbó, for example, caught them by complete surprise. When it occurred, Camilo quickly went to Masaya to try to put the FSLN stamp on the uprising, and the battle cost Camilo his life. Their failure to anticipate the uprising and Camilo's resulting death underscored the gap between where the Ortega brothers were and where they wanted to be as leaders of the insurrection, even as the events of early and mid-1978 showed that they were not yet in a position to lead the revolution, if indeed the revolution would ever come.

THE ORTEGA BROTHERS THEREFORE once again decided to act autonomously. Their plan involved nothing less than storming the National Palace and taking the entire government hostage. They put the plan into effect in late August 1978, and it was a sensational success. Led by the charismatic Edén Pastora (known during that operation as "Commander Zero"), with the smart and capable Dora María Téllez second in command, Sandinista guerrillas held over fifteen hundred government officials hostage in that raid. The negotiations for their release led to a five-hundred-thousand-dollar ransom, air transportation for the safe escape of the guerrillas (this time to Panama), the release of political prisoners (including Borge), and free news coverage of the FSLN's revolutionary aims. The bold act of the guerrillas captured global media attention and stimulated the hopes of the Nicaraguan people. Pastora, in a fit of daring egotism, defiantly ripped off his ski mask before he entered the escape plane, and the photograph of the gallant guerrilla swept the globe.

Taking the National Palace achieved what the Ortega brothers hoped it would: it stimulated the then-flagging popular insurrection. Spontaneous revolts erupted throughout the country in September—so many that Humberto worried about losing control of the insurrection, more or less the same way that the Monimbó uprising had caught him unprepared. The popular uprisings, though, were good for both the revolution and the Ortega brothers. With the battle once again in the streets, the pressure on all parties to reach a resolution quickly intensified. Protracted negotiations between Somoza and reform-minded opposition groups were infused with renewed urgency as men and women fought and died. Violent insurrection also augmented the Sandinistas' standing among the opposition groups, since they alone were the masters of military insurrection. As for the Ortega brothers, while there was no real secret about their role in the opposition, the taking of the National Palace was the first time the public at large became aware of their leadership. At the time, Pastora and the other guerrillas were allowed to take the credit for the siege, but those who were paying attention noticed that the signers of the Sandinista communiqué published in the newspaper after the raid were Daniel Ortega, Humberto Ortega, and Victor Tirado (the third leader of the Terceristas).[67]

The success of the takeover of the National Palace coupled with their named notoriety in connection with it did not immediately open a seat for the Ortega brothers at the public negotiating table. Neither of them, however, wanted such a seat, at least not yet. Humberto had his hands full running what for the next ten months would be a more or less continuous military campaign. This effort would tax his self-taught skills as a military strategist to their limits. His most controversial decision was the final offensive in late May 1979, which caught the National Guard in pinchers as the Sandinista armies moved in on Managua from the west, the north, and eventually the south. It was a bloodbath that some say was unnecessary, since by then it was likely that Somoza would fall anyway. Like most military strategists who make the tough decisions, Humberto always maintained that the carnage would have been worse had he allowed the insurrection to continue without the quickest possible victory. Whether he was correct or not, his role was to run the insurrection. To some extent, Daniel assisted him. Radio Sandino, the nexus of communication, was set up in Liberia, Costa Rica, with a transmitter obtained by Pastora in 1977, but with Murillo in charge of broadcasts.[68] There was also the matter of obtaining armaments, which involved negotiations with foreign suppliers as well as the government of Costa Rica, which had to permit the supply planes to land. Directly and through emissaries, Daniel helped to negotiate these arrangements. However, Daniel Ortega's main role was to organize the Front internally and to influence the plan for the government that would assume power once Humberto's military campaign succeeded. It was mostly behind-the-scenes political work.

AT FIRST GLANCE DANIEL Ortega's resumption of his role as a guerrilla commander in September 1978—after the taking of the National Palace—is curious. It seems to indicate that he had not yet come to grips with his responsibilities as the Front's principal political strategist, but still thirsted for the glory of military combat. However, there is another, more plausible, explanation. Ortega may have wanted to keep an eye on Edén Pastora. Since Pastora was a capable military commander and Ortega's capabilities were hampered by poor eyesight, there would not seem to be any military advantage in Ortega's assisting Pastora. Any advantage that accrued would have been political—and an advantage for Ortega.

Building a collegial relationship with Pastora—in part with the goal of controlling him—is an excellent example of the kind of work that Ortega increasingly focused on after the attack of the National Palace. He essentially inveigled personalities in the organization. By its very nature, a revolution attracts participants with a wide range of both abilities and shortcomings, and whose actions are unconstrained by predetermined institutionalized roles. The situation is probably something like prison in that an atmosphere of formal equality places a premium on carefully assessing people's unique characteristics and treating them according to the specific risks and opportunities they present. For the Sandinistas, Pastora was perhaps their most challenging collaborator. On the one hand, he was a tremendous asset to the Front. He was an able military commander, committed to the overthrow of Somoza, very charismatic, handsome, and daring, and moderate enough to appeal to a broad constituency. He insisted that he was a practicing Catholic and not a communist when those kinds of reassurances were helpful. He was also well connected politically. He was personal friends with Torrijos in Panama and Pérez in Venezuela, enjoyed cordial relations with Castro, and was a former high school classmate of Alfonso Robelo. He even charmed the United States and always turned up on the short list of those Washington considered when searching for a moderate Sandinista it might back. On the other hand, however, he was egotistical, undisciplined, and frankly uncommitted to a political creed much beyond his own self-promotion. He was more bluster than substance, and to no one's surprise ended up fathering almost two dozen children with multiple women.

His egotism even prompted him to claim that he was an original founder of the FSLN. Although he had been involved in insurrectional activities since the late 1950s and did have some connection with the Sandinistas early on, he was inconsistently involved with the Front and never deeply committed to its principles. He was a person the Sandinistas wanted to use but also needed to control.

During their time together, Ortega was able to make an ally out of Pastora, which presumably was his principal objective that September. Even after Pastora defected to the counterrevolution in 1982, he personally liked Daniel Ortega more than he did any of the other Sandinistas, and in fact he rejoined the Front years later when Ortega was reelected president in 2006.[69] Ortega was therefore able to exploit Pastora's political connections, suggesting, for example, that he meet with Torrijos and Pérez when negotiations with those leaders were required. Meanwhile, however, Humberto intentionally left Pastora's southern command undersupplied. Although Pastora remained unaware of it, Humberto used Pastora's forces to draw the National Guard south and keep them occupied there while equipping armies from the west and the north for victory.[70] The Ortega brothers simply did not trust Pastora with military victory, and therefore denied that to him. Their mistrust was warranted. On the eve of victory, Pastora contacted the United States and urged them to persuade Somoza to withdraw the National Guard from the south so that he, Pastora, could claim victory and deny it to the "radicals." The United States demurred, still hoping for a military stalemate that would enable it to control the outcome of the revolution.[71] It was obvious that Pastora was not loyal to the Sandinistas, although he was personally loyal to Daniel Ortega.

Managing Pastora remained challenging. His name was, for example, floated as a prospective member of the governing junta in late 1978 drafts of the post-revolution government, a candidacy that had to be quashed lest he gained too much power. In the end he was given a position subordinate to Borge in the Ministry of the Interior. This position did not suit Pastora's sense of his own importance, but the Sandinistas expected him to go over to the counterrevolution anyway and did not want to entrust him with significant power. Later, after he defected, someone tried to kill him by planting a bomb, although the blast only wounded Pastora while killing others.[72] Some believe the Sandinistas were behind the attempted assassination. Some say the CIA planted the bomb. The CIA was trying to run a counterrevolution and Pastora was a loose cannon for them, too. Everyone saw him as a man who had to be carefully managed, and Daniel Ortega assumed that responsibility.

Meanwhile, Ortega was managing others—like Sergio Ramírez. In fall 1978, Ramírez remained virtually the only link the Ortega brothers had to the high-level negotiations involving Nicaragua's regime change, then mediated by the Organization of American States with a prominent role assumed by the United States. Although Ortega's role was growing, and by December he was personally meeting with the international negotiators in Panama, he still needed to work through others, especially Ramírez.[73] At a crucial juncture that fall, for instance, Ramírez led a defiant opposition to a plan of government that would have included a reorganized National Guard. The retention of the Guard was a point that the Sandinistas refused to accept, although at the time they only had Ramírez and the Group of Twelve defending their position. The plan of government then being discussed was the Robelo plan, which would have excluded the FSLN and most of the left from governance anyway. It had to be stopped, and Ramírez did so. Later, even as Ortega himself was a participant at the negotiating table, at several junctures he relied upon Ramírez's largely secret support.

Ramírez later served as Ortega's vice president and then worked on behalf of the FSLN in the legislature during the early 1990s. However, Ramírez did eventually break with Ortega, bitterly, and complain that Ortega had used him. Many other Sandinistas eventually concluded that Ortega had used them as well. Belli writes, for example, that the Ortega brothers "felt superior" to their peers, "cannily manipulating" them until the brothers "situated themselves at the top of the heap," although in fact the Ortegas "usurped the legacy of our brave liberation struggle."[74] At the time, however, few of these resentments surfaced, and to some extent their eventual surfacing is predictable. Daniel Ortega's whole objective was to extract what he wanted out of others while preventing them from doing what he did not want.

Yet most of Ortega's efforts at personal persuasion were successful, seemingly because they were fair. One of his main goals in late 1978 and early 1979 was to negotiate a reunification of the FSLN. In part it was a personal goal. Since his teenage years, Ortega's whole life had been devoted to and enveloped by the FSLN, and he could not imagine winning a revolution without it. While he was obviously willing to act independently, he wanted the victory to be for the Sandinistas, not for the Terceristas alone. More practically, Castro conditioned substantial military aid on a reunification of the FSLN, since he remained hesitant to support a revolution whose leaders might stab each other in the back. In any event, a tentative agreement among the tendencies was reached in December 1978, and their formal reunification was announced on March 8, 1979. The plan for reunification was fair. Although the Terceristas had proven the merits of their strategy, they insisted upon no more power in the FSLN than the other tendencies. In the end, the reunification involved the FSLN being governed by a nine-person National Directorate, with three members appointed from each tendency. (Wheelock and Borge were thus appointed members of the National Directorate, for example, while the Terceristas were represented by Victor Tirado and the Ortega brothers.) For over a decade the Directorate operated with very little internal dissent, and usually by consensus. If there was animosity toward Daniel Ortega, it did not show. In fact, when it came time for the Directorate to name one of their members to the governing junta of the proposed new government, they chose him by consensus.

There remained, though, the challenge of securing a preeminent role for the FSLN in the plan for a new government of Nicaragua. The Sandinistas considered that they were the vanguard of the revolution, and as such were entitled to exercise ultimate authority. However, they did not intend to govern Nicaragua by fiat. Neither, of course, would the many other Nicaraguans who opposed Somoza welcome authoritarian rule by the Sandinistas. The widespread support for the revolution demanded a broadly representative government, and nothing less would merit the support of the international community. Indeed, the prominence of the business class and others on the center-right in the popular insurrection gave those interests a strong voice in the future government. The FSLN thus wanted a formal government beside itself, but wanted to leave a bold imprint on that government. In early 1979, the FSLN was still largely excluded from the formal negotiations for the future government. Together with their running the military component of the revolution and Daniel Ortega's sustained exertion of personal influence, the Sandinistas took steps to augment their power in negotiations for a new government. Specifically, they organized constituencies sympathetic to them into coalition groups that could counter the influence of Robelo's FAO as well as the political party formed and headed by him, the Nicaraguan Democratic Movement (MDN). In the summer of 1978 the Sandinistas coordinated fully twenty-two separate supportive groups into a single organization, the United People's Movement (MPU), headed by Moisés Hassan, and six months later created an even larger umbrella group, the National Patriotic Front (FPN), to absorb it and newcomers.[75] The goal was to provide a pro-Sandinista counterweight to the FAO and MDN. When the time came, the FSLN was in as strong a position as possible to shape the post-revolution government.

When the final plan of government was hammered out in an early summer 1979 meeting in Puntarenas, Costa Rica, Daniel Ortega was therefore in attendance. Along with the foreign governments (including the United States), Robelo, and the other interested groups that had participated in the negotiations the previous fall, the FSLN was now formally a part of the planning process for a new Nicaraguan government. The plan still resembled the one that Robelo had proposed under the auspices of the FAO the previous October. However, the composition of the proposed legislature, called the Council of State, was modified to represent a broader constituency than the overwhelmingly pro-business plan that Robelo had originally proposed, although the private sector retained majority representation. Then, instead of a three-member junta appointed by the Council of State, as Robelo had originally suggested, a five-member junta was appointed separately. The key members of the junta included Robelo and Ortega, one representing the private sector and the other the FSLN. Robelo's constituencies were further represented by Violeta Chamorro, the widow of Pedro Joaquín Chamorro. Ortega's were seconded by Moisés Hassan, who was head of the MPU and a Sandinista. The fifth member, and presumably its swing vote, was Sergio Ramírez, who at the time was still downplaying his allegiance to the Sandinistas. The result was thus a junta tilted three to two in favor of the Sandinistas, and a Council of State tilted in the opposite direction. All concerned were content with the compromises. In fact, when the United States pressured for an expanded junta in hopes of diluting the Sandinistas' strength, Robelo and Chamorro objected the most vociferously.[76] They were content with the junta they had. They were also content with Ortega, who they named their coordinator. Thus, in less than a year, Daniel Ortega went from an obscure guerrilla commander in a fragmented revolutionary group to the most powerful person in Nicaragua's proposed new government.

IT WAS PROBABLY SOMOZA'S obstinacy, coupled with Carter's refusal to interfere militarily, that allowed Ortega and the Sandinistas the revolutionary victory they desired. While Somoza had tried and failed to persuade the Carter administration to support his rule—a failure that prompted him to argue that he had been "betrayed" by the United States—the Carter administration did

try to intervene diplomatically.[77] By the fall of 1978, Carter officials finally realized that Nicaragua was on the brink of revolution and concluded that Somoza probably had to go. Empowered
by a resolution calling for mediation from the Organization of
American States, Carter therefore dispatched a team to Nicaragua,
headed by William Bowlder. The team was charged with negotiating a peaceful transfer of power between Somoza and a replacement, otherwise preserving the status quo. The United States, for
example, wanted the National Guard to remain. As it evolved, the
gist of the U.S. proposal was to encourage Somoza to stand for a
plebiscite, which if he lost would then set in motion democratic
procedures for his replacement. The details of the proposal were
intentionally left to the various parties to determine for themselves. The United States did not insist on a specific plan. The
only thing the United States wanted was a peaceful transfer of
power.

Had this diplomatic initiative of the United States succeeded,
the Nicaraguan Revolution would likely never have occurred. The
Sandinistas played only a minor role in the discussions—initially
they were only indirectly represented by Ramírez—and the odds
are that a successful outcome would have resulted in someone
like Robelo being elected president in a similarly structured but
more democratic Nicaragua. The obstacle to these initiatives was
Somoza himself. At first he disagreed, then he agreed with stipulations, then the stipulations were agreed to, then he disagreed
again. Months went by before the U.S. mediators recognized in
February 1979 that Somoza had no intention of relinquishing
power voluntarily and gave up. During this same period, however, Somoza and others recognized another reality, namely that
Carter would not back up his wishes with military power. Carter
asked, not ordered, Somoza to agree to an orderly relinquishing
of power, and Somoza said no. Interestingly, had Somoza had any
fear of "communists" taking over Nicaragua, he is the one who
walked away from the opportunity to prevent that. It was his
obstinacy at these negotiations that ensured he would be over-

thrown by force—led by those to the left of those with whom he refused to negotiate in good faith.

Some, especially in the later administration of Ronald Reagan, argued that Jimmy Carter "lost" Nicaragua. The argument amounts to faulting Carter for not backing up U.S. proposals with military force. The United States might well have been able to dictate the political outcome in Nicaragua had it been willing to use or convincingly threaten the use of force, and the tactic would hardly have been a new one in the history of the relations between the two countries. But Carter was morally opposed to using U.S. power in this way, and deeply committed to the sovereignty of Latin American countries. Indeed, in 1978 he expended what precious little political capital he had remaining to push the Panama Canal Treaties through Congress. He would seek to influence events in Nicaragua, but would not dictate them. Although this position earned Carter a great deal of respect and affection from some, it was perceived as weak by those accustomed to a more heavy-handed U.S. policy. Somoza himself referred derisively to Carter as a "middie"—an insulting diminutive for "midshipman," which as a graduate of the U.S. Naval Academy was the first rank Carter held as a career navy officer—to members of Congress.[78] Robelo fumed, "When the United States put it to Somoza that they wanted him out, they didn't expect him to say no. But what pressure did they use? They used no pressures."[79] These remarks revealed where Nicaraguans believed real power and real responsibility lay—and simultaneously betrayed their own reluctance to shoulder the responsibilities of national sovereignty themselves.

In any event, by early 1979, when the Carter administration realized that Somoza would not negotiate, it changed strategy. Instead of trying to ease Nicaragua through a peaceful and democratic regime change, it braced itself for the inevitability of Somoza's violent overthrow and worked to influence the nature of the government that would replace him. But by then it was too late for the administration to wield much influence. The United States favored the retention of the National Guard, pressured for junta, and called for the creation of an international force to maintain order during the transition. But ates stepped to the table too late. The Organization ....rican States, the countries of the Andean Pact (Bolivia, Colombia, Ecuador, Peru, and Venezuela), Cuba, and especially Costa Rica already backed the by then largely Sandinista-led revolution. At the same time, there were over 150 solidarity groups supporting the revolution throughout the world.[80] The widespread support for the revolution inside Nicaragua coupled with the savvy negotiating skills of people like Ortega had simply wooed the world community. Indeed, public sentiment turned in favor of the revolution inside the United States when an ABC television crew filmed the wanton murder of their own correspondent, Bill Stewart, by the National Guard on June 20. Only Israel continued to sell arms to the Somoza regime almost to the end. To insist on its preferences at this late date would bring the wrath of much of the world on the United States.

So the revolution came. When it did, it was most visibly led by *los muchachos* (the kids)—the men, women, and children who fought with rocks, .22 rifles, anything they had, in order to overthrow their hated dictator. Almost ten thousand Nicaraguans died in the final months, most of them civilians, while the death toll for the revolution as a whole reached forty-five thousand—80 percent of them civilians. Another 160,000 were wounded.[81] Combining these numbers, approximately one in every twenty Nicaraguans was killed or injured in the revolution, yet most fought on. In terms of formal military strategy, Dora María Téllez, the commander from the west, was the first to break through. León fell to her, the first major city claimed by the Sandinistas, and she pressed on to Managua. Estelí in the north fell, was recaptured by the National Guard, then fell again. To the south, Pastora was bogged down trying to claim a hilltop when the news of the Sandinista victory arrived by radio. But the Guard had put up a mighty fight everywhere. It left five hundred million dollars in war damages, mostly in bombed factories and neighborhoods.[82] Indeed,

Somoza had waged war on his own people, in the end indiscriminately bombing any place that posed a threat—but threats were everywhere. *Los muchachos* were from all over.

Then the National Guard disintegrated. Since most of the soldiers had only joined the Guard because it promised a way out of poverty, scant few had any loyalty to it or to Somoza at the moment of defeat. Rank-and-file Guardsmen stripped off their uniforms to reveal the civilian clothes they had been secretly wearing underneath in anticipation of their loss, then slipped into the general population. The Guard's leadership in the south commandeered boats at gunpoint and ordered the captains to take them to El Salvador, where they hoped they would be safe in defeat. Some Guardsmen in the north fled to Honduras. The Guard officers in Managua boarded planes to Miami. In the end, the highest official left in Managua to surrender to the Sandinistas on July 19 was the head of the traffic police, Fulgencia Largaespada.[83] Everyone else was gone. Somoza himself negotiated a safe escape with the junta and the United States, and he boarded a plane to Miami on July 17. He took suitcases full of cash with him. (He later took up residence in Paraguay, where he was killed a little over a year later, on September 17, 1980. The assumption is that the Sandinistas had him assassinated, although there is no hard evidence of this, and both Castro and drug lords have been blamed. His body was flown to Miami for burial.) There was some last-minute confusion when Francisco Urcuyo, the person who had been tapped to assume the presidency from Somoza just long enough to allow him to escape and then was supposed to turn power over to the revolutionaries, tried briefly to retain power himself. A phone call from Somoza, under pressure from the United States, put an end to those shenanigans. He promptly turned power over to the junta as agreed.

On July 15, Daniel Ortega flew to León with other members of the junta, preparing to enter Managua for the victory celebration. He was then the most powerful person in Nicaragua, and the only Latin American revolutionary to have won a revolution since

Fidel Castro. While in León, someone brought him film footage of Sandino. It was the first time that he had ever seen his political inspiration, and it moved him. Besides that, the victory celebration failed to excite him. Even after he was cheered by tens of thousands of grateful Nicaraguans four days later in Managua, he confessed that he felt less than enthusiastic.[84] Belli, who was much lower in the Sandinista hierarchy but nevertheless involved enough to have been forced into exile, may capture the emotional reaction of the Sandinistas to victory better than Ortega. When Belli tried to show the clerk at the Managua airport her passport, the clerk smiled and said, "You don't need a passport, compañera. This is your country."[85] Ortega was not like Belli, however, or like most people. His "prison personality" left him uncomfortable in freedom. He was under no illusion that the euphoria of the moment meant that Nicaragua was truly liberated. There was much to be done before he could feel confident in victory, and he felt an awesome responsibility.

4

GOVERNING AN
EMBATTLED REPUBLIC

ALFONSO ROBELO ADMITTED THAT it took him several months after the victory to notice that "someone in olive green" was always present at meetings of the governing junta.[1] He was not referring to Daniel Ortega, who often wore his commandante uniform; he was referring to various other members of the Sandinistas' National Directorate. It finally dawned on him that the FSLN expected to lead the government. Robelo's delayed awareness, however, must have been a result of his own wishful obliviousness. Arturo Cruz, a non-Sandinista member of the Group of Twelve who headed the Central Bank after the revolution, realized within weeks of the triumph that "the National Directorate was going to run the country."[2] The Sandinistas made no secret of their intentions in this regard, either. Daniel Ortega spoke directly to the issue on Nicaraguan television in late July. "There are many people asking, who is the government of Nicaragua, the Sandinista National Liberation Front or the Junta of National Reconstruction," he said. Then he answered the question directly: "It was wrong to think that the Sandinista Front was only a military organization. It was, is, and will continue to be a political organization. . . . We are going to stay until our program is fully accomplished."[3] The "we" Ortega referred to were the Sandinistas.

Most of what followed during Nicaragua's next long, dark decade can be traced to this issue of who—the Government of National Reconstruction or the Sandinista National Liberation Front—would really govern the country. Some can even be traced to the specific actions of Alfonso Robelo and Arturo Cruz. After realizing that the FSLN intended to play an active role in the government, Robelo wasted little time, resigning from the junta after ten months, on April 22, 1980, and going over to the counter-revolution (or the contras, as they came to be called) within two years. Cruz stuck with the new government a little longer. He briefly replaced Robelo on the junta, occupying one of the two seats intended for pro-business moderates, then served as Nicaragua's ambassador to the United States. He, too, soon became fed up, however, and in 1984 ran against Ortega for the presidency. Ironically, while the defections of men like Robelo and Cruz were prompted by their objections to the increasing concentration of power in the Sandinistas' National Directorate, their resignations augmented the very Sandinista power they opposed. As moderates defected from the government, the vacuum that was created could only be filled by the National Directorate. Obviously, the FSLN wanted a great deal of power, but they were handed it by the departures of non-Sandinistas.

The question of which body exercised power in post-revolution Nicaragua paralleled the question of how the country would develop economically. At the time of the victory, the economy was in shambles. In addition to the dead and the wounded, some 250,000 Nicaraguans were displaced by the fighting, and an estimated quarter of the population was hungry.[4] Nearly two-thirds of the citizenry was classified as poor by United Nations' standards, half the children under five years old suffered from malnourishment, and half the population consumed an average of only 1,571 calories per day.[5] With an annual GDP hovering at only around two billion dollars in the best of times, Nicaragua's

GDP had declined by a quarter, or by around five hundred million. Somoza had left the country not only with over five hundred million dollars in war damages but also with over $1.5 billion in foreign debt and only $3.5 million in the treasury.[6] More ominously, an estimated quarter of all private business owners had fled the country, taking some five hundred million in investment dollars with them.[7] This capital flight, followed by continuing divestments from Nicaragua's economy on the part of nervous business owners, gutted the country's private sector while virtually guaranteeing that it could not recover. Just as the defection by moderates from the government had augmented the Sandinistas' political power, the defection of business owners pushed economic policy to the left to a degree that it would not have otherwise gone. The Sandinistas may not have been communists, but without private capital there could be no capitalism.

The story of Nicaragua during the 1980s is of course more complicated than this. These events did not occur in a global vacuum. The United States increasingly had become a player, and before long was the major player. After Robelo resigned from the junta and joined the contras, and when Cruz left the country only to return to run against Ortega for the presidency, they were not merely switching sides. They were joining an opposition largely created, managed, and funded by the United States. Robelo himself ended up receiving a ten-thousand-dollar-per-month retainer from the United States for his anti-Sandinista activities, Cruz seven thousand per month.[8] Both were welcome visitors to the White House, which recruited Cruz to run for the presidency against Ortega and then directed his campaign. By contrast, neither Ronald Reagan nor George H. W. Bush ever so much as met with Daniel Ortega (although Jimmy Carter had). Reagan even ordered the U.S. delegation to the United Nations to walk out before Ortega addressed the assembly, and, when Henry Kissinger spent all of one day in Nicaragua in 1984 to "investigate" the situation there, he could not be bothered to talk much with Ortega. "Let's not listen to this son of a bitch," whispered an aide to Kissinger, and that was that.[9] Meanwhile, the business owners who divested from Nicaragua were welcomed with open arms by the United States. Tens of thousands were granted U.S. residency, often as political refugees, while the south Florida banks handled their capital outflows with experience honed by having provided similar services for Cuban immigrants. By contrast, Tomás Borge, then Nicaragua's minister of the interior, was denied a visa to visit the United States in 1983 to lecture at Harvard University. Even after Ortega was elected president, his visa was once mysteriously delayed.[10] Events in Nicaragua did not unfold the way they might have if Nicaraguans had been left to slog it out among themselves.

Daniel Ortega's predicament was that he was the person positioned in the center of the cyclone. As the only member of the Sandinista National Directorate to serve on the governing junta, he was charged with holding that uneasy alliance together. As a leader of the Tercerista tendency that had forged alliances with the private sector, he was charged with building a vibrant private sector within an overall socialist framework. As the Front's chief personal negotiator, he was charged with maintaining good relations with the international community. Then, as events unfolded, he was increasingly charged with defending the very national sovereignty that the revolution had won for Nicaragua. It is no wonder that by 1983 he was already quipping, "Why didn't anyone ever tell me that it was easier to run a revolution than a country?"[11] Wisecracks aside, Ortega failed in all his responsibilities. However, the challenges were daunting and success elusive. He was pitted against a mighty opposition, achieved occasional successes against incredible odds, and fought tenaciously as the United States systematically undermined the Nicaraguan Revolution. As it had happened, he was even out of the country during the junta meeting at which Robelo tendered his resignation, and thus was unable to use his powers of personal persuasion to prevent the rift that ultimately destroyed the government.

Governing Tensions

FOR THE FIRST FIVE years following the revolutionary victory, Nicaragua's official government consisted of a ruling junta (the Governing Junta of National Reconstruction, or JGRN), and a Council of State. The JGRN was the executive branch, and its membership initially included Daniel Ortega, Sergio Ramírez, and Moisés Hassan, all more or less affiliated with the FSLN, as well as Alfonso Robelo and Violeta Chamorro from the private sector. Again, the junta was tilted in favor of the Sandinistas, in part because Ramírez's allegiance to the Front had not been fully disclosed. However, Hassan was not an uncritical supporter of the Sandinistas, and in fact had reservations. His reservations led to his leaving the junta after about a year, although he served as the Sandinistas' mayor of Managua for a few years afterward before leaving the Front altogether and becoming a critic of it.[12] The Sandinista tilt of the initial junta was therefore not particularly pronounced, and it never really became so. New appointees replaced Robelo and Chamorro, who resigned at about the same time, apparently for similar reasons though without stating them. But they did not work out and the junta was reduced to three members. Even so, Sandinista control of the junta was still not absolute. While Ortega and Ramírez remained part of the three-member junta, Hassan was replaced by Rafael Córdova, a conservative lawyer. Córdova did tend to align himself with the FSLN, but was not himself a Sandinista. The idea was always for the junta to broadly represent Nicaraguan society, not merely act as a rubber stamp of the FSLN.

The idea was similar for the Council of State, which functioned as the legislature (albeit a fairly weak one). Initially planned to have thirty-three members, its membership was quickly expanded to forty-seven and then to fifty-one. The aim was for it to represent all walks of Nicaraguan life in rough proportion to each one's prevalence in the population. As such, it was essentially a democratic body. Initially FSLN members or sympathizers held a dozen seats on the Council of State, almost 40 percent, although after being expanded twice the FSLN counted thirty-two of the fifty-one members as supporters or sympathizers, about 60 percent. The increased representation of the Sandinistas on the Council was the reason Robelo gave for resigning from the junta. When Nicaragua held its first elections in 1984, however, and both the JGRN and the Council of State were replaced with a president and vice president (the executive) and a National Assembly (the legislature), the party affiliations of those elected mirrored those of the previous unelected government. Daniel Ortega was elected president and Sergio Ramírez vice president with 63 percent of the vote. In the National Assembly, which replaced the Council of State as the legislative branch, the Sandinistas garnered sixty-one out of ninety-six seats, about a two-thirds majority. This elected representation was actually slightly higher than the appointed representation. Meanwhile, 75 percent of registered voters (and 94 percent of eligible voters were registered) cast ballots in that election, a turnout that would be considered high in the United States.[13] Thus, while the Sandinistas had a numerical advantage in both the appointed and the elected governments, that advantage reflected the democratic will of the Nicaraguan people. Both formal governments were broadly democratic, at least in structure and intent.

Following the 1984 elections, when the National Assembly was elected and convened, it got busy writing a formal constitution. The constitution more or less codified the democratic form of government that had existed prior to its writing. The draft constitution was presented at numerous public forums throughout Nicaragua, where public input was solicited and occasionally resulted in modifications. As it emerged, Nicaragua's formal post-revolution government arguably reflected a commitment to loftier Western political ideals than even the United States embraced. To be sure, as a predominately Roman Catholic country, the Nicaraguan constitution did not go to the lengths that the U.S. constitution does in insisting upon the separation of church and state, although freedom of religion was enshrined in the document. Nicaragua also abolished the death penalty (although the provisional government had abolished it by decree prior to the writing of the constitution), a ban commonly believed to be a core tenet of human rights values by Western Europeans and others. In like manner, Nicaragua extended formal rights to women at a time when the United States could not pass an equal rights amendment for women. Structurally, the government incorporated a couple of features that are generally looked upon favorably by democratically minded thinkers. These included a system of proportional rather than geographic representation in the legislature, an electoral process that is more likely to include minority voices, and a fourth independent branch of government for monitoring elections and ensuring that they are fair, the Supreme Electoral Council. Throughout the process, a lot of informal emphasis was placed on governing through consensus—the JGRN and Council of State usually worked harmoniously together, as did the president and the National Assembly—as well as including citizen input. Top government officials, including Ortega, regularly appeared at "Face the People" meetings held throughout the country where average citizens could voice their concerns and express their opinions.

In terms of political philosophy, Nicaragua's formal government rested upon three pillars: political pluralism, a mixed economy, and international nonalignment. Political pluralism meant that Nicaragua would welcome political parties from across the ideological spectrum and allow voters to choose the parties and candidates they preferred in fair, democratic elections. A mixed economy would include a mix of private and state businesses, and the state would strive to maintain a vibrant private sector tempered by a slate of social welfare benefits and worker guarantees. International nonalignment meant that Nicaragua would retain the sovereign right to maintain friendly relations with whatever other countries it chose to. It would not automatically ally with either side of the Cold War foes, but would go its own way. Taken together, this political philosophy reflected the Western democratic ideals of countries like Sweden—one of the models that Nicaragua looked toward for guidance[14]—and it was in turn anchored in a governmental structure that seemed capable of expressing and sustaining these ideals.

This, though, was only Nicaragua's formal post-revolution government. Behind it lay the nine-person National Directorate of the FSLN. The members of this body were not elected by the public at large, and in fact the public did not initially know who all of them were. The members included Bayardo Arce, Tomás Borge, Luís Carrión, Carlos Nuñez, Daniel Ortega, Humberto Ortega, Henry Ruíz, Victor Tirado, and Jaime Wheelock. They were all stalwarts of the Front, chosen by their peers in the manner in which the Front had always operated, namely by insiders agreeing among themselves on other members. In fact, the membership on the Directorate had been carefully negotiated by the three tendencies in connection with their reunification. The bulk of Nicaraguans had no idea about the three tendencies or much else about the Front. Of course, neither the meetings nor the decisions of the National Directorate were open to public input. Although the Directorate met weekly as well as in special called sessions, and the meetings typically ran six hours or longer, no member of the press or the public was ever apprised of them or invited to attend. It was even the case that, while members of the Directorate were often accompanied by aides at the meetings, aides were only allowed to speak if specifically addressed by a member. It was a decidedly undemocratic, clandestine body, although the Directorate itself internally worked through discussions leading to consensus.[15]

The National Directorate was enormously powerful vis-à-vis the formal government. It had been involved in negotiating the plan of government prior to the victory of the revolution, and then increasingly assumed appointment powers in that government through Ortega. Replacements to the governing junta following resignations, for example, were chosen by the National Directorate. There was no other body to consult; the Council of State did not even convene until after Robelo and Chamorro resigned. It was also the National Directorate that decided to expand representation on the Council of State. Meanwhile, the National Directorate assumed appointment powers for the various government ministries. This resulted in four of nineteen ministerial positions held by members of the Directorate, all powerful positions: the Ministry of the Interior, in charge of the state police force, court system, and prisons, headed by Tomás Borge; the Ministry of Defense, headed by Humberto Ortega; the Ministry of Planning, charged with managing the economy, headed by Henry Ruíz; and the Ministry of Agriculture, headed by Jaime Wheelock. Nicaragua's economy was largely agrarian, making agriculture policy a key component of economic policy. Humberto Ortega's appointment as Minister of Defense illustrates the growing power of the Directorate. It was not made until December 1979, largely because an earlier appointment would have been met with the objection that it smacked of too much intermingling of military and political power. By December, few other voices were empowered to object to decisions of the Directorate, so it quietly replaced the existing minister with Humberto. Meanwhile, all the other ministerial positions were held by loyal Sandinistas, albeit not members of the National Directorate. Of course, Directorate member Daniel Ortega was also coordinator of the governing junta.

Sandinista political philosophy was also at some odds with that of the formal government, although it was not the communist authoritarianism that their critics alleged. Both characterizations—communism and authoritarianism—obscure more than they reveal. With respect to communism, the Sandinistas who managed the economy were openly Marxist-Leninists— Wheelock had published a book offering a Marxist interpretation of Nicaraguan history and Ruíz was educated in the Soviet Union—while the Sandinistas as a whole looked upon Castro with special affection and respect. But even Wheelock readily discarded Marxist orthodoxy in favor of reality. "Economic doctrines and romantic ideas are no good if people are hungry," he said, quickly emerging as one of the Front's chief advocates of a genuinely mixed economy.[16] "The middle and upper strata feel that we respect their property and that they can live somewhat affluently," he later announced, because "we allow them the possibility of owning some of the means of production."[17] It was the same with private business in general. The National Directorate was genuinely committed to a vibrant private sector and went to considerable lengths to nurture one. They did veer toward more socialist policies, but even Robelo had said, "We should all understand that our revolution is socialist."[18] With respect to Castro, Cuban advisors did arrive to assist the new government. Immediately after the triumph, the National Directorate convened not in Nicaragua but in Cuba.[19] Cubans never had more than advisory roles, however, and in most cases they served as teachers and medical workers. In other areas, most notably regarding communism's rejection of religious faith, the Sandinistas were emphatically not communists. In fact, early on the Front had a problem: the Church did not allow priests to voluntarily serve in the government. It insisted that the priests resign, the priests refused, and eventually a compromise was reached in which the priests were allowed to continue in government service as long as they did not administer the sacraments.[20] In reality, although all members of the Directorate were informed by Marxist-Leninist thought, all considered themselves Sandinistas first, and Sandinismo had long before abandoned many tenets of that school.

With respect to the characterization of the Sandinistas as authoritarians, the reality was more complicated. They plainly considered themselves the vanguard of the revolution, and as such believed themselves Nicaragua's ultimate political authority. As they understood it, their role was more to establish an overall framework within which Nicaraguan politics would operate than to directly govern the society themselves. The country needed a new governmental system, based on core values, and the Sandinistas took on the task of defining these structures. Moreover, the framework they championed was, in their minds, a democratic rather than an authoritarian one. There is some confusion about this, because the Sandinistas understood democracy more in terms of French than of British traditions.[21] The Directorate viewed the will of the people as better expressed in collaborative action and discussion than through elections. The notion was of "participatory democracy" more than of "electoral democracy," and on occasion individual members of the Directorate even voiced the opinion that elections were sometimes merely "raffles." Indeed, when they were finally persuaded to hold their first elections in 1984, they did so mainly to placate the United States and other critics. In their opinion, elections were more of a nuisance than a mark of democracy. Their main goal was to establish a deeper and more communitarian democracy in Nicaragua than one that, in the words of one rank-and-file Front member, could be realized when voters simply supported the candidate who promised "toothpaste and toilet paper for all."[22]

Daniel Ortega's views reflected the Sandinista consensus. Regarding the authority of the National Directorate vis-à-vis the formal government, for example, he explained: "The revolution has established a framework within which different political, economic, and social forces can be active," and "the Sandinista National Liberation Front was the organization, the party, that carried out revolutionary change." It followed for him that whereas the FSLN was committed to "political pluralism" and opposed to "a one-party state," the Sandinistas had the right as well as the duty to establish the overall system within which Nicaragua's political pluralism would be permitted. To illustrate what he meant, he compared Nicaragua under the Sandinistas to the United States. "In the United States, if some political force were to attempt to alter the political system, that force would be destroyed by the system. In the United States, other political forces can participate, they can present opinions, and they can dissent so long as there is no attempt against the system itself. In Nicaragua we are doing something similar." And, cognizant of comparison cases, he added that the Sandinista efforts to establish a framework within which democracy can operate was more restrictive than Chile under Allende, which proved too weak to preserve Allende's government against the coup supported by the United States, but that it was more lax than Castro's Cuba and other socialist states. Nicaragua "has its own characteristics," he admonished.[23]

Elsewhere Ortega commented on his understanding of freedom. "I always think of freedom in the plural," he said. "There is room for the rights of the individual," but freedom involves "the action of the individual within society which organizes the rights of each to the benefit of all." This view of freedom, he agreed, stood in some contrast with the prevailing view of that value in the United States. The United States' version of freedom "made America prosperous," he conceded, but in Nicaragua this same view of freedom "tossed up a few millionaires and left everyone else impoverished." Acknowledging that he was "educated" in "Marxist thought" and that it provides "a certain guidance," Ortega nevertheless insisted, "Our idea of freedom itself comes to us directly in a deeply Christian sense, deeply Catholic." Again contrasting his view with that of the United States, he explained: "In the United States you began with the individual and worked out to the people as a whole. This was the Protestant way to salvation. . . . In our case we start from the people as a whole, as a group, the way Christ considered humanity as a flock. His crucifixion was for the salvation of the whole flock, not just the strong ones. . . . You proceed outward from the individual to the group, we work inward from the group toward the individual."[24]

Ortega is not on record speaking as reflectively about the value of democracy, but his public orations leave little doubt that he understood it in terms similar to those of the other Sandinista leaders. "They say we're anti-democratic," he once said, referring to the United States (which he accused of sending "gangs of criminal mercenaries to attack us"), "but we know what real democracy means. Democracy is literacy, democracy is land reform, democracy is education and public health! That is what we have always stood for, and what we stand for today."[25] This was not a description of a democracy with simply the right to vote, but of a democracy with the right to tangible goods. Interestingly, he made these remarks at a 1984 campaign rally when he was running for president, and to that point he had never been elected to any office in his life. This setting, though, did not prevent him from presenting his more complicated views of democracy—or from the cheering crowd affirming them.

THERE WERE THEREFORE REASONS for moderates like Robelo and Cruz to be wary of the extra-legal power of the Sandinista National Directorate. However, to some extent, its exertion of authority was a practical necessity—and remarkably restrained. One example is Tomás Borge's initiatives as the minister of the interior. Immediately after the triumph, angry mobs hunted down and killed many former National Guardsmen and Somoza collaborators (while looting and other acts of lawlessness were common). There was so much vengeful violence that no one has ever been able to count all the victims, much less identify all their killers. Had the Carter administration's proposal for an international peacekeeping force been accepted by the various parties negotiating the new government, that force might have quelled the violence and stopped the looting. But there was no such force, and it fell to Borge to create one overnight. There was no time to wait for the government to be established, and then wait for it to create a civil service police system to replace the National Guard, a new and impartial court system, and all the rest. Indeed, as was common in other ministries, Borge's first task was simply to find the relevant government buildings, get keys to their doors, introduce himself to the remaining staff members, and so on. It was a chaotic situation, yet there was blood in the streets and he had to act fast.

Borge's actions remain a subject of some controversy. He immediately accepted an offer of help from communist-bloc East

Germany (which even provided free uniforms to Nicaragua's state police) and built a tough state police force under their guidance, yet he relegated the Panamanian police who offered similar assistance to traffic control.[26] This made Borge's Ministry of the Interior appear to be heavy-handed from the start, and it was. Rumors of political imprisonments, torture, and even assassinations persist, and there may be some truth to them. It is true, at minimum, that under Borge groups called "divine mobs" were created for political purposes. These "divine mobs" were (and still are) groups of ordinary citizens sympathetic to the FSLN that can be called upon to disrupt opposition political rallies and otherwise engage in street actions, all the while appearing to be merely spontaneous outbursts of citizen sentiment. Clearly the creation and deployment of these mobs reveals that Borge was not above the use of repressive tactics for political ends. With respect to the courts, Borge quickly established a system of "people's tribunals" in which accused collaborators with Somoza could be given speedy trials. However, the "people" who presided over these tribunals were almost always Sandinista sympathizers with limited or no legal training. Opponents judged these "people's tribunals" to be little more than kangaroo courts in which the Sandinistas' thirst for vengeance was lent a veneer of legality.

Despite its excesses, the imperative to act swiftly and decisively in a climate of violence cannot be overlooked. Similarly, the Sandinistas showed more mercy toward their former enemies than is customarily the case when revolutions succeed. There were no state-supported death squads, no guillotines, and the examples of excesses are all piecemeal. Borge's stated view was that the Sandinistas should behave more morally than their predecessors. "Why did we make this revolution if we are going to do the same thing they used to do?" he asked rhetorically.[27] Coming from Borge, who had been a torture victim himself (and if rumors are believed was partially castrated in a Somoza prison), this opinion has a ring of credibility, although the human rights standards of the Somoza regime were not hard to exceed. In any event, the excesses appear

Augusto César Sandino, with the
Colombian Rubén Ardila Gómez and
the Mexican José de Paredes, 1929.

Courtesy of Father Alvaro Argüello/Instituto de Historia
de Nicaragua y Centroamérica

Battle of San Jacinto: A print of this painting, which depicts the defeat of William Walker, hangs in many government buildings.

Tim Rogers/*Nica Times*

Anastasio Somoza García with his sons Luís and Anastas Somoza Debayle, c. 1949. Instituto de Historia de Nicaragua y Centroamér

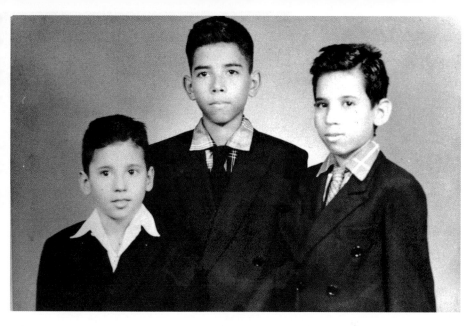

The Ortega brothers (Camilo, Daniel, and Humberto). Instituto de Historia de Nicaragua y Centroamérica

(below) Humberto and Daniel Ortega. Instituto de Historia de Nicaragua y Centroamérica

Daniel Ortega at the time of one of his arrests, no date.
Instituto de Historia de Nicaragua y Centroamérica

Daniel Ortega, Tomás Borge, and Edén Pastora, 1979.
Instituto de Historia de Nicaragua y Centroamérica

Daniel Ortega and his mother, Lydia Saavedra, visiting the graves of Daniel Ortega Cerda and Camilo Ortega.
Instituto de Historia de Nicaragua y Centroamérica

Sergio Ramírez and Daniel Ortega. Instituto de Historia de Nicaragua y Centroamérica

Daniel Ortega and Cardinal Miguel Obando y Bravo. Instituto de Historia de Nicaragua y Centroamérica

The Sandinista National Directorate, without Daniel Ortega, 1984. Left to right in uniform: Tomás Borge, Víctor Tirado, Humberto Ortega, Henry Ruiz, Jaime Wheelock, Bayardo Arce, Carlos Núñez, and Luis Carrión.

Chavarría/ Instituto de Historia de Nicaragua y Centroamérica

Daniel Ortega and Fidel Castro. Instituto de Historia de Nicaragua y Centroamérica

Daniel Ortega speaking at a ceremony celebrating the fifth anniversary of the Revolution, 1984.
Chavarría/ Instituto de Historia de Nicaragua y Centroamérica

Daniel Ortega visiting the Sandinista soldiers. Instituto de Historia de Nicaragua y Centroamérica

Daniel Ortega at a ceremony inaugurating electrification in a rural area.
Instituto de Historia de Nicaragua y Centroamérica

Daniel Ortega with José Azcona (Honduras), Vinicio Cerezo (Guatemala), and Oscar Arias (Costa Rica).
Instituto de Historia de Nicaragua y Centroamérica

Daniel Ortega and Oscar Arias.
Instituto de Historia de Nicaragua y Centroamérica.

Daniel Ortega at a celebration of the tenth anniversary of the revolution.
Instituto de Historia de Nicaragua y Centroamérica

Daniel Ortega presented with flowers by some of the vendors in Managua's Oriental Market in appreciation for his support, 1993.
Instituto de Historia de Nicaragua y Centroamérica

Alfonso Robelo, 1994.
Germán/ Instituto de Historia de
Nicaragua y Centroamérica

Arnoldo Alemán.
Tim Rogers/*Nica Times*

Enrique Bolaños.
Tim Rogers/*Nica Times*

Antonio Lacayo, Daniel Ortega, and Violeta Chamorro. Instituto de Historia de Nicaragua y Centroamérica

Rosario Murillo.
Tim Rogers/*Nica Times*

Gioconda Belli.
Tim Rogers/*Nica Times*

Hugo Chávez and
Daniel Ortega.
Eric Sabo/*Nica Times*

A billboard announcing a new oil refinery depicting Hugo Chávez and Daniel Ortega with Simón Bolívar in the background. The billboard reads: "Rise up poor of the world" and "Refinery, the supreme dream of Bolívar."
Eric Sabo/*Nica Times*

Protesters carrying a banner objecting to the Councils of Citizen Power. Sam Jacoby/*Nica Times*

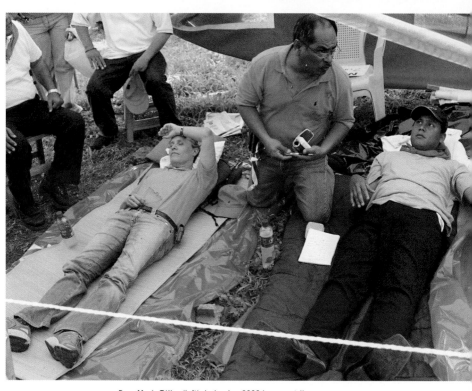

Dora María Téllez (left) during her 2008 hunger strike. Tim Rogers/*Nica Times*.
(below) A protester carrying a sign denouncing Ortega as a dictator. Tim Rogers/*Nica Times*.

A typical 2008 FSLN banner. It reads: "This power is of the people. This power is Sandinista."
Blake Schmidt/*Nica Times*

Eduardo Montealegre. Tim Rogers/*Nica Times*

Alexis Argüello. Tim Rogers/*Nica Times*

Daniel Ortega speaking to a reporter from the Sandinista-controlled media while guards block reporters from other media. Tim Rogers/*Nica Times*

Protesters wearing masks depicting Rosario Murillo and Daniel Ortega. Tim Rogers/*Nica Times*

to have been episodic rather than systemic. The use of "divine mobs" for political purposes, for instance, rarely resulted in more than fisticuffs (killings were rare), and to some extent they were simply ordinary citizens expressing their views in public demonstrations. They were not employees of the Ministry of the Interior, though the Ministry may have helped to organize them. Neither does the pattern of convictions and sentences meted out by the "people's tribunals" demonstrate systematic bias. Out of 4,250 cases, almost 300 resulted in acquittals or dropped charges, almost 40 percent of those convicted received sentences of five years or less, and fewer than 30 percent were sentenced to over twenty years. In addition, some convictions were later overturned on appeal and several hundred of those convicted were granted clemency.[28] On the balance, Borge's initiatives were comparatively restrained. In fact, it can be argued that he was too lenient, since he permitted plenty of former National Guardsmen and others enough liberties to mount a counterrevolution.

There were many other decisions that needed to be made, and actions that needed to be taken, for which there was no formal government entity in a position to assume responsibility. In theory, the governing junta had authority over these matters, but three of its members essentially agreed to whatever the National Directorate decided and its other two members resigned, as did their replacements. Most powers not seized by the Sandinistas accrued to them by default. Ironically, these included the power to establish and implement an electoral democracy. When critics of Sandinista authoritarianism increasingly called for elections, they called upon the Directorate to hold and organize them. It was a little bizarre for the extra-legal FSLN to be tacitly empowered even by its critics to decide whether, when, and how elections for the formal government would be held.

As the concentration of political authority in the Directorate steered the country further away from what its critics considered a democracy, the Directorate quickly displayed its commitment to democracy as the Sandinistas understood it. They saw democracy as participatory and collectivist, involving equal access to tangible goods more than access to formal procedural rights. A first step involved organizing a network of neighborhood associations throughout the society and empowering them with responsibilities ranging from organizing childcare and adult education classes to policing the streets and identifying sewer lines needing repair. These neighborhood associations were called Sandinista Defense Committees, owing to the role they played in national defense. Of course, their opponents complained that these committees were really instruments of Sandinista authoritarian control, since they were organized by the Front and ultimately answered to it. There is anecdotal evidence of Sandinista Defense Committees operating as the critics charged, becoming little fiefdoms in which local leaders used their positions to further the powers of the Front (and themselves) more than the needs of the neighborhood. Even so, however susceptible they might have been to political corruption, the rationale for and to some extent the functioning of these committees was to further participatory democracy in a country that had only known dictatorships.

The Directorate also understood that generations of repression had deprived Nicaraguans of the rudimentary requirements of democratic self-rule. Among other obstacles was a population in which over half the adults were illiterate. How can a populace that cannot read and write vote? Accordingly, a main early initiative—and an "authoritarian" initiative if a label must be attached to it—of the National Directorate was to launch a literacy crusade that relied upon tens of thousands of volunteers to teach approximately four hundred thousand adults how to read and write. The crusade was a sensational success, garnering an award in 1980 from UNESCO for the best program of its kind in the world, and it reduced the illiteracy rate from over half the population to around 13 percent. It did not stop there. A spin-off anti-malaria campaign was launched with corresponding success, and public school enrollments were twice as high in 1982 as they had been in 1978.[29] Not surprisingly, the literacy crusade was challenged because some critics felt that under the guise of teaching basic literacy the Sandinistas fostered ideological indoctrination. Some examples from 1983, from formal instructional materials used in the public schools, show passages from primary school readers that were decidedly tainted by Sandinista ideology. Sentences told the children how happy they would be as members of the Association of Sandinista Children, of the heroism of Carlos Fonseca, and even how crowds in the plaza cheer the FSLN.[30] During the literacy crusade Cuban teachers were also accused of instilling atheism in their students.[31] In addition, the National Directorate passed on accepting Peace Corps volunteers (alleging that they would be undercover CIA agents) from the United States but welcomed volunteers from Cuba.[32] However, it is arguably impossible to teach even basic literacy without some implicit ideological agenda, and the National Directorate's championing of literacy reveals how radically they departed from Somoza's genuinely authoritarian views. "I don't want educated people," said Somoza, "I want oxen."[33]

In these ways and others, the Sandinista National Directorate displayed their commitment to democracy as they understood it. Although they waited five years to hold the first elections and then called them only under pressure, by handily winning those elections the Sandinistas demonstrated that there was little conflict between their and their opponents' understandings of democracy. Nevertheless, they did display an attitude of entitlement about their right to rule that struck opponents as arrogantly authoritarian, and they did believe themselves to be the transcendent political authority in Nicaragua. In case there was any doubt about this Sandinista self-conception, they put it in writing at a September 1979 meeting. Their thirty-six-page report, "Analysis of the Situation and the Tasks of the Sandinista People's Revolution" but informally known as "The Seventy-Two Hour Document," expressed the Sandinista belief that they had won the revolution and were accordingly the country's preeminent political authority. But the report did not stop there. It explicitly described the Front's relations with the bourgeoisie, the Group of Twelve, and even the formal government as "alliances of convenience" that after an "intermediate period" would be dissolved. Although the document was intended only as an internal party platform and attended to details like the structure of the Front as a party (including, for example, an internal voting Sandinista Assembly), when copies of it got into the hands of outsiders a few months later, many were enraged. The document looked like a blueprint for an intended takeover of Nicaragua by a militaristic party of Marxist authoritarians. The excesses of "The Seventy-Two Hour Document" may be partially explained by the heady atmosphere of victory in which it was written, and it may merit emphasis that its most radical portions were dreamily futuristic. There were no plans to dissolve any "alliances of convenience" soon. Even so, the document expressed the Sandinistas' belief that they alone were the ultimate authority in Nicaragua, and this belief understandably struck their opponents as dangerously undemocratic.[34]

When Robelo resigned from the junta, followed immediately by Chamorro, the reason was the expansion of the Council of State. Robelo had valid objections: not only did the expansion augment Sandinista representation on the Council, but it also did so by decree from the National Directorate in direct violation of the plan of government that had been agreed to in Puntarenas. Ironically, however, the expansion can be viewed as a democratic initiative. In the aftermath of victory, many new civic groups formed in Nicaragua, and the Directorate believed that they should be included on the Council of State too. Their inclusion did make the Council more reflective of the society as a whole. Granted, many of these groups were formed by the Sandinistas. Even so, opposing forces could have formed groups supportive of them, and citizens did voluntarily join the pro-Sandinista groups. Granted also, the addition of the pro-Sandinistas groups diluted the influence of the private sector on the Council. But as a proportion of the population, the private sector had been grossly overrepresented on the initially proposed Council, and after it was expanded the private sector was still overrepresented.[35]

The Stampede of the Buffaloes

IT IS POSSIBLE THAT Nicaragua's business people would have begun referring to themselves as "buffaloes"—animals too dumb to fall in their tracks after being shot—no matter what.[36] There was certainly provocation, at least in rhetoric and personal behaviors. After his resignation from the junta, for example, the Sandinistas denigrated Robelo as just another wealthy capitalist who never had the people's interests at heart.[37] There was enough Marxist-style rhetoric in Nicaragua's post-revolution air to make business people shudder. The word "bourgeoisie," for example, became a popular insult. And the departure of Somoza and his allies had left a good deal of propertied wealth in the country for the new government to claim. Any post-revolution government would have inherited the wealth of the ousted dictator and his allies, so the Sandinistas were not unusual in this regard. But the transfer of so much wealth to a government that even moderates like Robelo insisted would be socialist gave business interests pause. Their fears then escalated when the government confiscated additional private properties—usually because they had been de-capitalized and their owners had fled the country, although occasionally out of mere greed or vindictiveness. Nor was the business class reassured by the lavish lifestyle members of the National Directorate enjoyed, made possible by their expropriation of others' wealth rather than the humble three-hundred-dollars-per-month salaries they paid themselves. Although Directorate members criticized each other for ostentatious displays of wealth—Humberto Ortega, for example, took Borge to task for an Olympic-size swimming pool—the Sandinistas found it difficult to restrain themselves. Humberto himself took over three houses, spent nearly a hundred thousand dollars remodeling them into a single compound, and had seventeen personal employees, including a chauffeur.[38] There were ample reasons for the business class to worry.

Contrary to both stereotypes and expectations, however, the National Directorate did not nationalize vast sectors of the economy and place them under socialist state control. Indeed, in May 1983, almost four years after the victory, *Business Week* magazine evaluated the Sandinistas' "performance" as "mixed," noting for example that 70 percent of business remained in private hands.[39] In fact, the Sandinistas even took the risky but responsible step of assuming rather than repudiating the national debt that the country inherited from Somoza. Their objective was to reassure global investors and thus to retain and even to attract capital investments. Similarly, they negotiated "production accords" with private industries that resulted in the state pumping $230 million into them during 1979–1980 alone, while they also established favorable currency exchange rates for the private sector.[40] Meanwhile, the National Directorate systematically fought against union demands for wage increases, preferring instead to subsidize food staples so that workers could buy essential goods at below-market prices. In these ways and others, the Sandinistas demonstrated a genuine commitment to the kind of private sector economic development that was consistent with their promise of a mixed economy.

The situation was similar, albeit more complicated, in the agrarian sector. The overthrow of Somoza immediately put nearly two million acres of farmland and some two thousand farms and ranches—approximately 20 percent of Nicaragua's agricultural sector—under state ownership. The question was what to do with it.[41] The stereotypical command economy solution of establishing large, collectively owned state farms was only one part of Sandinista agricultural policy, and one they embraced only out of necessity. By 1983, 23 percent of the cultivated land was on state farms, another 7 percent on cooperative farms (a public-private arrangement the Sandinistas tended to prefer).[42] Motivating the establishment of the state farms and cooperatives was the very

real problem of efficiently producing cash crops for export. Sandinista sympathies, like many others in the world at the time,
leaned toward "land reform" policies that placed ownership of
small- and medium-sized farms in the private hands of the workers, which would in turn allow for a self-sustaining agricultural
sector fueled by pride of ownership. The Sandinistas pursued this
policy, and the percentage of cultivated land on privately owned
small farms increased from 15 to 18 percent during the first four
years after the revolution.[43] In fact, Nicaragua's emphasis on private ownership of small farms may have influenced Gorbachev's
reforms in the Soviet Union.[44] However, a dimension of the agricultural problem that Nicaragua confronted, and in turn a dimension of its economic problem, involved the necessity of producing cash crops for export. Only by doing this could Nicaragua
attract the currencies necessary to buy goods it did not produce,
like tractors. Moreover, while morally compelling, the reality is
that small farms are rarely as efficient as highly mechanized large
farms. Thus Nicaragua needed to retain a large-farm sector producing for export. While cooperatives were a preferred solution,
state farms were the easiest. The result was a public-private mix-
ture that, despite more than a few problems, increased agricultural production and struck a U.S. ambassador in the region as
one of the most sensible land reform policies in Latin America.[45]

In addition to periodic flourishes of left-wing rhetoric, the
Sandinista leaders were also frequently inept in their economic
policies. "This is hardly what we would call socialism," explained
a diplomat from the Soviet bloc during the early 1980s. "It is much
too undisciplined, much too chaotic."[46] Henry Ruíz in the Ministry
of Planning struck Ortega as in so far over his head that he quietly
eliminated the ministry as soon as he was elected president and
turned to Lance Taylor of the Massachusetts Institute of Technol-
ogy for more realistic economic advice.[47] The whole idea of subsidizing a basic basket of goods for consumers, for instance, had
sounded good, but in reality these goods were often not available
on the store shelves, either because the government purchase price

was too low to motivate farms to produce the goods or because a black market quickly developed in which producers, wholesalers, and retailers made more money bypassing government channels. Meanwhile, hoarding goods—both as a hedge against later shortages and in the hopes that their black market prices would rise (which they usually did)—became common practice, while the poor who stood in line to purchase their subsidized government allotment often turned right around and sold it to wealthier people who wanted more than their share and did not want to stand in line. In the agricultural sector, Wheelock tried to influence which crops would be cultivated by setting government prices for them while simultaneously establishing a government farm-credit system at lower interest rates than the private system. Like most such plans, Wheelock's probably looked great on paper, but it met resistance among farmers and ranchers who had to live with it. Noncompliance was routine, as peasant-farmers balked at state edicts, and many of the farmers even appeared to prefer the higher interest rates offered and lower wholesale prices paid by the agricultural middlemen who had preceded the state's involvement. These "bloodsucking" middlemen, as the Sandinistas regarded them, at least knew their customers' needs and catered to them. The state seemed remote, inefficient, and a little clueless. In all, market forces tended to trump even the best intentioned of Sandinista policies, and anyone looking for evidence of dysfunctional Sandinista economic management can find plenty of examples.

The divestment of the Nicaraguan business class from the country's economy had created the loss of the kind of business expertise that might have prevented some of the Sandinistas' blunders, and this continued for years after the revolution. Instead of plowing profits back into their businesses with an eye toward growing them, many business owners intentionally bled their firms of capital, which they then shifted into private accounts abroad where they expected to wait out the post-revolution government with their personal wealth intact. The National Directorate tried to stop this outflow of capital by decreeing that any business found divesting in Nicaragua would be subject to confiscation by the state. The problem with this decree was threefold. First, it is very difficult to prove that a business is divesting, and to distinguish that from mere poor management. Second, nationalizing businesses sent exactly the opposite message to the private sector that the Sandinistas wanted to send. The Directorate did not want to threaten private business, which would only provide business owners with an even greater incentive to divest, but wanted to encourage businesses to remain and grow. Third, the Sandinistas did not want to own or run the businesses. They earnestly wanted a mixed economy, and thus a vibrant private sector too.[48]

A more insidious problem followed: Nicaragua became the immediate and then long-term recipient of enormous amounts of foreign aid. Especially in the early years, hundreds of millions of dollars flowed into Nicaragua from dozens of foreign countries (including the United States) as the world community locked arms to assist this tiny, poor country that had against all odds thrown off the yoke of dictatorship. Later, Ortega, always at his best in personal negotiations, became something of Nicaragua's top salesman-beggar, regularly traveling the globe to seek and usually to secure generous aid from foreign governments. Like any form of charity, however, foreign aid is a two-edged sword. Whereas temporary emergency aid of the sort that Nicaragua immediately received is helpful, and targeted longer-term aid may be advantageous, dependence upon it rather than a growing economy is very dangerous. It fuels corruption among political and economic power brokers, who skim aid dollars off for themselves, and it encourages an entitlement mentality among the general public, who come to expect the aid. Few recognized it at the time, and there were reasons to accept it then, but the divestment from Nicaragua's economy coupled with the massive influx of foreign aid effectively replaced the country's dependency on a foreign-backed dictator with dependency on global charity.

In the end—that is, by the middle- to late 1980s—it was inflation that destroyed the Sandinistas' hopes of economic improvement. "We are waging the battle for military defense with great effectiveness," Ortega declared optimistically in February 1986, "but the economy is more complex and difficult."[49] Then he announced a 100 percent increase in interest rates and a 150 percent devaluation of the córdoba, the Nicaraguan currency. In the worst years, inflation topped 3,000 percent. The córdoba was for all practical purposes worthless. Stacks of large-denomination bills were required to buy lunch at a restaurant. There was a constant shortage of nearly all goods (except seemingly weapons). Customers at McDonald's had to return their paper cups so that they could be washed and reused—that is, if the water worked that day, which most days it did not. Housewives would go shopping with AK-47s strapped over their shoulders, but there was rarely much in the stores to buy and few had enough of the inflated currency to buy much anyway.

The problem by this time was that Nicaragua was at war. Shortly after the inauguration of President Ronald Reagan in January 1981, officials in the administration began to organize, direct, and rapidly escalate a counterrevolution against the Sandinistas. The United States not only inflicted direct war damages on Nicaragua—by bombing its bridges and hospitals, for example, as well as by mining its harbors—while forcing the country to divert its meager resources to military defense, but it also placed an economic embargo on the country and actively lobbied against Nicaragua's loan applications with institutions like the International Monetary Fund. In fact, part of the United States' strategy against Nicaragua during the 1980s was to strangle the country economically, which in turn would presumably pressure the people to oust the Sandinistas. Because of this U.S. aggression, it is very difficult to disentangle the Sandinistas' economic mistakes from the suffering inflicted upon Nicaragua by the northern superpower. Perhaps more ominously, with the United States pressing for a regime change in Nicaragua, the country's business class had little incentive to remain in the country and slog it out with their adversaries. It made more sense for the buffaloes to stampede to Florida, where they could wait out a war that they were certain the United States would eventually win.

Ronald Reagan's Dark Hobby

SOME ARGUE THAT THE Sandinistas brought on the war by their own missteps. During the Carter administration, Congress joined the world community in earmarking aid to Nicaragua, but stipulated that the aid was conditioned upon Nicaraguan not "exporting" its revolution elsewhere, in particular to El Salvador. The United States opposed the leftist revolutionaries in El Salvador, the Farabundo Martí National Liberation Front, or FMLN. Although Sandinistas, including Daniel Ortega, steadfastly denied involvement in the shipment of arms to the FMLN, the truth lay elsewhere. By early 1981, Carter's intelligence provided him with enough information to convince him that arms were being transported through Nicaragua to El Salvador, and the U.S. president who many Sandinistas regarded as a "good gringo" had no choice according to the terms stipulated by Congress other than to suspend the aid payments. Two months later, after President Ronald Reagan had taken office, the arms transfers were used as a pretext to launch war against Nicaragua.

The decision by the National Directorate to assist the FMLN was thus a fateful one, and no doubt one that few members of the Directorate would make again today. However, at the time the Sandinistas believed it was the right decision. At minimum, as an explicitly nonaligned sovereign country, Nicaragua had the right to make its own foreign policy decisions. The Sandinistas supported the revolutionaries in El Salvador ideologically and reasoned that Nicaragua would be better off with a more like-minded government in El Salvador. Then, too, the FMLN had lent crucial assistance to the FSLN during its revolution, while in January 1981 the FMLN was preparing to launch a final offensive that many believed would succeed. Since the Sandinistas were not asked to do much—only to allow arms to be shipped through their country—the Directorate leaned in favor of assisting the Salvadoran revolutionaries. The Directorate was unsure, however, and Ortega in particular was tempted to acquiesce to U.S. pressure. To settle the matter, he turned to Castro for advice. Castro said, "No, chico, you don't have to make a deal yet. The Salvadorans are like the Russian missiles we once had in Cuba. Don't bargain them away until you have to."[50] Thus it was ultimately practical politics that led the Sandinistas to assist the Salvadorans. They calculated that doing so would put them in a stronger bargaining position with the United States, not start a war.

The issue came to a diplomatic head during late summer and early fall 1981 when Assistant Secretary of State Thomas Enders presented Daniel Ortega with the United States' offer: in exchange for ending the arms flow to the Salvadoran revolutionaries and reducing Nicaragua's own military from twenty-three thousand to fifteen thousand, the United States pledged not to intervene in Nicaragua, to renew economic aid, and to expand cultural relations. Ortega, the negotiator, rejected the offer. "We have an historic prejudice toward the United States," he explained, "which makes us fear attack from it, and look for all possible means of defense." He then added the clincher that was pertinent at the moment: "We see that there is no good will in the United States toward us." That perception was grounded in fact. The United States was already permitting paramilitary groups preparing to "oust the communists" from Nicaragua to train in Florida and California (in violation of its own neutrality laws), was beginning threatening military maneuvers of its own, and had canceled aid that it had previously promised only to hold in suspension. In fact, Ronald Reagan had already essentially launched the war against Nicaragua five months before Ortega rejected Enders's offer. On March 9, 1981, Reagan signed a "Presidential Finding" authorizing the CIA to engage in covert actions in Central America to interdict arms destined for Salvadoran guerrillas. It was an open secret that the president wanted the CIA to topple the Sandinista regime too.[51]

DANIEL ORTEGA NEVER FULLY understood Ronald Reagan. He did believe that he understood the United States, and therefore politicians like Reagan. "People say that we're like the boy who cried wolf," he explained about his mistrust of the United States. "The problem is that Nicaragua is a country that has already been invaded on several occasions by the United States. Unlike the boy in the fable, Nicaragua has already had the wolf come. And now we have the same wolf showing us his teeth and sticking out his claws at us."[52] He and the other Sandinistas also believed that Reagan's election in particular meant war for Nicaragua. Not only was Reagan a cold warrior who tended to see Nicaragua as "another Cuba,"[53] but he had also made his basic position on Latin America plain when he proudly declared his opposition to the Panama Canal Treaties during his unsuccessful 1976 run for the Republican nomination. "We bought it, we paid for it, it's ours," thundered Reagan, apparently reasserting the U. S. claim to domination over Latin America rather than stating its interests.[54] Then the 1980 Republican Party platform declared, "We deplore the Marxist Sandinista takeover of Nicaragua." It was obvious to the Sandinistas where Reagan's ideological proclivities lay, and that his foreign policy views were "uncluttered with the complexities" that prevent others from reaching simplistic solutions.[55] Even so, the depth of Reagan's animosity toward them puzzled the Sandinistas. Eventually Ortega could only muse: "He's taken us as his thing, like a little kid with his toys, making a little war. The only thing he can talk about is Nicaragua, because it is his hobby. And it's a dark hobby."[56]

It was essentially a "hobby," albeit a hobby of the most powerful man in the world. The war against Nicaragua was never really waged by the U.S. government, but rather by Reagan and a handful of his like-minded associates. Public opinion in the United States never supported it, despite Reagan's repeated attempts to rally the public to his side, and in fact so many U.S. citizens voluntarily flocked to Nicaragua to assist the Sandinistas that they earned the nickname "Sandalistas," referencing their footwear. Congress did not fully support the war either. Although it did periodically acquiesce to Reagan's requests for funds, it often rejected his requests. When it did approve them, Congress tended to attach restrictions that required the funds to be used for only "humanitarian" purposes. Indeed, after discovering that the $19.5 million it had approved in November 1981 for arms interdiction had gone to training and equipping right-wing Argentinean mercenaries bent on overthrowing the Sandinistas, Congress passed the Boland Amendment in December 1982 forbidding the funds they appropriated from being used to undermine any foreign government. Had it been up to Congress or the people of the United States, there would have been no war against Nicaragua.

But Reagan was committed to war, and waged it anyway. In order to finance it, he charged Lieutenant Colonel Oliver North of the National Security Council with the primary responsibility of raising the necessary funds, although North was assisted by others. North performed brilliantly. He proceeded in the usual government manner by simply using existing appropriations in ways that had not been specifically intended. The funds that went for training the Argentinean mercenaries, who in turn were used by the CIA for an initial combat operation, for example, were appropriated by Congress, just not used exactly as Congress had intended.[57] Soon, though, CIA Director William Casey instructed North in the art of establishing a series of dummy corporations, which could serve as conduits for government contracts from which profits could be skimmed. The corporate labyrinth constructed by North has never been completely unraveled, in part because he shredded documents once some of his illegal activities came to light. North was accused and eventually convicted of diverting $3.8 million from an arms sale to Iran to the contras in

Nicaragua. His conviction was eventually overturned on appeal owing to his Fifth Amendment rights against self-incrimination having been violated. However, the amount raised by this deal was a minuscule fraction of the total. He persuaded Saudi Arabia to kick in eight million dollars per month, while South Africa, Taiwan, and even the Sultan of Brunei were pressured to contribute what they could. If these "third country" payments had been routed through the United States, North would have been in violation of the law, but he handled the risk by using unnamed Swiss bank accounts. He also raised more money through donations. North organized fund-raisers and solicited donations from such right-wing stalwarts as Joseph Coors (who bought an airplane for the contras) and Pat Boone. *The 700 Club*, an evangelical television show, raised money from its viewers and sent it in. The evidence is also fairly clear that North, apparently with the knowledge of then Vice President George H. W. Bush and others, entered into unsavory deals with Colombian drug kingpins to allow them to bring their cocaine cargo into the United States unmolested in exchange for carrying arms from the United States to Nicaragua on their return flights.

In North and others, Reagan also found like-minded ideologues—people whose minds were equally uncluttered by complexities. As a senior U.S. Foreign Service officer put it, none of the White House war-makers knew "a damned thing about Latin America."[58] North was an especially tragic case. After being hospitalized at Bethesda Naval Hospital for emotional problems for several weeks in December 1974 and January 1975, he appeared to survive emotionally by leaning on the crutch of ideology, which he called patriotism.[59] It was not patriotism the way most people would define it, since it involved open contempt for the law. "If it weren't for those liberals in Congress," he once complained, "we wouldn't be doing half of what we do illegally."[60] He also did not know much about the country on which he was waging war. Toward the end of his tenure, he assumed that a baseball diamond in Nicaragua proved that Cubans were there, since he was unaware that Nicaraguans are baseball enthusiasts. He thought Nicaraguans only liked soccer.[61] When asked about North, Ortega said that he felt mostly "compassion" for him.[62] But North was not alone in his ignorance of and hostility toward Nicaragua. CIA Director Casey, who largely directed the covert war, could not even pronounce the name of the country, saying "Nicarga" or "Nigara" instead. "Casey wanted a rollback of communism," commented a government official, but "the place itself didn't seem to matter to him."[63] Neither did it matter to anyone to find out if Sandinista Nicaragua really was communist. Mikhail Gorbachev of the Soviet Union told George H. W. Bush point-blank that Ortega was "not a Marxist." Bush's notes of that meeting indicate that he considered Gorbachev's opinion "weak."[64] About the same time, he justified his "strong" opposition to the Sandinistas by telling Diane Sawyer on *60 Minutes* that "I really feel viscerally on this."[65] It was a war waged by those who relied upon their feelings more than facts. Or, as Reagan once put it to North, "Your work will make a great movie one day."[66] Ortega also guessed correctly that cinematic fiction rather than reality drove the Reagan war and responded in kind in a speech to the United Nations. He pointed out that *Rambo* was a movie, not a real-life adventure to be enacted on Nicaragua's sovereign soil.[67]

Run as it was by a cabal of well-funded, powerful, but ignorant men, it is no wonder that the war was fought mostly by paid professionals, mercenaries, and others for whom pecuniary motives were paramount. This was true of both U.S. fighters and Nicaraguans. The U.S. involvement was spearheaded by professionals from the CIA. By 1982, neighboring Honduras, the principal site of U.S. counterrevolutionary activity, swarmed with 150 CIA agents, and experts admitted that their intelligence was so good that they "could hear a toilet flush in Managua."[68] It was thus no surprise when the first major attack on Nicaragua, a March 14, 1982, bombing of two bridges, was found to have been committed by former National Guardsmen who had been trained by the CIA and used CIA-supplied components.[69] A Green Beret officer shared his opinion about the motives of the professional military personnel charged with managing the war. Most soldiers saw it as a "rebound from Vietnam," he said, while most officers saw it as a chance to "cap off their careers with a victory" after losing that war. "I don't think we give a shit about the Central Americans," he added.[70] Among the civilians and mercenaries, there were a few, like John Hull, who were true believers. Hull provided the contras with an illegal airstrip in Costa Rica and otherwise contributed to their cause. Hull once explained his politics pithily by saying, "If it were within my power people like [Edward] Kennedy and [John] Kerry would be lined up against a wall and shot tomorrow at sunrise." Although clarifying that he was not himself an "assassin"—a clarification that might have been required in that context—Hull was plainly no fan of the liberal senators from Massachusetts who had helped to lead the fight against U.S. aggression in Nicaragua.[71] Hull, though, appears to have been an ideological exception. One three-thousand-dollar-per-month mercenary pilot (who received a seven-hundred-dollar bonus for each flight into Nicaragua) wryly quipped, "Every time there is a war the same dammed people always show up."[72] When one U.S. cargo plane transporting weapons to the contras was finally shot down on October 2, 1986, and crew member Eugene Hasenfus miraculously survived, Hasenfus cut an almost sympathetic profile. He was simply an unemployed fellow from Wisconsin trying to support his family, he explained. He did not even know the true identities of those who recruited him, much less have an opinion about the war. A month after he was convicted of terrorism in a Nicaraguan court and sentenced to the maximum thirty years in prison, President Ortega pardoned him. It was December, and Ortega called the pardon a "Christmas and New Year message to the American people," a "message of peace."[73]

The story was similar with regard to the Nicaraguans who joined the contras, though somewhat more complicated. Some men and women of conscience joined the counterrevolution— people perhaps like Robelo and Pastora—and as the war esca-

lated, more and more Nicaraguans found themselves on the contra side. Many were indigenous Miskitos, whom the Sandinistas
removed from their homeland near the Honduran border on the
Caribbean coast in order, they said, to avoid having them become
casualties of the early contra attacks. The Miskitos resented their
forced relocation, and some chose to join the contras in Honduras
instead. However, this happened after the war was underway, and
among a population that had never felt strong ties to a culturally different country headquartered on the Pacific coast anyway.
In the main, the original contras were simply disaffected former
National Guardsmen. Lawrence Walsh, who served as the Independent Counsel in the Iran-contra scandal, estimated that only
"a few hundred" former National Guardsmen who made their
way to Honduras after the revolution formed the nucleus of the
contras.[74] The number may have been slightly larger, especially
since some fled to El Salvador and others made their way into
Guatemala, where in the fall of 1980 they formed a "September
15th Legion" of hired guns available for "special operations" like
robbery, kidnapping, and assassination.[75] There were also former
Guardsmen, the more elite among them, exiled in south Florida.
Together with the expatriates from the business class who shared
their disgruntlement with the Sandinistas, these former Guardsmen offered ideological and financial support to the contras in
Honduras. Most contras were former Guardsmen, and as late as
1986, twelve of thirteen top contra commanders were identified
as former Guardsmen in a U.S. congressional report.[76]

Even the contras, however, knew that they were largely a creation of the United States, not an indigenous counterrevolutionary force, and most behaved accordingly. According to one former contra, the "collection of small, disorganized, and ineffectual
bands of ex-National Guardsmen" grew to a "well-organized,
well-armed, well-equipped, and well-trained fighting force of
approximately 4,000 . . . entirely due to the C.I.A., which organized, armed, equipped, trained, and supplied us."[77] Many of the
contras even admitted that theirs was a business decision, not a

matter of political principle, and even called the U.S. ambassador to Honduras, John Negroponte, "the boss."[78] Robert Owen, Oliver North's aide, understood this and told North, "The war has become a business to many of them."[79] After their ranks had swelled, a few years into the war, one contra commented on the pecuniary motivations of the contras. "You've got estimates of between five thousand and thirty thousand tough contra soldiers on this border, yet they hold not one inch of dirt. The only progress they've made is in purchasing condominiums." A mid-level mercenary, Jack Terrell, who worked with Owen, embellished that the contras would pick up canned goods donated by Miami Cubans "like they were shopping at Safeway," and cynically opined that "the closest thing that the leadership have to a combat situation is when they put on their pinstripe uniforms and come to Washington to do combat for money."[80] Or, as a critic of Reagan's war policies noted, "The only town the contra mercenaries ever held was Washington."[81] Indeed, while there is little doubt that the contras shared an antipathy toward the Sandinistas, not much besides that and U.S. payments united them. The main contra political organization was created by the United States and its leaders were recruited by the CIA, yet it was never able to ally successfully with other contra groups, like Edén Pastora's in the south.[82] This was despite that fact that CIA operatives paid six of Pastora's top commanders five thousand dollars each to ally with the U.S.-controlled contras in the north.[83] The contras knew, even if Reagan officials pretended otherwise, that they were at most quixotic adventurers, at worst simply mercenaries going about the well-paid business of war.

Neither was there significant support within Nicaragua for a counterrevolution. A 1983 U.S. Defense Department report flatly stated, "Support for the democratic resistance within Nicaragua does not exist," although it spun the truth by referring to the contras as a "democratic resistance" when the report itself concluded that they did not have "democratic" support.[84] Again, the 1984 elections were a landslide for the Sandinistas. Moreover, the

Front issued weapons to ordinary Nicaraguans for the purpose of their own defense, and built a defense strategy premised in part upon local citizen militias, often organized through the Sandinista Defense Committees. Whereas this practice can be exaggerated—the Sandinistas did not issue weapons to all takers, but only to those it was reasonably certain were supporters—the fact is that the citizenry was knowingly armed by the Sandinistas in order to participate in its common national defense. The myth that Sandinista Nicaragua was a repressive Soviet-style state from which the people yearned for liberation was simply concocted by Reagan and his like-minded ideologues. There were no watchtowers like those in East Berlin, and during the early 1980s the staff of the Soviet embassy in Nicaragua was no larger than the staff of the U.S. embassy. Also, unlike Cuba, anyone who wanted to obtain a passport and leave Nicaragua could, and many did. [85] "If Nicaragua was a Soviet-style state," concluded Salman Rushdie after his visit there, "I was a monkey's uncle."[86] In reality, most Nicaraguans favored the Sandinistas, wanted the FSLN to succeed, and prepared themselves for a defensive war against the United States.

As might be expected, the White House did not lack a detailed plan for invading Nicaragua. By early 1985, if not before, Reagan was presented with a plan by the country's top military commanders, and by 1987 a version of that plan was published by the Center for Defense Information in *The Defense Monitor.* The plans of course only provided estimates. The first plan assumed that 125,000 U.S. troops would be required for a successful invasion and that casualties would number between three and four thousand a month. The second plan was more optimistic in its estimate of likely U.S. casualties, but as published was more refined overall. It assumed a smaller invading force of only around 50,000 troops, but a larger backup force of 100,000 to 150,000 troops. It also recommended sophisticated techniques of psychological warfare and placed a cost estimate on the entire war. Part of the plan, for example, was for graffiti to appear suggesting that the

United States' invasion was intended to "Restore the Revolution." The total cost, including reconstruction after the fighting, was estimated to be between thirteen and fourteen billion dollars. By comparison, the United States had earlier estimated that the cost of assisting Sandinista Nicaragua in rebuilding its economy would only be eight hundred million dollars up front and about two hundred million per year for a few years afterward. Basically, the cost of war was ten times the cost of peace.[87]

Yet the Reagan administration never launched a direct invasion. This frustrated some Nicaraguans. Bridges, hospitals, and grain storage warehouses were blown up, mines were placed in Nicaragua's harbors, and people were killed—most of it under U.S. direction, using U.S. materials, financed by U.S. dollars. Indeed, atrocities abounded. An eleven-year-old village girl was used for target practice by invading contras, who tried only to wing her and make her spin rather than kill her. They succeeded; the wounded girl survived.[88] A man was photographed with his throat slashed after being forced to dig and then lie in his own grave. He did not survive. Contras raped two women and a girl and left them for dead with their throats cut. By 1986 it was estimated that the contras had killed thirty-six hundred civilians wantonly, although adding the combat casualties increased the death toll tenfold.[89] But the enemy was largely a phantom one, because the United States refused to invade. On a November morning in 1984 over breakfast, an exasperated twenty-five-year-old Nicaraguan woman blurted out, "I wish Reagan would just get it over with and send in the Marines. We are ready to fight."[90] The remark was occasioned by the window-rattling sonic boom of a U.S. spy plane breaking the sound barrier overhead, by then a regular occurrence.

The United States never invaded because the Reagan administration lacked both public and Congressional support for it. Support declined even more in November 1986, when allegations of White House wrongdoings in the Iran-contra affair came to light. Reagan's approval ratings dropped over twenty points almost overnight and never recovered. Although North's subsequent testimony before Congress endeared him to many in the United States, who saw him as the patriot he believed he was, his support does not appear to have ever reached a majority. He and others involved in the scandal were convicted of criminal wrongdoings (although President Bush pardoned everyone except North, who had his convictions overturned on appeal). North was defeated in his 1994 run for the Senate from Virginia, despite having raised an astonishing twenty million dollars for his campaign. In any event, only a minority in the United States had the stomach for a war against Nicaragua after the Iran-contra scandal erupted. Meanwhile, there remained the gnawing problem of too little support inside Nicaragua to overthrow the Sandinistas. Even the Pentagon's own war plans revealed this. The pro-U.S. graffiti would be clandestinely scrawled by U.S. operatives, not by Nicaraguan citizens, and it would be phrased as support for the revolution (such as "Restore the Revolution").

The White House hawks had known all along that they lacked support for a U.S. invasion of Nicaragua, and the plans for one were only drawn up as a contingency. The Reagan administration's strategy had always been for what it called a "low intensity" war. The idea was not for the United States to overthrow the Sandinistas directly, but to recruit and equip others who would. The administration would assist the contras in any way possible, and even sabotage the Nicaraguan economy, but it drew the line at a direct U.S. invasion. The strategy thus included heavy use of propaganda. North hired a public relations firm to plant op-eds in various newspapers, eight Costa Rican journalists were put on the CIA payroll, and Chamorro's *La Prensa* was subsidized. The emphasis was on getting out the media message that the Reagan administration wanted, and suppressing other messages. But the strategy was even craftier than this. By subsidizing *La Prensa*, the White House also wanted the Sandinistas to censor the paper. After they did (and *La Prensa* was heavily censored), the United States and others could accuse the Sandinistas of infringing upon freedom of the press, even though the press that was censored had been financed by a wartime enemy. The strategies were similar in other areas. The United States paid up to eight hundred thousand dollars for high-level Sandinista officials to defect, and then implied that they had defected over matters of principle. It also invited anti-Sandinista priests to address Congress and complain that the Sandinistas were atheists, which was not true. In these and other ways the Reagan administration's war strategy emphasized the manipulative and the covert over direct military engagement. Nowhere was this strategy more egregiously applied than when the Reagan administration undermined the very Nicaraguan elections that it insisted the Sandinistas call.[91]

El Presidente

"ONE BY ONE, WE'VE been eliminating the pretexts used by Washington," explained National Directorate member Bayardo Arce about the Sandinistas' decision to hold national elections in 1984 rather than later as they had planned. "The only argument they have left is that we are . . . governing without a popular mandate." Thus the Directorate decided to move up scheduled elections.[92] The goal was to diffuse the main remaining criticism that the Reagan administration had of the Sandinista government, and to end the war. That goal was frustrated by the Reagan administration.

Interestingly, it was by no means clear that Daniel Ortega would be the presidential candidate of the Sandinistas in the 1984 elections. In the memoir in which he recounts his time as a foreign correspondent in Nicaragua, Stephen Kinzer writes of how he and his fellow reporters handicapped the National Directorate's selection of its presidential candidate. They were not certain that the Directorate would tap Ortega for the job, although they were able to narrow the field down to him and three others.[93] While Ortega was from the beginning the most powerful person in post-revolution Nicaragua, it was not until he ran for the presidency and won the 1984 election, Kinzer writes, that he was the "man on the move" in the country's leadership circles, and not until two years later that he appeared to be emerging as the country's top leader.[94] Ortega's slow but steady emergence reflected Sandinista philosophy. The National Directorate opposed any strong personality arising from their ranks. In the words of Borge, they believed ardently in "collective leadership," and even after Ortega was elected president they considered him merely the "spokesman" in a difficult job.[95] Since Borge was Ortega's most likely competitor for the top position, his willingness to set aside his personal ambitions is telling about his commitment to his stated principles. (However, Humberto Ortega's position as the minister of defense provided a check on Borge's power as minister of the interior, should Borge have contemplated asserting himself by force.) Yet, Borge continued to explain, "Unity is the magic formula, the greatest secret we Sandinistas have."[96]

Incredibly, no cult of personality ever developed around Ortega, at least to any significant degree. Even after he was elected president and continuing to this day, such basic personal facts about him as the number of his children have generally been successfully kept out of public view. All Salman Rushdie was able to conclude after visiting with him during the mid-1980s was that "children's toys, and indeed children, were everywhere. There was no shortage of little Ortegas."[97] (Ortega's first child—a son—with Rosario Murillo was born on January 30, 1980, and the couple had three more children—daughters—together. This information was only reluctantly provided in 2008 by the son of another member of the National Directorate, who asked that details about the children not be revealed.) Meanwhile, if Ortega emerged as first among equals in the Directorate, the accent should be on "equals." He was chastised by the other members for arriving late to meetings, for example, an act that they regarded as egotistical, and he soon started arriving on time.[98] He was the person his peers chose to run for the presidency, no doubt because he had already proved himself in the vortex of power. Edén Pastora fleshed out the Directorate's reasoning from a different perspective when he opined that Ortega was the "least bad" Sandinista. The difference between him and the others, commented Pastora, is that Ortega "feels."[99] There were therefore good reasons that Ortega was chosen to be the Sandinistas' presidential candidate.

The Reagan administration nevertheless maneuvered to deprive Ortega's campaign and subsequent election of legitimacy. This was all that it could do. After labeling the Sandinistas authoritarians for failing to hold elections, Reagan officials faced the embarrassing prospect of the Sandinistas not only holding elections but also winning them. To prevent this, the Reagan administration recruited Arturo Cruz. By that time, Cruz had left the Front to return to his job at the Washington, D.C.–based Inter-American Development Bank (where, minus his 1979–1981 participation in the Sandinista government, he had been a career employee since the early 1970s). They set him up to run for the presidency against Ortega. The United States also helped forge a coalition of anti-FSLN groups, referred to as the Coordinadora, to support Cruz. The idea was never for Cruz to actually run, though, since if he did he would probably lose. Rather, according to a senior official in the Reagan administration, the idea was for Cruz to occupy the position of "oppositional candidate" and then "either not to enter the race, or, if he did, to withdraw before the election, claiming the conditions were unfair."[100] In order to do this, the Cruz forces insisted upon so many conditions for their participation in the elections that even Robert Pastor, who goes easy with his criticisms of the Coordinadora–Reagan administration strategy for the 1984 elections, concedes that the conditions were simply impossible for the Sandinistas to meet.[101] In the end, Cruz did as instructed and withdrew from the race so that the opposition could claim that the Sandinista victories in 1984 were illegitimate. To this day the State Department's Nicaraguan Web site states that it was not until 1990 (when Ortega lost) that the country held its first free and fair elections.

There are those, including Robert Pastor, who agree with the State Department's official position: the 1984 presidential election in Nicaragua was not democratic. Others, such as the Latin American Studies Association and various foreign observers, hold the opposite opinion. Moreover, Holly Sklar quotes a member of the Coordinadora coalition saying that there were so few members in three of the so-called parties in that coalition that he could have "fit them all in a bus," as well as a Central American ambassador's opinion that if Cruz had remained in the race he would have only "shaved three or four points off the Sandinistas."[102] Meanwhile, since the Sandinistas overwhelmingly won in the National Assembly too, and the legitimacy of those elections has never been called into question, it can be inferred that the presidential elections were equivalently legitimate. Even so, Reagan administration initiatives prevent anyone from being certain. This was the intent: to make the Sandinistas appear to be an undemocratic, totalitarian regime, and thus to justify the war against Nicaragua.

ALTHOUGH THE LEGITIMACY OF his election was cast into doubt, Daniel Ortega was the elected president of Nicaragua. He proceeded to act like it, too—even replacing his olive green commandante uniform with a business suit when the occasion demanded. In reality, however, his role changed very little; it only became more visible. He was still the Front's main personal negotiator—and now Nicaragua's main personal negotiator as well—and it was to these tasks that he devoted the bulk of his energies. And there was much to negotiate. On one hand, as a desperately poor country at war, Ortega had to negotiate for arms as well as for general economic aid. On the other hand, as the head of state in a country that wanted to end its war, Ortega had to negotiate for peace. As part of this latter objective especially, it was also incumbent upon Ortega to win as many friends in powerful positions as he could.

Ortega was quite successful in soliciting military aid, in particular from the Soviet Union. Soviet military aid mushroomed from only a few million dollars' worth of armaments in 1979 and 1980 to as much as $160 million in 1981, between $250 million and $370 million per year in 1983–1985, and $500 million or more per year between 1986 and 1988.[103] But the Soviet Union faced its own problems, which made it an increasingly unreliable military supplier, and it appears that some promised Soviet aid never arrived. There was a controversy, for instance, in 1984 about Nicaragua receiving MIG-21 fighter planes from the Soviet Union. The United States' concern was that if Nicaragua obtained these planes it would have offensive military capabilities, when even the Pentagon acknowledged that Nicaragua's military preparedness to that point was overwhelmingly defensive. It appears that there was some consideration of giving Nicaragua MIG-21s or even a tentative commitment to do so, but the Soviet Union reneged on its commitment at about the same time that the FSLN National Directorate decided that they preferred to maintain a defensive military posture anyway. By then the war was winding down. Fortunately, Ortega could also rely upon his brother Humberto, who in fact did manage defense well enough to keep the battles out of the major cities and confined to the border regions.

Ortega thus focused on ending the war. Toward this end, he was desperate to get his message to the public in the United States, who he hoped would pressure the Reagan administration to end the war. In 1985, for example, he issued an open invitation to the members of the House and Senate to visit Nicaragua "with no type of restrictions."[104] He then accepted numerous speaking engagements in the United States, appearing for instance on *Donahue*, addressing church congregations, and showing up at an event for Jesse Jackson's Operation PUSH in Chicago, while of course speaking at the United Nations on behalf of Sandinista Nicaragua. Yet his public relations initiatives in the United States were hamstrung by the propaganda campaign that the Reagan administration had successfully waged against him, and there were times when he was forced to cancel scheduled speaking engagements owing to mysterious delays in obtaining a visa. As a

result, even the *New York Times* adopted the practice of referring
to him as a Marxist in passing, and was otherwise not always fair
to him. In a 1985 article headlined "Nicaragua's President Praises
Moscow as Friend," for example, Ortega is quoted as saying, "We
would like the same relationship with the United States that we
have with the Soviet Union." Nobody reading the headline would
have expected to read this quote, or to learn that Ortega's trip
to Moscow also included visits to France, Italy, Sweden, Finland,
and Spain, or to read the Spanish prime minister's favorable comments about Sandinista Nicaragua.[105] When, during a 1988 visit to
the United Nations, Ortega's motorcade stopped at Cohen's Fashion Optical store on the Upper East Side and he used a Diner's
Club credit card to purchase six pairs of eyeglasses for a total of
thirty-five hundred dollars, even the left-leaning Maureen Dowd
of the *New York Times* poked fun at this so-called egalitarian with
high-toned tastes, adding that his motorcade that day was seventeen cars long.[106] This event prompted Reagan to nickname Ortega
a "dictator in designer glasses," and made him something of a
laughingstock. Ortega later explained the glasses were a gift, paid
for by a New York supporter, and many were for his children.
They were not all for him (although he did have poor eyesight and
benefited from high-quality glasses, and at the time polycarbonate
lenses were expensive). As for the seventeen-car motorcade, perhaps that was excessive, but it is rare for an article in the *New York
Times* or elsewhere to mention the number of cars in any foreign
president's motorcade—or in a U.S. president's motorcade, for
that matter—and the article neglected to mention that, the year
before, two men from the United States were charged in a plot
to assassinate Ortega for a five-million-dollar fee.[107] He was not a
man who could very well hail a taxi and stay alive.

Ortega's efforts to woo the Catholic Church were also fraught
with difficulties. It is not clear what turned Miguel Obando y
Bravo, who was by this time a cardinal, against Ortega and the
Sandinistas. Odds are that Obando y Bravo was in part genuinely
disturbed by the authoritarian strains evidenced by the Sandini-

stas and in part simply protecting his own power. He had led the charge against the priests who served in the Sandinista government, for instance, which in reality signaled a victory for the popular church and a diminishment of his own authority. In any event, Obando y Bravo had a sympathetic ear in Pope John Paul II, who had endured Soviet satellite rule in his native Poland and was staunchly anti-communist. Worse, when the pope visited Nicaragua in 1983, he was actually shouted down by angry FSLN supporters. Some allege that the demonstration was engineered by the Sandinistas, and the fact that the pope's microphone went dead suggests that someone did pull the plug, but whether the protest was real or manufactured (or more likely in what combination) will never be known. Then the National Directorate expelled sixteen priests from the country and shut down a Catholic radio station. Ortega explained it was for treason—the highest crime there is. The priests and the radio station were calling for the violent overthrow of the government. "Going over the boundary of the law, siding with those who are committing an aggression against our country is punishable in Nicaragua or any other country," he explained unapologetically. But the expulsions and the censure of the radio station played into the hands of opponents who wanted the Sandinistas to appear to be anti-Catholic atheists. Meanwhile, although Obando y Bravo and other Nicaraguan priests opposed to the Sandinistas enjoyed private meetings with the pope (as well as with members of the U.S. Congress), Ortega's request for a personal meeting with the pope was denied.[108]

Ortega, however, persevered. He won many friends for Nicaragua, including the "Sandalistas" who continued to pour in to offer help. Benjamin Linder, a U.S. volunteer, was helping a village obtain electrical power when he was killed by a grenade in a contra attack. Ortega himself was a pallbearer at Linder's funeral, and he choked back tears to speak briefly about the "American citizen who . . . gave his life for the poor people of Nicaragua."[109] Nicaragua also took the United States to the World Court for mining its harbors in violation of international law, and won. Filed in

April 1984, the case prompted the Court to issue an immediate injunction against the United States, ordering it in May that year to cease all hostilities against Nicaragua. After the full case was heard two years later, the Court ruled that the United States was guilty and ordered it to pay reparations to Nicaragua. Before the case came before the Court, though, the Reagan administration elected for the only time in U.S. history to deny that the Court had jurisdiction over the United States. To be sure, the United States had used the World Court when doing so was to its advantage, but when it knew it would lose, it denied the Court's authority. The Court rejected this claim and others presented by the United States, but in the end the superpower refused to pay the reparations and the war continued.

Ortega therefore turned to what he did best—personal negotiations—and to the astonishment of all, ended the war. Ronald Reagan was furious, but Ortega checkmated him.

RECEIVED OPINION IS THAT Ortega was ultimately led by the scruff of the neck to peace by the newly elected president of Costa Rica, Oscar Arias. An heir to Costa Rica's pacifist tradition who believed that peace is a process requiring work to maintain rather than a state to be enjoyed passively, in 1987 Arias called the presidents of all five Central American countries (Costa Rica, Guatemala, Honduras, Nicaragua, and El Salvador) to a series of summits where they took versions of the Central American peace plans that had been floating around for a few years and discussed them in earnest. Indeed, Arias was committed to a locked-door style of negotiations, namely a strategy of putting the principals in a room and discouraging any of them from leaving before consensus was reached, and implemented this strategy. Even better from Nicaragua's standpoint was that Arias displayed real toughness in his dealings with the United States. A sticking point of all previous peace negotiations, from Nicaragua's perspective, was that the United States had not directly participated but rather insisted that

Nicaragua negotiate with the contras instead. To this insistence, the Sandinistas had a stock reply: "We want to negotiate with the owners of the circus, not the clowns."[110] Arias did not get the United States to the negotiating table, nor did he want it there. The peace agreement being negotiated forbade any member country from hosting a foreign military presence or any "irregular forces." These were clear enough, albeit indirect, references to the United States and the contras. What made Arias trustworthy is that he had personally stood up to Reagan by insisting that a contra airfield in neutral Costa Rica be closed. In so doing he risked losing a third of his country's budget, then provided by the United States, and in fact was told that he could "never set foot in the White House" again or get another "five cents" from the United States.[111] Despite the risks Arias took, Ortega never believed that Arias deserved the credit he received for engineering the peace (credit that included receiving the Nobel Peace Prize). The terms of the peace plan were not significantly different from previous ones, and Nicaragua was still not able to negotiate with the circus owners. Even so, Arias displayed a resolve that prompted all involved, including Daniel Ortega, to hope that this time peace might actually materialize.[112]

So on August 6, 1987, Ortega joined the other Central American presidents and signed the Central American Peace Plan. Reagan was furious, claiming that the agreement undermined U.S. policy in Nicaragua, but he was trapped.[113] Reagan could not very well violate an agreement signed by all five Central American presidents, or one that garnered its author the Nobel Peace Prize. As Arias put it, to the White House the agreement was "a kick in the balls."[114] The agreement allowed the Sandinistas to remain in power and forbade the United States from intervening. In short, it ended the war without removing the Sandinistas: a victory for Ortega and a defeat for Reagan.

The Sandinista National Directorate was also shocked. It had empowered Ortega to attend the negotiations but never expected him to sign an agreement they regarded as involving too many

concessions. An emergency meeting of the National Directorate was called, and Ortega was grilled by his comrades for a full
day. Still deadlocked, Ortega flew to Cuba that night to present
the issue to Castro. The old man agreed with Ortega. He viewed
the treaty as a way to end the war, and worth the tradeoffs. The
National Directorate was satisfied and the next day publicly
endorsed the treaty.[115] Ortega, the Sandinista in the middle, had
accomplished the near impossible. He had beaten Ronald Reagan
at war and managed to persuade his fellow Sandinista leaders of
the wisdom of his strategy.

But the practical challenge of bringing an end to the war had
yet to be confronted. This included reconciling with the contras,
who by then had sufficient numbers of ordinary Nicaraguans
within their ranks to turn the conflict into a genuine civil war,
not merely a war of Yankee aggression. Ortega broached the matter in a November 5, 1987, speech at a rally where he announced
his intention to enter into negotiations with the contras with
the aim of achieving a cease-fire.[116] This was the first time that a
Sandinista leader had agreed to negotiate with the contras. Previously the Sandinistas had always dismissed the contras as agents
of the United States and denied that they were fellow Nicaraguans with a different political opinion. Ortega's announcement
was accordingly met with shock and anger. Those assembled for
the rally had neither expected nor wanted to hear that the administration would negotiate with the enemy. But Ortega's resolve
was strong, and the next day he met with Cardinal Obando y
Bravo to attempt to persuade him to preside over the negotiations. Obando y Bravo hesitated, and introduced some conditions
of his own, and eventually the Sandinistas passed on his help. In
lieu of Obando y Bravo, Ortega then offered that the Front would
negotiate without an intermediary, and that Humberto Ortega
himself would represent the Sandinistas. The village of Sapoá on
the Costa Rican border was chosen as the site for the talks, and,
as it happened, Daniel Ortega joined his brother Humberto in
the negotiations while even Cardinal Obando y Bravo partici-

pated. Late in the evening of March 23, 1988, the Sandinista and contra leaders emerged to sing the Nicaraguan national anthem together.[117] "Brother Nicaraguans," Ortega began. "I speak to you as constitutional president of the nation of Sandino and Darío. We have reached an agreement based on the spirit of peace that is within all Nicaraguans, and we are determined to bury the weapons of war and raise the olive branch of peace."[118]

The fact that the U.S. Congress had recently voted against another Reagan request for aid to the contras, this one carrying a price tag of $270 million, did influence the contra's willingness to negotiate, admitted contra leaders privately. They had little to lose by disarming and agreeing not to accept any future military assistance, since none would be forthcoming anyway. However, they did extract concessions from the Sandinistas, including unrestricted freedoms for dissent, the right of exiles to return to Nicaragua without reprisal, and even freedom for contra prisoners. One of the prisoners freed under the Sapoá accord was the former Guardsman who had killed Camilo Ortega. Daniel Ortega was present for the occasion, but he stood in stoic silence as he watched the killer of his brother exit the prison. What Ortega got out of the negotiations at Sapoá was peace—and in important respects he considered all Nicaraguans to be his brothers and sisters.

He was the "least bad" Sandinista, and probably the cleverest. Arias got the credit and he got the blame, but Daniel Ortega outfoxed Ronald Reagan and extracted his country from war when no one believed that possible. Even so, in this final year of his second term, Reagan was still privately telling his aides that he wanted the Sandinistas out by the time he left office.[119] He would not succeed, but his successor would.

The Indirect Invasion

PRESIDENT GEORGE H. W. BUSH, who took office in January 1989, finished the job that Reagan started. He may have had personal as well as political motives for doing so. Some believe that if Oliver North's congressional testimony had not provoked a public outcry on his behalf—*Time* magazine wrote of "Olliemania" as ordinary citizens wore Ollie T-shirts and put Ollie bumper stickers on their cars—a fuller investigation into the Iran-contra scandal would have been launched that would have implicated Bush.[120] The vice president, who had himself formerly headed the CIA, was simply too close to too many misdeeds not to have participated in some of them. In particular, Bush was well aware that Panama's Manuel Noriega was involved in the drug trade, even knew that he was working as a double agent for both Castro and the CIA, and knew that he had funneled ten million dollars in drug profits to the contras with the Reagan administration's knowledge. Since Noriega was craftily helping the Reagan administration fight the Sandinistas while at the same time enriching himself, Reagan officials decided to eliminate the Sandinistas first, then go after Noriega.[121] Bush, however, had more of a personal incentive to eliminate Noriega, although he felt "viscerally" about eliminating the Sandinistas too. He therefore alighted upon a plan that allowed him to oust the Sandinistas, not by invading Nicaragua but by invading Panama.

Timing was crucial. Although there remained skirmishes, and the possibility existed that the by-then civil war would be reignited, the war in Nicaragua was essentially over. It was time for the country to reclaim the promise of its revolution. In part to get a fresh start, elections were called for February 1990. Daniel Ortega together with Vice President Sergio Ramírez ran for reelection, the polls showed them ahead, and the Sandinistas had every reason to believe that they would be swept into victory. Ortega's opponent turned out to be Violeta Chamorro. She was fairly formidable. The wife of slain journalist Pedro Joaquín Chamorro who had briefly served on the governing junta, Chamorro made no secret of her opposition to the Sandinistas. However, she drew the line at going over to the contras. One of her sons, who edited *La Prensa*, was a contra sympathizer, while another edited the

Sandinista newspaper, *Barricada*, and was a Sandinista. Chamorro was thus able to present herself as a symbol of reconciliation in that war-torn country. That she frequently dressed in white and campaigned from a wheelchair may have helped to strengthen this image. Nevertheless, she was merely the consensus candidate for a collection of fourteen different parties, temporarily united as the National Opposition Union, or UNO, for the elections, rather than the nominee of a party with an ideology of its own. The United States of course backed Chamorro and the UNO—the Bush administration pumped more money per vote into her election than it had spent on its own 1988 presidential campaign and admitted to "micromanaging" it—yet many of the campaign dollars were dispersed too late to be of much help, and in fact many observers believe that the Sandinistas had the edge in the elections from the standpoint of organization, funding, and other variables that win races.[122] In all, Bush faced the real prospect that Nicaragua's 1990 elections would be a repeat performance of the 1984 elections, when the Sandinistas won handily.

So, on December 20, 1989, Bush sent an invading force of over fifty-seven thousand troops supported by three hundred aircraft into Panama. During the fighting that extended to January 12, 1990, upward of four thousand civilians were slain while over twenty thousand Panamanians were displaced, many by fires that appear to have been intentionally set by U.S. soldiers. To the principal justification for the invasion—the capture and arrest of Panamanian leader Manuel Noriega for drug trafficking—the Bush administration appended others, including the usual one of defending American life and property as well as protecting the canal. Although these justifications had merit—Noriega's involvement in the drug trade was an open secret while tensions between U.S. soldiers stationed in Panama and the Panamanians had resulted in the killing of one Marine—the invasion inflicted casualties so far out of proportion to its justifications that many wondered what Bush's real motivations were. Nicaraguans, though, believed they knew. The Bush administration was obviously backing Chamorro and had even promised renewed aid to Nicaragua if she were elected. Nicaraguans therefore interpreted the invasion of Panama as a warning of what would befall them if they voted for the Sandinistas. They did not take that warning with indifference. In the words of a journalist at the time, Nicaraguans "feel like they are voting with a gun to their heads. They know that if they vote for the Sandinistas, the war will continue. . . . They don't want any more war."[123]

Daniel Ortega therefore captured only 41 percent of the vote against Chamorro's 55 percent, and lost the election. The vote was not a repudiation of him personally, but rather of the Sandinistas as a whole. The FSLN won only thirty-nine seats in the National Assembly while the UNO took fifty-one, pretty much the same proportion as the Chamorro/Ortega split. Indeed, the striking feature of the 1990 elections may be that over four in ten voters still thumbed their noses at the United States, determined to fight on in their own way in their own country. Even so, most Nicaraguans assumed that they would be better off voting in the way that the gringo president wanted them to vote, and did so.

Of course, there are always myriad factors that explain the outcomes of elections. Material deprivations surely played a role in dissuading Nicaragua's voters from granting Ortega another term.[124] Although Ortega's campaign slogan that year was "Everything Will Be Better," it was a difficult slogan for the voters to believe. The rationing of toilet paper seemed best to symbolize the wearying deprivations that ordinary Nicaraguans unwillingly endured. Everyone mentioned it. First it was one roll per person a month, then six, then three, then two. The government could not even keep toilet paper on the store shelves. Neither could it keep soap or meat or sometimes even beans there. Most days store shelves were virtually empty. But it may not have mattered, since the outrageous inflation rate prevented most Nicaraguans from being able to buy much anyway. Indeed, Nicaragua had the distinct misfortune and dishonor of being the poorest country in the Western Hemisphere on the day that Ortega was denied reelection.[125] Granted, the government subsidized a basic set of goods—as well as bus service, health care, schools, and so on—but people noticed what they did not have as well as what they did have. Managua went without running water two days a week and suffered frequent electrical outages; there were lines at gas stations, lines almost everywhere. In fact, Belli writes that if the United States would have simply dropped candy bars instead of bombs, the country would have surrendered on the spot.[126]

The Sandinista leaders undertook their own postmortem of the elections, and they identified their troubled relations with the Church together with their having instituted mandatory military conscription in 1984 as the key reasons for their defeat. They were probably right on both counts, but the two explanations overlapped. The Church had taken a strong position against a draft, largely because it opposed the Sandinistas and at minimum favored reconciliation between them and the contras instead of war. Indeed, as the war had increasingly become a civil war, ordinary Nicaraguans resisted conscription in an army they were beginning to believe narrowly represented the Sandinistas more than it did Nicaraguans. At the same time, Nicaragua had no tradition of a citizen military. Its tradition was rather one of subjugation by repressive forces on the one hand, and romantic guerrillas on the other. Whereas the citizen militias of the Sandinista Defense Committees were consistent with this tradition, conscription into a regular army was not. In any event, while the Sandinistas' postmortem properly included separate emphasis on their troubled relations with the Church, their main diagnosis was the same as everyone else's. The problem had been the war. With a death toll that approached forty thousand and the number permanently disabled almost as high, one out of every seventy-five or so Nicaraguans—an extended family in this culture—was dead or maimed in the war.[127] Nicaraguans were tired of having newspapers delivered by twelve-year-old boys armed with assault rifles, tired of the carnage.[128] They therefore voted for the presidential candidate who promised reconciliation over the one who was a magnet for more Yankee aggression.

JIMMY CARTER, WHO MONITORED the 1990 elections in Nicaragua under the auspices of the Carter Center, was with Daniel Ortega and other Sandinista leaders on what turned out to be a long, sleepless election night. Carter had expected Ortega to win reelection.[129] His mistaken prediction was in part a product of the polls, which had shown Ortega ahead, although it may have been rooted in part in the fact that Carter frankly liked Ortega. The two had squared off during a September 1979 visit to the White House, when Carter finally told Ortega, "If you don't hold me responsible for everything that occurred under my predecessors, I will not hold you responsible for everything that occurred under your predecessors."[130] It seemed to clear the air. Ortega could in no way be appreciative of Carter's policy toward Nicaragua during the revolution, but in person it was difficult for him not to regard Carter as a "good gringo." Carter's basic moral sentiments were sound and his attitude toward Latin America fair. Thus it transpired that at a crucial juncture in Nicaragua's history—February 25, 1990, election night—Ortega put his cautious trust in Carter.

Carter tried to encourage Ortega by telling him that the FSLN had accomplished a great deal about which it could be proud, that its leaders were still relatively young men (Ortega was only forty-four years old), and that losing an election was not the worst thing that could happen. When he said that, though, Rosalynn Carter could not help herself from interjecting, "But I thought it was!"[131] Laughter burst out, tensions eased, and the institutionalization of democracy in Nicaragua, British style, was underway. No one seemed genuinely to fear that Ortega would refuse to accept defeat and attempt to retain power by force, but that was frankly a risk. With his brother Humberto as the head of the military, and Borge as the minister of the interior, Ortega theoretically could have clung to power in a manner that might have plunged the country right back into war. More practically, there were things that Ortega could do to smooth the transition to a Chamorro administration, as well as things he could do to sabotage it. (As it happened, a sticking point arose when Humberto

Ortega attempted to negotiate an arrangement whereby be retained as minister of defense in the Chamorro admin tion, a bit of political maneuvering Carter vehemently opposed.) Democracy, even in the British tradition, is after all not measured merely by the ballot but also by how much respect and goodwill winners and losers show to one another. Carter counseled concession, with respect and goodwill.

So Ortega and Chamorro met briefly and hugged. They were opposing candidates, but fellow Nicaraguans who had worked together when they could, opposed each other when they had to, but throughout had genuine affection for each other. Chamorro herself resisted claiming victory, believing that decorum required her to wait for Ortega to concede, and that is what Ortega did. At 6:20 A.M., after a sleepless night, Ortega emerged to concede the loss of everything he had devoted his life to up to that point. Many believe it was the speech of his life, and it impressed even his opponents. He thanked those who voted for the Front, but then turned to "the majority of those who voted for the UNO" and stunned listeners by insisting that they "did not do so because they are counterrevolutionaries." He was careful to explain that, while there were a few people like Judas who will sell out the revolution, "the majority of these people are neither unscrupulous nor extremist, nor do they dislike the Revolution." As a whole, Ortega said, "the people do not sell out." They may "make mistakes," implying that they had in the election, "but they also know how to correct them and I'm sure that they will soon discover the truth." Reinforcing his investment of democratic faith in the people, he added, "All the people, the people who voted for the Sandinista Front and the people who voted for UNO, will never vote for anything contrary to the people's interests." It was just unimaginable, in the long run, that the people would oppose themselves. Correspondingly, it was unimaginable to him that they would turn away from the FSLN. "The Sandinista Front was born in the people, lives in the people and will never cease to be of the people."

ⁿne undetected in Ortega's oratory at the
ⁿterpretation he gave to democracy. He con-
ᵣaciously, but did not concede that the ballot
asure of the people's will. He plainly said that
ᶦ people had made a "mistake" that they would
ᵢs faith in democracy was unwavering, but it was
a pₑᵣ   ᵖaradoxically elitist faith that could not be accurately measuᵣₑⱼ by a mere vote. The people, in his opinion, could
never truly oppose the Sandinista Front. Accordingly—and what
is most remembered about this speech—he vowed to fight on, to
"govern from below." In his words on that Managua morning:

> We are accustomed to confronting difficult moments, to
> living in difficult situations. We were not born at the top,
> we were born at the bottom and we're used to fighting
> from below. We're used to struggling, to fighting from
> below. We're used to struggling and fighting in the face of
> our executioners and torturers. We're used to struggling
> and fighting from prisons. So, now that people's power,
> revolutionary power exists in this country, we have much
> better conditions in the short term to return to governing
> this country from above. . . . I tell you that the day will
> come when we return to governing from above because the
> Sandinista National Liberation Front, with the Nicaraguan
> people, will continue governing from below. We will con-
> tinue governing from below.[132]

5

GOVERNING FROM BELOW

In 1990 DANIEL ORTEGA found himself in new political territory. He was no longer a revolutionary, entitled by an illegitimate dictatorial regime to violate the laws in pursuit of his revolutionary objectives, but instead the defeated candidate of a party that had lost at the polls in a democratic republic. Neither was he invested with much formal power. As an ex-president he retained a seat in the National Assembly, according to the rules of the Nicaraguan constitution, and he remained the head of the FSLN. He also had solid ties to several pro-Sandinista unions, which he immediately helped to organize into a coalition, the National Workers' Front (FNT). This became perhaps his strongest political base from 1990 onward. These various platforms of power, however, were not especially satisfying to a man who had become accustomed to exercising considerably greater authority. It therefore comes as no surprise to learn that when Jimmy Carter's entourage returned to Managua in March 1991 to help mediate a dispute between Ortega and the Chamorro administration, they had the impression that Ortega was suffering an identity crisis, not sure how he would become a constructive opposition to his successor's administration. Ortega even privately confessed to Carter that, although he had no alternative to acquiescing to the Chamorro administration's policies, he was looking for "political cover" from Carter before doing so.[1]

Ortega floundered. To some extent he reveled in
one point early on he vacationed with supporters
lite Upper East Side, where he negotiated a book
ever wrote the book.[2] A few years later he was
... New York, this time slipping out of a dinner party with a
Brazilian bombshell he fancied after a few dances.[3] He was still a
relatively young man, and he had never pretended to be faithful to
his wife. During the middle 1990s he and Murillo even temporarily separated.[4] He traveled often to Cuba, where he would receive
whatever medical treatments were necessary. Fidel's friendship
and protection provided him with a security that eluded him
everywhere else in the world. It is not known what the problems
or the procedures were, but it appears that Ortega received extensive treatments for serious ailments during the 1990s. He may
have heart problems, although he is also rumored to have lupus.
No one knows but him and his Cuban doctors—and they are not
talking. His sister, Germania, died unexpectedly in Cuba in 1999,
and that coupled with various reports of his mother living there
(until she died in 2005 at ninety-eight years old) prompts the
conjecture that Ortega did more than visit often. Cuba became
something of his second home.

But Ortega was not the kind of person who could enjoy a life
of leisure, whether at home or abroad, and he had few interests
outside of politics. Unlike his brother Humberto, who took some
interest in business affairs, or his former vice president Ramírez,
who could and eventually did return to his vocation as a writer,
Ortega's passions were exclusively directed toward politics. He
would not—could not—amuse himself very long outside of
that realm. Insofar as he floundered, it was because his passions
encountered obstacles. He wanted nothing less than to reclaim the
presidency of Nicaragua, but in the meantime he had to content
himself with being as influential as he could be while battling his
way back into office. That battle would drag on much longer than
he expected it to—over sixteen years, in fact—and require considerable moral and political compromises.

The Challenge of the Chamorro Administration

WHILE DANIEL ORTEGA AND Violeta Chamorro remained on cordial terms personally, and he was even happy to welcome her son, Carlos Fernando Chamorro, as the editor of the Sandinista newspaper, *Barricada*, Ortega vociferously opposed Chamorro's 1990–1997 presidential administration. Two features of it in particular disturbed him. One was that the Chamorro administration championed the "neoliberal" economic model, also known as the "Washington consensus," and brought it to Nicaragua. This was the prevailing economic ideology of the World Bank, the International Monetary Fund, and other global financial institutions that was then being foisted upon Latin America. Ortega believed that it was a simplistic, one-size-fits-all economic ideology devised by and for global capitalists. The poor, he believed, unfairly bore the burden of these policies. His other objection was that the administration welcomed the rise within its midst of a corrupt economic elite that was largely indifferent to the country's struggling poor. This elite, a hodgepodge of legislators, political appointees, and hangers-on, brazenly misdirected funds earmarked for the country's development to their own private business concerns. Moreover, in his mind his two main objections to the Chamorro administration were flip sides of the same coin. Accepting the "Washington consensus" was pretty much tantamount to accepting the rule of economic elites, since only a fool could believe that kowtowing to capitalist interests does not come at the price of welcoming capitalist corruption too.

Since this issue continues to confront Nicaragua, it is important to understand why Ortega objects to the neoliberal economic model, and argues that it leads to "exclusion and poverty for millions of human beings" by, for instance, encouraging the conversion of corn harvests into biofuel when the people in whose country the corn is grown are starving.[5] The objection is not to the model's core economic idea. This idea is that inflation in poor countries is a serious problem for the poor as well as the rich (and perhaps even more harmful to the poor, who rarely have easy access to more stable foreign currencies). Inflation, in turn, is largely created by governments spending in excess of their incomes. This spending is often directed to programs to help the poor, but the resulting inflation often does more harm than the programs do good. The route to economic recovery for these countries is therefore to adopt an "austerity" program in which the governments spend no more than they take in. Ortega was well aware that his own Sandinista government's deficit spending, made necessary by the contra war and the economic stranglehold that the United States had placed on Nicaragua, caused inflation to spiral out of control. He also understood that there was no alternative to slashing government spending to halt this hideous inflationary spiral. In fact, he himself had made a tentative move in this direction in 1985, and then a more ambitious one in 1988. The 1988 plan did in fact reduce Nicaragua's inflation rate dramatically—it dropped from 33,657 percent in 1988 to 1,689 percent the next year—but of course 1,689 percent was still ridiculously high.[6] Ortega knew that more needed to be done to bring inflation under control. Indeed, he knew that austerity measures were typically mandated by foreign creditors, leaving Nicaragua little choice but to comply if it wanted aid.

However, Ortega could not countenance the specific ways in which these austerity plans are usually implemented, in particular the effect they have on the poor. "Austerity" invariably involves the poor accepting even lower wages and higher unemployment rates as the government withdraws funding from various state-sponsored enterprises. At the same time, it requires the poor to endure cuts in social welfare services that are also justified by government budget-cutting. To Ortega, like others on the left, however necessary it may be for government to reduce spending, the budgetary ax should never fall in a way that victimizes the poor. Funds simply must be set aside for such staples as food, public education, and health care, even if other objectives of the austerity plan may not be met. Granted, it may be difficult to persuade global lenders to approve funding to a country that refuses to slash aid to the poor, but whenever Ortega found himself in a position to negotiate these kinds of loans, he never allowed budget cuts that would harm the poor even to be put on the negotiating table (and he usually secured the loans).[7]

Of greater concern than the immediate impact on the poor of government austerity plans, however, is the model of future economic development that these austerity plans unthinkingly assume. In order to reduce its expenditures and obligations, a state that institutes an austerity plan must privatize some of its state-owned enterprises. The idea is not only to reduce the government's fiscal burden, which is often made worse by its unprofitable attempt to operate businesses according to a host of social objectives rather than according to the clearer business criterion of profitability. It also frees up these businesses to become profitable, which presumably many can be when placed in private hands. In the long run, the theory is, societies benefit more from successful private businesses than from unsuccessful public ones. However, while this line of reasoning is economically persuasive as far as it goes, it overlooks the fact that the most profitable way to operate a business in a poor country is usually to replicate the historic pattern of successful businesses there, a pattern in which profitability depends upon the continuing availability of a low-wage workforce. Traditionally, the comparative economic advantage of doing business in a poor country is a low-wage workforce, not much else. (Obviously access to raw materials, like the gold in Nicaragua's mines, provides another incentive for doing business in poor countries.) Thus, to privatize businesses in a country like Nicaragua is to invite the perpetuation of the classic "banana republic" dependency economic model in which a low-wage peasantry sustains local and foreign elites, while remaining poor itself. If political leaders in impoverished countries hope to improve conditions for their countries' poor, that is, to develop their economies in a manner that does not lead to continuing economic dependency, they must therefore usually resist wholesale privatization and insist upon some ongoing state involvement in the business sector. In addition, in the rush to privatize, governments tend to sell off state-owned enterprises at fire-sale prices, often sweetening the sales by offering various financial inducements and guarantees, to purchasers who are already economic elites. This process essentially replicates the cronyism of elites that, coupled with the exploitation of the poor masses, has long been characteristic of the world's poor countries.

There is also the issue—never far from the forefront of Ortega's economic thinking—of what impoverished countries like Nicaragua are owed by their historic exploiters. For a free-market philosophy to pass moral muster, it must after all assume a more or less level playing field—or at least the ability of the weaker party to act autonomously in the marketplace. These conditions often do not apply to poor countries, and did not apply to Nicaragua. In 1990 Nicaragua had the highest per capita national debt in the Western Hemisphere, while it was simultaneously the hemisphere's poorest country. (In fact, although the Chamorro administration managed to attract over a billion dollars in foreign aid in 1991, almost half of that went right back to foreign creditors for payments on the national debt.[8]) If Nicaragua was to be thrust into the global capitalist free-for-all, should it be compelled to shoulder such enormous debt? Since some of that debt had been inherited from the Somoza dictatorship and most of the rest of it was incurred in a defensive war against a superpower that sought to destroy Nicaragua's economy, it never struck Ortega as fair to force a capitalist austerity plan onto Nicaragua without forgiving the country's debt. At minimum, there was the issue of the unpaid reparations that the World Court had ordered the United States to pay to Nicaragua.

Unfortunately, as Ortega watched economic events unfold under the Chamorro administration, all his reservations about neoliberalism became reality. Inflation was brought under control, dropping to less than a tenth its rate between 1990 and 1991 and then registering only 3.5 percent in 1992 (after which it increased a little, but remained manageable). However, unemployment shot up from 8 percent in 1989 to over 20 percent in 1993, which, combined with the lingering problem of underemployment, effectively prevented over half of the workforce from being able to support itself, even marginally. Meanwhile, wages for those with jobs actually fell. Half the population lived below a poverty line of $428.94 per year, while 20 percent lived in extreme, life-threatening poverty. Almost a third of all children under five suffered from malnutrition. Owing to the fees instituted for health care—another "austerity" initiative—medical consultations declined 21 percent between 1990 and 1994, and public health deteriorated. Because fees were also instituted for public schools—a bizarre condition the International Monetary Fund typically placed on loan recipients—school attendance declined and illiteracy rates rose. While approximately 350 state-owned businesses were privatized and top tax rates were reduced, Nicaragua emerged as a country with one of the most unequal income distributions in the world. The highest-earning fifth of the population received 65 percent of the income while the lowest-earning fifth received a paltry 3 percent—and it was not a very affluent pie before it was divided up. Meanwhile, the economic growth promised by neoliberalism never came. Per capita GDP growth remained negative from 1990 to 1994, and only showed marginal aggregate improvement in 1994 because of a temporary increase in world coffee prices. Neither did the Chamorro administration reduce Nicaragua's foreign debt. It increased during her term. More outrageously, she settled the seventeen-billion-dollar claim Nicaragua made against the United States in the World Court for reparations for a fraction of the amount owed.[9]

Ortega was infuriated. He had not devoted his life to the revolution because of some abstract disagreement over political philosophy with the Somoza regime, but because of the poverty and exploitation he saw all around him in his native country. It was all well and good that the Chamorro administration was popularly regarded as democratic while the Somoza regime had been a dictatorship, but if the material fruits were no better, debating these systems' merits is a meaningless academic exercise. Indeed, in such a debate, it might even be easier to defend a dictatorship than a modern capitalist democracy. At least a dictator is a person and as such is capable of compassion. The impersonal marketplace lacks this capacity. Beholden as they are to the supposed laws of the marketplace, modern capitalist democracies conveniently attribute the hardships they impose on the people to impersonal economic forces, which as forces rather than persons are by definition incapable of compassion and therefore immune from moral responsibility. Never a champion of democracy in the British sense anyway—and knowing that he had been defeated for reelection in large part because of U.S. interference—Ortega was incensed over the consequences of his defeat in the name of democracy. Worse, he had firsthand knowledge of the Chamorro administration's descent into corruption and cronyism and its hypocritical and routine disregard for the rule of law, a cornerstone of democracy.

VIOLETA CHAMORRO'S STRENGTH AS a political leader was her ability to present herself as a figure of reconciliation in that war-torn country, and in this she succeeded. A flare-up of the war was always a possibility, especially when various "recontras" surfaced and threatened to spark a resurgence of the fighting, yet for the most part Chamorro quelled the uprisings and defused the hostilities. However, Chamorro had two crippling weaknesses as a political leader. Although few described the first weakness as succinctly as one Nicaraguan did when she privately opined, "Violeta is stupid," others indirectly identified the same problem. Salman Rushdie, for example, noted that "she wore a great deal of jewelry," implying that she lacked cerebral substance, although admitted that he found her "very unconvincing" as a political leader more because her upper-class demeanor was out of sync with the lives of most Nicaraguans than because she gave little evidence of mental agility.[10] Interestingly, Chamorro herself did not apparently believe that she was up to the job of the presidency either—or at least was not especially interested in shouldering its responsibilities—because she turned the day-to-day operations of the office over to her son-in-law, Antonio Lacayo, whom she appointed minister to the president. But Chamorro's second weakness as a political leader, at least in that still-idealistic post-revolution environment, was that she simply assumed that corruption was an essential ingredient of political success. In fact, under her, well over half the members of the National Assembly received regular bribe payments, about a hundred other public officials (including judges) were put on the president's private payroll, and development dollars were routinely misdirected from their intended use to insiders' business dealings. According to Antonio Ibarra Rojas, who served as vice minister of the presidency in her administration and was personally aware of the rampant corruption within it, Chamorro believed that it was "natural" and "simply politics" for presidential administrations to pay off supporters, and in fact she regarded the legislators and other public officials as "employees" who needed to be paid.[11]

Ortega was well aware of Chamorro's easy corruptibility, and in fact helped to negotiate a behind-the-scenes pact with her and Lacayo during the transition period. The pact was basically between Humberto Ortega and Lacayo, and at its core was Humberto's promise to bankroll a slush fund that Layaco could use to further his political objectives. The amount of money was substantial—over three hundred thousand dollars per week in U.S. currency—and Humberto had this amount regularly hand-delivered to Layaco's office. This was not all the unaccounted-for money that Lacayo had at his disposal. He managed to skim additional funds from various foreign aid donations, and received regular cash allotments in the hundred-thousand-dollar range from the Nicaraguan embassy in Miami. It is frankly not clear how much money ran through the safe in Lacayo's office, but it is clear that the three hundred thousand that Humberto had delivered weekly was a substantial amount—enough to persuade Lacayo and Chamorro to agree to the terms of the pact that the Ortega brothers negotiated.[12]

Humberto Ortega could generate this kind of money because under his command the military had been turned into a very profitable enterprise. Humberto appears to have been originally motivated by his need to finance Nicaragua's defense in the face of declining and uncertain Soviet aid. By 1990, however, he had a humming operation. Most of the income was generated by the navy, which extracted payments from foreign vessels fishing Nicaraguan waters and helped Colombian drug traffickers launder money. The navy managed the money laundering by arranging to buy fish catches on behalf of the Colombians with their money, and then the Colombians would sell the fish catches on the wholesale market. In this way, their drug profits could appear to be the legitimately earned profits from successful fishing expeditions. The air force provided Colombian drug dealers with similar services, although the operations were more complicated (involving dummy land-based businesses and fleets of currency traders working the streets) and the profits were lower. The army was the least lucrative branch of the military because, although it was heavily involved in cattle rustling, it was forced to share its profits with local police forces and border officials. Taken together, the "defense industry" generated enough income for Humberto to be able to contribute the promised three hundred thousand dollars a week to Lacayo after everyone else, including presumably Humberto himself, had also been paid.[13]

The most obvious benefit of the pact for the Ortega brothers involved securing protections for themselves and their fellow Sandinistas in exchange for the cash payments. Chamorro's agreement to retain Humberto Ortega as minister of defense, for example—the idea that had struck Jimmy Carter as outrageous[14]—was a tenet of the agreement. Chamorro was able to pass this off as a gesture of reconciliation, although it was essentially a business decision. In like manner, Chamorro agreed to support an increase in the government's military budget, despite the expectations that the budget would be scaled back in peacetime. Humberto Ortega also extracted the Chamorro administration's support in opposing legislation intended to roll back what was by then known as *la piñata*. This was the popular term for the highly unpopular last-minute transfer of wealth from the state to the Sandinista leadership following their electoral defeat in 1990. Believing they were public servants and never expecting to lose the 1990 elections, the Sandinistas had simply never gotten around to transferring ownership of the property they used during the 1980s from the state to themselves, much less passing a pension law that would sustain them after a defeat. Although most observers are probably correct to criticize the scale of the *piñata*—Daniel Ortega and other FSLN leaders became very wealthy as a result of this last-minute property grab—it was in part simply a matter of correcting an oversight. People like Ortega could not, after all, simply go out and get jobs, and as a practical matter they remained vulnerable to political opponents, some of whom may have put prices on their heads. Surely they were entitled to some security following their defeat. Their opponents, however, saw this wealth transfer as blatant thievery, and initiatives in the National Assembly were designed to nullify it.[15]

Meanwhile, the pact had a political rationale. The UNO coalition that had been created to elect Chamorro had been united only by its opposition to the FSLN. In reality, Chamorro had no political constituency of her own. At the same time, the FSLN had thirty-nine seats in the legislature—not a majority, but a sizeable voting bloc—and Lacayo knew that his principal political objective had to be to create a governing coalition. For that he needed the FSLN. Thus, Lacayo and the Ortega brothers agreed to work together to forge a political coalition that would enable each of their interests to be served. Accordingly, some of the payments that Humberto funneled to Lacayo went right back to the FSLN. It was agreed, for instance, that former vice president Sergio Ramírez would be the point man for directing legislative votes and be put in charge of maintaining discipline in the ranks of the FSLN legislators. For the latter service, Lacayo provided Ramírez with a $150,000 monthly stipend, which Ramírez then distributed to FSLN legislators as he saw fit. With the FSLN bloc managed by Ramírez, Lacayo was then free to devote most of his energies to wooing other legislators into his coalition and securing favors from other public officials. In the end, Lacayo managed to buy the loyalty of about a dozen legislators, which combined with the FSLN bloc was an ample majority.[16]

While the agreement bought protection for the Sandinistas and helped Lacayo forge a governing coalition, it simultaneously advanced another objective of the Ortega brothers, namely the political destruction of Antonio Lacayo. The strategy was basically to give Lacayo enough rope to hang himself, and then to watch him dangle. Buying the legislature, for example, proved to be an expensive proposition for Lacayo, and it was not as easily accomplished as he hoped. Legislators who accepted two-thousand-dollar-per-month stipends quickly asked for more, which put Lacayo in the position of regularly purchasing cars for lawmakers, buying a farm for one, arranging bogus business loans for others, finding a job for another's niece, and so on. Indeed, one legislator even managed to run up thousand-dollar-a-week bar and restaurant tabs, which he expected the president's office to pay. What neither Lacayo nor, through him, Chamorro adequately understood is that there are limits to the amount of influence money can have in politics. At the end of the day, even politicians are motivated by morality and principle as well as avarice. By treating legislators and other public officials like "employees," Lacayo appealed to their selfish interests, not their nobler aspirations, and thus he fueled their greed and invited their resentment. The result was that Lacayo became increasingly caught up in the web of corruption that he himself spun, and this was the apparent objective of the Ortega brothers.[17]

Inevitably Lacayo took the steps that follow when politicians travel the low road he was on: he began to order an escalating series of violent acts that eventually included political assassinations. It all started innocently enough when he turned to Lenín Cerna of the FSLN to provide security services on behalf of friendly legislators who requested them. By calling upon Cerna, though, Lacayo was playing with fire. Cerna is a shadowy figure in the Sandinista story, and intentionally so. The son of Nicaraguan communists whose parents named him after the leader of the Russian Revolution, Cerna was an early supporter of the FSLN. He was one of only two surviving men who had served the seven years in the Somoza prison with Daniel Ortega. Cerna was fiercely and personally loyal to the Ortega brothers. He was also probably the toughest member of the Sandinistas' inner circle. Although nothing was ever proved, it is assumed that Cerna was the coordinator of the "divine mobs" and behind other unsavory acts of the Sandinistas. He is rumored to have personally skinned opponents alive, to have tortured others, and to have developed one of the most extensive intelligence networks in the world. Whether or to what extent these rumors are true is unknown to outsiders, but it is known that insofar as the FSLN ever developed a secret police, Lenín Cerna was its head. When Lacayo began to call upon Cerna, he stepped onto a slippery slope that descended into a real moral quagmire. Matters escalated rapidly, and the man who had started out only trying to help his mother-in-law forge a governing coalition ended up ordering assassinations. Of course, the Ortega brothers had set this trap for Lacayo. They expected him to be enticed by the prospect of wielding this kind of power, and then to lack restraint and forego caution when using it.[18]

Lacayo blundered badly, proving no match for the Ortega brothers. Humberto Ortega, for example, never once personally delivered the weekly payments to Lacayo's office, but always sent senior military officials with the money instead. Meanwhile, Daniel Ortega was never even formally a partner to the pact, which his brother handled. In these ways and others, the Ortega brothers wisely avoided any direct complicity in the corruption of the Chamorro administration. Similarly, while Cerna's personal loyalty to Daniel Ortega is known, only once was either of the Ortega brothers anywhere near an act of political violence—and that was by accident. Lacayo kept his slush fund in his office safe, personally kept handwritten records of it, and even helped to count the money. He also ordered political assassinations and approved acts of political terrorism within earshot of those who could not be trusted to keep quiet, and in fact did not. It is no wonder that, although the full extent of his misdeeds never became known and he managed to avoid conviction, Lacayo was indicted on charges of corruption. Neither is it any wonder that his goal of building a center-governing coalition failed, or that the trial balloons that he floated on behalf of his own presidential ambitions in 1996 remained stuck on the ground. Lacayo left politics a wealthier man than he entered it—bogus loans he never intended to repay helped him expand a shrimp farm and other businesses into profitability—but a political failure.[19]

ALTHOUGH THE ORTEGA BROTHERS proved that they were better political operatives than their opponents in the Chamorro administration, that knowledge provided Daniel Ortega with limited comfort. While he and his brother outfoxed Lacayo, they did not win any prizes that Ortega cared passionately about. They were winning access to power and retaining their personal wealth, but they were not shaping policy. Indeed, Ortega's most successful political initiatives during the Chamorro years involved helping to organize strikes and then negotiating concessions for workers that tempered the pain that neoliberal economic policy inflicted. These were achievements, but minor ones. Daniel Ortega wanted to direct policy, not to have to fight against policies he opposed.

Ortega therefore spent the bulk of the Chamorro administration eagerly looking forward to the 1996 presidential election. He assumed that he would be the candidate of the FSLN and believed that he would win the election. This would provide him with the legitimate power that he craved, and would allow him to right the course that Nicaragua was on. And again, in his opinion, the voters had simply made a mistake in 1990—a mistake that had been heavily influenced by the contra war and then the United States' dramatic invasion of Panama. Surely the voters would not make the same mistake a second time, and the United States would not intervene so dramatically. Ortega believed the revolution would be recovered.

The 1996 Election

As the election approached, two ominous political currents swept over Nicaragua's political landscape that together swelled into a virtual tsunami that drowned Ortega's hope for a quick political comeback. One, which had been festering for years, reached the crisis point in 1995 when the bulk of the FSLN leadership abandoned the Front and formed an opposition Sandinista party, the Sandinista Renovation Movement (MRS). With them went all but two of the thirty-nine FSLN members of the National Assembly; fully thirty-five former FSLN representatives switched to the MRS.[20] Daniel Ortega found himself left at the head of a party that was for all practical purposes defunct, and which former friends began to disparage as "Danielista" rather than "Sandinista." The other current involved the formation of a liberal alliance in opposition to the Sandinistas (in either of their FLSN or MRS incarnations) under the leadership of Managua's popular mayor, Arnoldo Alemán. Indeed, Alemán succeeded in accomplishing what Lacayo tried and failed to accomplish when he set his sights on creating a governing coalition. Though not quite a center coalition— "liberalism" in Nicaragua is closer to center-right than to the center, and in fact is the former nominal political creed of the Somozas—the liberal alliance that Alemán forged emerged as perhaps the majority political coalition in Nicaragua. To this day, although the specific party affiliations remain in some flux, approximately half of Nicaraguans loosely self-identify as "liberals."

The reason why many of the leaders of the FSLN abandoned the Front in 1995 and formed the rival MRS party is frankly because Ortega lost the 1990 election. This is not a reason cited by any of the defectors, and the majority would likely deny it. But ever since the FSLN had split into the three tendencies— only to reunite on the eve of revolutionary victory—Daniel and Humberto Ortega were suspected of being unprincipled political opportunists rather than principled political visionaries. It was only by winning that they were able to coax the recalcitrant into rejoining them and then to lead the revolution. The 1990 loss eliminated the incentive for others to remain loyal to the Ortega brothers, and few did. Accordingly, it was not one event at one time that prompted the division of the Sandinistas during the early 1990s, but rather a series of escalating reservations about the Ortega brothers, which festered in that atmosphere of defeat. The other Sandinistas began to grumble among themselves, and the process started early.

Of course, there were specific complaints. One involved Ortega's increasingly autocratic style. He would not permit the members of the National Directorate to be elected individually, for example, but insisted that they be elected as a slate. This ensured that they could continue to be hand-picked by insiders, of which he was one. He also changed his own title to the ominous-sounding Secretary General. That smacked of Soviet-style authoritarian ambitions. Then there was the growing awareness of his behind-the-scenes political deal making. To the more idealistic members of the FSLN, plunging into this old-style political corruption was not why the revolution had been fought. They wanted a cleaner form of politics. Meanwhile, there were personal rivalries. Ortega insisted that he once again be the Front's presidential candidate, even though there was other talent in the party; Sergio Ramírez in particular wanted the nomination. At the same time, there was envy over the fact that the spoils of the *piñata* had mainly gone to the senior leadership, when lower-ranked members believed that they were entitled to a larger share. As these things tend to happen, the acrimony sometimes became quite personal. After the break, which Sergio Ramírez essentially led, Ramírez's eyes sometimes noticeably moistened when he recalled his long association with Ortega and the caustic comments that ended it. Even so, there was a split, it was final, and Ortega would run for president without the support of, and even in opposition to, many of his former comrades. Ramírez got his wish: he became the 1996 presidential nominee of the MRS.[21]

Meanwhile, there was the problem of Arnoldo Alemán and his liberal alliance. Alemán was an affluent pro-business lawyer who had worked in the Somoza regime during the 1970s and had various friendly ties to the United States. He believed in the free enterprise system, not socialism, obviously had no qualms about serving a U.S.-backed dictator, and rarely met a neoliberal program he did not like. Indeed, Alemán was not even very ideological. He was only politicized after the Sandinistas confiscated some of his property during the 1980s and he spent nine months in a Sandinista prison on suspicion of counterrevolutionary activity. Upon his release, he threw his energies into COSEP, the business consortium that usually opposed the Sandinistas. Prior to the 1996 election he served as mayor of Managua, perhaps the second most visible position in Nicaraguan politics next to the presidency. As mayor, Alemán tended to promote the kinds of visible public works projects that constituents noticed, and which allowed them to see that their elected officials were "at least doing something." Alemán for instance paved a lot of roads. How these public works projects fitted with his political creed—if they did fit—is unclear. It is not clear that Alemán even had a coherent political creed. Alemán's political popularity appears to have been premised more on his personality than on his ideology. Affectionately known as "The Fat One" ("El Gordo" in Spanish) owing to his girth, Alemán was simply a gregarious, likeable fellow. Commentators began calling his brand of politics "neo-populism" in an attempt to account for his wide following in sectors of the population that would not normally be predicted to support a right-leaning leader. Add that he was able to forge a liberal alliance in opposition to the Sandinistas out of the political disarray of Nicaragua during the early 1990s and Alemán became the natural leader of the roughly half the population that wanted an alternative to them.[22]

Alemán also had no intention of fighting fairly in the 1996 election. The report from the Carter Center, which monitored the election, frankly states that the election was riddled with irregularities that favored Alemán.[23] In the end, 7 percent of the votes simply had to be nullified, since their authenticity was impossible to ascertain. Both the United States and the Catholic Church also aided the Alemán forces in their legitimate and illegitimate politicking. There was not a lot of U.S. involvement in the 1996 elections, and the nine million dollars it spent was for the most part nonpartisan, yet Nicholas Burns of the State Department did publicly question Ortega's commitment to democracy in a press briefing two weeks before the election. The possibility that the pro-U.S. liberal alliance would prove to be less enthusiastic about democracy as measured by transparent elections did not seem to occur to the State Department. Although Ortega had changed his campaign song from the FSLN anthem, which openly pronounced the Yankee as "the enemy of humanity," to Beethoven's "Ode to Joy," and had selected a conservative businessman, Juan Manuel Caldera, for his vice presidential running mate, he was obviously still suspect by the United States. Worse, he was still suspect within the Church. Shortly before the voting, Cardinal Obando y Bravo invited Alemán to join him in a mass where the influential Church leader preached a sermon that metaphorically described Ortega as a poisonous snake poised to strike. The country's electorate did not misunderstand the parable, as evidenced by the appearance on Election Day of the message "Kill the Viper" on beepers throughout the country.[24]

Daniel Ortega lost the October 20, 1996, presidential election to Arnoldo Alemán decisively. The final vote tally was 38 percent for Ortega and 51 percent for Alemán, with the remaining votes divided up among minority candidates. The margin of Ortega's loss was large enough to make challenging the outcome pointless. Even though the pattern of voting irregularities suggested that he had been the victim of rampant fraud—fraud that, again, the Carter Center essentially recognized in its final report on the election—challenging the accuracy of the vote count would not close a thirteen-point gap. Ortega knew this, and knew that he had lost. Accordingly, he feigned a respect for the democratic process that he did not necessarily possess by politely questioning the accuracy of the results but not stridently decrying the fraud. It was time, once again, for him to behave publicly like a senior statesman—and prepare for a comeback while continuing to "govern from below."

DESPITE ORTEGA'S DISADVANTAGES GOING into the elections and his eventual loss, astute political observers immediately realized that he had pulled off a near political miracle. His 38 percent of the vote—a solid second-place finish—put him far ahead of where his political opponents expected him to be. He was after all running without the support of most of his former friends in the FSLN, who had openly denounced him as "Danielista" rather than Sandinista. Ortega proved that "Danielismo" remained surprisingly popular in Nicaragua, and that he could attract about the same share of the vote running without the support of his former comrades as he could running with it. More than this, Ortega led the FSLN to a thirty-six-seat victory in the National Assembly. The liberal alliance captured forty-two legislative seats, six more than the FSLN, but the now "Danielista" FSLN had gone into the election with only a single seat and came out with thirty-five more. For all its heady idealism, and after having persuaded almost all of the sitting FSLN legislators to change their allegiance to the new MRS prior to the elections, the MRS won only a single seat in the National Assembly. Ramírez, heading the MRS ticket as its presidential nominee, tallied only 2 percent of the popular vote. Daniel Ortega demonstrated that he was a formidable political force at a time when many assumed that his political career was finished.

Still, he lost. Ortega's hopes to govern Nicaragua were dashed again, and he was forced to the sidelines. He was not politically irrelevant, however. He had trounced the MRS—revealing it to be a perhaps idealistic but impractical party—and had showed that he remained a political force to be reckoned with. He had a lot of personal supporters inside Nicaragua, especially among the poor and working class. One person who reckoned with Ortega's political clout was Arnoldo Alemán. He had to.

El Pacto

WITH FORTY-TWO SEATS IN the National Assembly, Alemán did not have a governing majority. He was in more solid political shape than Chamorro and Lacayo had been in—at least Alemán had a constituency—but he was not in a position to govern effectively on the basis of his liberal supporters alone. He also knew that Ortega's supporters, primarily in the unions, could and would fight him every step of the way. Even as it was, Ortega helped to organize union demonstrations against Alemán's policies—this was part of "governing from below"—that threatened to cripple his administration several times. Though Ortega's legislative position in the National Assembly was little more than a courtesy role, and his position as secretary general of the FSLN was just as figurehead of his own fiefdom, he remained politically potent. Alemán quickly realized that he had to negotiate with Ortega. Of course, he reasoned that he was in the stronger position, and like most who had dealt with Ortega, assumed that he could get the best of him in the end. Accordingly, the two men met over thirty times, mostly in private (if Ortega was accompanied by anyone it was usually his brother Humberto), over a concentrated period of three months immediately following the elections, and then continued to meet periodically thereafter. These meetings were all secret, but their outcome would soon not be. The outcome was a pact—"El Pacto" in Spanish—that every Nicaraguan soon learned about, and quickly discovered would define their country's political future for a long time.[25]

The specific terms of the pact remain largely unknown, and there is no evidence that they included the kinds of cash payments on which the agreement between Humberto Ortega and the Chamorro administration had rested. By 1996, Humberto Ortega had stepped down as minister of defense, and while clouds of scandal gathered over Alemán's administration, neither of the Ortega brothers was ever implicated in the corruption. It appeared that Daniel Ortega kept the negotiations focused on politics, and over thirty meetings a lot of specific points were surely hammered out. In early 2000, the first noteworthy results of the pact became public, when changes to the Nicaraguan constitution that augmented each man's power were pushed through the National Assembly and when Daniel Ortega retained his immunity from prosecution on charges of child molestation. The constitutional changes involved expanding the membership of the Supreme Court, the Supreme Electoral Council, and the Comptroller General's office. These expansions allowed Alemán and Ortega each to appoint new members loyal to them and thus to have joint influence, if not control over, these important bodies. Another change, important to Ortega, was lowering the threshold of votes that a winning presidential candidate needed to garner in a general election in order to claim victory without a runoff to 35 percent. Ortega realized that he was not likely to attract over 45 percent of the vote in a general election, or over 50 percent of a runoff election, as the Nicaraguan constitution then required for a presidential candidate to claim victory, so he needed the threshold lowered to a percentage that he could foreseeably attain. Similarly, after his stepdaughter's allegations of sexual molestation were made public in March 1998, Ortega needed Alemán's help to retain his immunity from prosecution. As the second-place finisher in the presidential election as well as a former president, Ortega was entitled by the Nicaraguan constitution to a seat in the National Assembly, and in this capacity he was granted immunity from criminal prosecution. However, the National Assembly could have voted to strip him of his immunity, and to prevent this from happening Ortega needed support from Alemán's liberal legislators.

Since Ortega was the weaker party to the pact yet appears to have benefited the most from it, the question of what he offered to Alemán arises. The inference is that Ortega agreed to remain silent about Alemán's extensive financial corruption. Ortega had to have been aware of it. When in late 2003 a Nicaraguan court finally convicted Alemán on charges of embezzlement, money laundering, and corruption, he had personally stolen upward of a hundred million dollars during his 1997–2002 presidential term. At this amount, he entered the ranks of the most corrupt politicians in the world—despite the fact that he governed one of its poorest and smallest countries.[26] Ortega could not have been unaware of Alemán's corruption, yet he remained silent about it (while evidently not gaining from it). Surely this was his concession to Alemán in the pact. Just as surely, Ortega calculated that Alemán's appetite for avarice coupled with the kind of hubris that allows a politician to believe that he can get away with colossal corruption would ultimately be Alemán's undoing. Ortega would not have to blow the whistle himself, but simply wait for someone else to do so. In this way, he reasoned that he would eventually end up with the upper hand in the pact.

THE 2001 PRESIDENTIAL ELECTION offered a brief interlude to the pact, since Ortega ran—and ran to win—against Alemán's hand-picked successor, Vice President Enrique Bolaños. It was an open battle between opposing parties and ideologies, not a negotiated deal between two power brokers. Ortega was more realistic about his chances for victory than he had been in either 1990 or 1996. Despite the MRS begrudgingly supporting his candidacy, he had,

as usual, both the Catholic Church and the United State
him. The United States helped to suppress support for (
labeling him a "terrorist" in the post-9/11 climate, for
At the same time, Ortega campaigned under the cloud of accusations that he had sexually molested his stepdaughter and dodged
having to stand trial for it. This drove many feminists and other
good people away from the FSLN. More than this, Ortega obviously understood that he was unlikely to win a majority of the
vote in a two-way race. He could simply not attract enough votes,
and it was in recognition of this reality that he had gotten the
threshold required for victory reduced to 35 percent. He needed
a divided opposition in order to win an election. He almost got
his wish when the former Conservative Party reconstituted itself
and prepared to do battle against Alemán's liberals. The Conservatives even tried to convince Violeta Chamorro to be their nominee. Negotiations with Chamorro fell apart and the United States
stepped in to pressure the Conservatives to abandon their ambitions. The United States did not want Ortega to face a divided
opposition for the same reason that Ortega wanted to—it would
allow Ortega to win. In the end, Ortega's opponents did rally
behind Bolaños, although it was perhaps a sign of their lack of
enthusiasm for Bolaños more than support for Ortega that the
final vote tally was 54 percent for Bolaños against 46 percent for
Ortega, while the liberals captured forty-nine seats in the National
Assembly against thirty-nine for the FSLN. In short, Ortega and
the FSLN once again did surprisingly well, just not well enough
to garner a majority.

The real action went on behind the scenes. Alemán, then with
the upper hand in the pact, worked to preserve both his power
and his recently acquired ill-gotten fortune. The contest was never
really between Ortega and Bolaños but rather between Ortega
and Alemán, with others in cameo roles. Bolaños's role was a
supporting one. He had served as vice president in the Alemán
administration, had remained loyally silent about the corruption within it, and was already in his seventies. Alemán reasoned

that by promoting Bolaños's presidential bid, he could install a president who would threaten neither his fortune nor his power. Indeed, Alemán appears to have viewed Bolaños as almost his puppet, who would at least do little damage while Alemán himself plotted his recapture of the presidency in the 2006 election. (The Nicaraguan constitution forbade the consecutive reelection of a president.) In the meantime, Bolaños would tend the store. It was perhaps because others understood Alemán's transparent strategy that many were reluctant to support Bolaños. Another reason may have been that Bolaños did not have the degree of personal support that men like Alemán and Ortega had learned to cultivate. Bolaños was a man of the right, or center-right, with a background typical of those with this political leaning. He had attended college in the United States, been a businessman his whole life, and had experienced the Sandinista rule following the revolution as a personal financial setback. However, he was a man of relatively modest means, and perhaps in part because of his age was not given to the coalition building required to the extent that others were. The upshot was that Bolaños was a stand-in for Alemán, and everyone knew that.

As fate had it, Alemán made a politically disastrous miscalculation. He overlooked that Bolaños had some fairly unusual character traits for Nicaragua's political life, namely a penchant for honesty and fairness. No sooner, in fact, did Bolaños take office in 2002 than he called for a full-scale ethics investigation into allegations of corruption during the Alemán administration. Alemán was of course stunned, and this investigation led to his prosecution and conviction. Nevertheless, Bolaños publicly said, "Arnoldo, you took the pensions from the retirees, medicine from the sick, salaries from the teachers."[27] A shrewd politician may have calculated that by getting rid of Alemán he could rise to the leadership of the liberal alliance, but Bolaños does not appear to have been this calculating or ambitious. Bolaños called for the investigation because he believed it was the right thing to do—a rarity in Nicaraguan politics.

But if Bolaños or anyone else believed that the
Alemán this easily, they underestimated the pov
Although Alemán was sentenced to twenty yea
spent barely a day behind bars. Instead, express
over his supposedly frail health—frailties that did ...
Alemán from giving speeches and granting interviews, nor from
posturing for another presidential run as a convicted criminal—
the court allowed the former president to serve his sentence
under house arrest. The court did not keep Alemán in his pala-
tial estate for very long; he was soon free to come and go at will
as long as he did not leave the country. That was no matter to
Alemán, and in fact there were some countries where he could
face criminal charges. Clearly the pact, which had allowed him to
pack the courts, protected Alemán. But Ortega had played hard-
ball against him. There was no immunity from prosecution like
that Ortega had negotiated for when he was faced with his criminal charges, and the twenty-year sentence remained officially in
force (although it was eventually reduced to five years and then,
in a renegotiation of the pact, vacated altogether). Ortega could
yank Alemán in any direction he wanted to with that sentence in
force—or have something to offer the criminal president the next
time he needed a favor. The tables had turned, and Ortega was
now the stronger party to the pact.

Another measure of the pact's importance is what happened—
or rather did not happen—during the Bolaños administration.
Even Nicaraguans of the center-right shake their heads in dismay
over those years. The problem, they maintain, was not Bolaños.
To be sure, he was accused of corruption too, but then most politicians are accused of corruption; few Nicaraguans believe that
Bolaños was corrupt. The problem was that Bolaños was simply
ineffectual. He had next to no influence in the National Assembly, the courts, or anywhere else. These important political bodies
were for the most part controlled by Alemán and Ortega, making the president little more than a figurehead. In reality, power
in Nicaragua did not reside in the ballot or the courts or in any

er democratic institution. The people could elect whomever they wanted and the courts could even convict an ex-president of colossal corruption, but this did not change the fact that power really resided in a pact between two powerful men, Arnoldo Alemán and Daniel Ortega.

This was nothing new for Nicaragua. In the old style of Nicaraguan politics—born even before the Somoza era—power was a product of pacts between two or more savvy and powerful players, usually backed by foreign interests, typically the United States. These pacts functioned to exclude others from gaining access to power by ensuring that most serious matters would be resolved privately by power brokers, with elections and other democratic institutions providing a veneer of legitimacy. Indeed, this pattern had never really been altered in Nicaragua, only the participants had changed. The United States had interfered in the 1984 election with the goal of depriving Ortega's election of legitimacy, and then had interfered in the 1990 election with the goal of helping Chamorro defeat Ortega. Real power was in Washington, D.C., during these elections, not in the Nicaraguan ballot box. The 1996 election was perhaps the freest and fairest of any, since participants to a pact had not yet surfaced and the United States played a minor role, but even it was riddled with fraud and its outcome influenced by both the United States and the Catholic Church. By 2001, though, internal actors had largely replaced external ones, as that election was essentially a contest between participants in the Alemán-Ortega pact. All that really happened in Nicaragua around the turn of the millennium was that the country's internal political culture reverted to its old ways.

Political Values

THE PACT BETWEEN ALEMÁN and Ortega was the kind of political shenanigan that ordinary Nicaraguans found distasteful, especially in light of the ideals of their revolution. By 1999 neither man was very popular, and polls showed that support for both the liberals and the FSLN hovered around an anemic 20 percent each. Sixty percent of Nicaraguans had little use for either man or either party.[28] However, a 2001 poll revealed something else that may be more important about Nicaraguans' political values. Fully 73 percent of those surveyed said that they believed an "authoritarian" president was necessary in their country, while an astonishing 57 percent even said that it is proper for a president to bribe legislators and other political figures. These results do not suggest a political culture committed to democracy and the rule of law, nor do they suggest that many Nicaraguans overly concerned themselves about the pact between Alemán and Ortega. Indeed, Nicaraguans were not even especially upset by Alemán's corruption. Although over three-quarters of the citizens believed that Alemán's administration was the "most corrupt government in Nicaragua's history," only 7 percent replied "corruption" when asked to name their country's top political problems. Instead, 27 percent named "poverty" as their country's main problem and 47 percent the closely related problem of "unemployment." Nicaraguans in effect told pollsters that they did not care how a politician got the job done or even how much he personally stole in the process of doing it. What they wanted was relief from their intense poverty, ideally by the dignified means of a job.[29]

The political idealists, who inside Nicaragua include many of the elites on both the left and the right and outside Nicaragua include most of the world's opinion leaders, routinely misunderstand this reality of Nicaraguan life. The finger-pointers rail against the backroom deal making of the caudillos and their authoritarian ways, as if the main thing that matters about Nicaragua is how well or poorly its political culture conforms to the blueprint for democracies described in high school civics textbooks. But few Nicaraguans care—or can afford to care—about any of this. Few of them ever attend a high school civics class anyway—or even high school. As recently as the Bolaños administration (2002–2007), only half of the Nicaraguan children who started the first grade finished primary school. The rest dropped out, in part because their parents could not afford the nominal school fees and in part because their labors were needed to help support the family. Of course, with a 60 percent unemployment rate, it may not be immediately obvious to outsiders how children can get jobs when their parents cannot. The reality is harsh: children are often more successful beggars and street hustlers than adults, there are a lot of children laboring illegally in the farms and the mines of Nicaragua, and the country is frankly a global supplier of child prostitutes. The half of Nicaraguans who live below the poverty level and the 16 percent who endure the intense poverty of eking by on less than $1.25 per day have more pressing concerns than political philosophy. Indeed, almost a third of the country's GDP is made up of remittances returned to families by the 12.5 percent of Nicaraguans working abroad, mostly in next-door Costa Rica, where they comprise the bulk of farm laborers, construction workers, and service personnel. If this supplies the country with much needed financial support, it deprives the country of its ablest and most industrious workers. Moreover, despite these remittances (as well as hundreds of millions of dollars of foreign aid, often channeled through NGOs rather than the government), 27 percent of the Nicaraguan population remains malnourished. This, not political philosophy, is what concerns most Nicaraguans.[30]

Political idealists will argue that a cleaner and more transparent government is a precondition for economic and social development, and they make a strong point. A continuing obstacle to economic development in Nicaragua, for example, is that the legal ownership of close to thirty thousand pieces of property remains uncertain. This is in part a lingering consequence of the expropriation of property by the Sandinistas after the revolution, though in larger part a consequence of the rampant corruption of the local courts and other public officials since then. Obviously, without clear and assured title to a piece of property, there is a disincentive to invest in developing the property in a way that generates profits and creates jobs. It is also plausible to argue that the culture of corruption starts at the top, and that if top-level officials changed their practices, the changes would filter down through the ranks. This line of argument has the whiff of naïveté about it, at least in the context of current and recent Nicaraguan realities. Ortega watched—and we can watch—what happened to the idealists in the MRS. They lost. In like manner, Enrique Bolaños on the right ran a clean administration, but was an ineffectual president. Those who attempted to play by the rules of good governance were simply crushed in Nicaragua. Whatever the theory, the reality was that political success depended upon making major ethical compromises—and without political success, a person lacked the power to develop anything.

Nor was Ortega persuaded by even the theory of a linkage between transparent democratic governance and a society's economic and social development. In his understanding of history, Western powers had become wealthy primarily through plunder—plunder that had victimized his own country—and all the prattle about ethical governance was mostly an ideological gloss pasted over historic aggression. With respect to the United States specifically, he refused to believe that it had ever changed its imperialist ways or that it abided by the rules of transparent democracy that it preached. He had firsthand experience of the United States waging a secret war on his country without the "democratic" support of either Congress or the voters and in defiance of international law. He then watched the United States work to install the supposedly "democratic" Chamorro administration, but knew firsthand that it was utterly corrupt. He was no longer surprised when the United States supported Arnoldo Alemán's presidential bid on the grounds that he was democratic while Ortega was not, when in reality Alemán was one of the least democratic and most corrupt politicians in the world. The United States simply did not practice the transparent democracy it preached, and neither was its affluence premised upon practicing it.

But if Ortega had reason to question the purported linkage between transparent democratic governance and economic development when he considered the example of the wealthy but undemocratic United States, he was also not sure that he favored democracy for other philosophical reasons. As he told an audience in Cuba in 2009, democracy as practiced in countries like the United States tends to divide a population into opposing political parties, when it is preferable for a people to be united in common purpose. His argument recalled the one made by James Madison in the *Federalist Papers* (#10) where it was discussed in terms of the problem of "factionalism"—or what today might be called "special interests"—in a democracy. Madison resolved the problem by maintaining that a large enough country would diminish its tendencies toward factionalism, although this solution ran counter to the historic one advanced by Thomas Hobbes, which insists that a strong central authority is required to prevent factional strife. It is also not an altogether convincing argument, since it would appear that factionalism is every bit the divisive force in large countries that it is in small countries, and perhaps even more divisive in large countries since the factions are themselves larger and more powerful. Whatever the criticisms of Madison's solution to the problem of factionalism may be, that solution could not apply to Nicaragua since it was a small country. Interestingly, Ortega could have invoked one of the United States' founding fathers in defense of his criticisms of democracy and preference for a more authoritarian political system. However, Ortega did not elaborate at the time, but simply mentioned the point and then added his usual dig against democracy as practiced by the United States. If it were committed to democracy, he asked rhetorically, why did it refuse to abide by the overwhelming majority vote in the United Nations urging it to lift its trade embargo against Cuba?[31]

The issue for Ortega—and if the polls are to be believed, for the majority of his compatriots—was not how political power is acquired and exercised, but to what ends it is devoted. The question of means is secondary, the question of ends primary. He and Alemán were roughly equivalent in their willingness to flout the democratic process, including transparency, the rule of law, and all that accompanies it. They had equivalent indifference to the political means, and their pact signaled this. The difference was in the ends. Alemán was out primarily for himself; he thought little about those from whom he stole. Ortega's means may have been identical, but the ends he sought were different. He wanted political power not merely for himself but also to help Nicaragua's poor. In this conviction he stood squarely in the center of his country's political culture. Authoritarianism was not welcome, but it was acceptable if it got the job done. Many believed it was necessary to getting the job done.

Two Final Pacts

ORTEGA NEEDED TO NEGOTIATE two more pacts in order to become president—although even with them he still had to get lucky and face a divided opposition. One pact was with his wife, Rosario Murillo, the other with the Catholic Church. Murillo had stood by him (and against her daughter) while the allegations of sexual molestation swirled around him, and for this she wanted compensation in the form of a renegotiated pact granting her greater political power. The Church was a more difficult pact to negotiate, since it was not clear what it would demand of Ortega to stop opposing his candidacies. However, Ortega had grown tired of the Church throwing its institutional weight against him in every election, and he was determined to do whatever it took to placate it.

The terms of the renegotiated pact between Ortega and Murillo can only be inferred from details that surfaced later, after Ortega was finally reelected president, although its effects are fairly clear. Murillo was put in charge of the reconstituted neighborhood organizations, renamed Councils of Citizens Power, which gave her control over the FSLN at the grassroots level, including municipal and other local offices. She was also made head of the FSLN media, enabling her to control its public relations messages. It also appears that she negotiated successor rights. Whereas few seriously believe that she will run for president herself, in part because she is decidedly unpopular in Nicaragua (where she is nicknamed a *bruja*, or witch, owing to her dabbling in various New Age spiritualities), her son Rafael regularly appears in public with Ortega. It appears that he is being groomed for the role of successor. As for Ortega, he has remained free to pursue the political objectives he cares about, and if rumors are to be believed has even remained free to philander as often as he wants to. (It is said that he fathered another child in 2009 with the daughter of one of his security guards.) However, he now dresses in pastels, which Murillo believes are more soothing to the spirits than the old Sandinista colors of red and black. There may be other aspects to the pact—and the couple appears genuinely to get along—but it is common knowledge in Nicaragua that an Ortega-Murillo pact exists alongside the Ortega-Alemán pact.

One step that Ortega took to mollify the Church was to get married. After twenty-seven years of living together in a common-law union, Ortega and Murillo were formally married in a church ceremony presided over by Cardinal Obando y Bravo himself in 2005. This and other outward signs of piety helped Ortega curry the Church's favor, but they were not enough. The Church demanded more. Specifically, it wanted the government's unequivocal opposition to abortion. Ever the pragmatist, Ortega had always deferred to popular opinion on the abortion issue. In Nicaragua, popular opinion strongly opposes abortion, so even during the 1980s the Sandinistas allowed it to remain illegal. Neither Ortega nor the Sandinistas, however, had ever stood in the way of therapeutic abortions, namely those performed to save the life of the mother, and permitting them had been the law of the land. To the Church, though, this was too weak a position, so ten days before the 2006 presidential election an old nineteenth-century statute prohibiting abortion in any circumstances was resurrected and passed by the National Assembly with Ortega's open support. This meant that even therapeutic abortions were outlawed. In turn, it meant that poor women would suffer and even die, since the affluent could always travel to a nearby country to have their abortions performed. This was not the kind of social policy that Ortega favored, and it ultimately stimulated considerable animosity toward his later administration. Feminists and others strongly objected to the total ban on abortions, and European governments even cited it as a reason for canceling aid to Nicaragua. Ortega later argued, probably more or less correctly, that his administration was not enforcing the ban against therapeutic abortions, thus in effect decriminalizing them if not making them legal. Nevertheless, he did formally support the ban, it was Nicaraguan law, and his support for the ban was part of a transparent pact he made with the Church for his political gain. Not only did Ortega avoid having the Church oppose his 2006 presidential bid, but Nicaragua also received special praise from Pope Benedict for taking the strong stand it did.[32]

With the pacts negotiated, Alemán weakened, and with his reliable if minority constituency behind him, Ortega was ready for victory in the 2006 presidential election. He still of course needed to get lucky in order to win. Specifically, he needed to face a divided opposition. However, it was not merely a matter of luck in 2006. Ortega had played rough against Alemán, brought him down, and fractured the liberal alliance in the process. This was all it took to divide his opposition and finally win reelection to the presidency.

6

TOWARD A DYNASTY
OF THE LEFT

In 2005, Nicaragua's liberal alliance splintered into two main parties. Eduardo Montealegre, a businessman who had occupied various senior positions in the Bolaños administration and had been educated at Brown and Harvard in the United States, caused the fissure by creating the Nicaraguan Liberal Alliance (ALN). Montealegre justified his breakaway party by arguing that liberals should dissociate themselves from Alemán's Liberal Constitutional Party (PLC) both because of Alemán's corruption and because of his pact with Ortega. The renegade liberal persuaded many Nicaraguans, 29 percent of whom voted for Montealegre in the 2006 presidential election. The party also persuaded the United States, which openly supported Montealegre's candidacy. Alemán's PLC, however, remained strong too. Its presidential nominee, José Rizo, served as vice president under Bolaños and was reasonably popular. Complicating matters was that Oliver North, then a conservative commentator for FOX News, showed up in Nicaragua to endorse Rizo on the eve of the election. Whether North's endorsement helped or hurt Rizo is unknown, but it left the impression that the United States did not have a preferred candidate. When the votes were counted, Rizo garnered 26 percent, only slightly lower than Montealegre. This left Daniel Ortega, who attracted 38 percent of the vote, in the position that he had planned for when he pushed through the lower 35 percent threshold for a win without a runoff: the victor, and president-elect of Nicaragua.

As it happened, Ortega came perilously close to losing the 2006 election anyway. The threat came from Herty Lewites, the nominee of the MRS. Lewites was a popular figure in Nicaragua among the center-left. His revolutionary credentials could be traced to his having run guns out of the United States during the revolution on behalf of the Sandinistas, an activity for which he served time in a U.S. prison. He subsequently served in various capacities in Nicaragua's government, including a term as mayor of Managua. He was also thought to have a sound business mind, which added a special feather to the cap of a leftist. While Lewites had not faithfully identified himself with the FSLN after the defections from the Front during the 1990s, he did not formally leave it until he was expelled for challenging Ortega for its 2006 presidential nomination. When that happened, the MRS welcomed him as their nominee. Early polling showed him running second to Montealegre, and well ahead of Ortega. No one knows what would have happened if Lewites had remained in the race, but a likely scenario is that he and Montealegre would have ended up in a runoff. Four months before the election, however, Lewites dropped dead of a heart attack. There were rumors that he had been poisoned, although nothing was ever proved. The MRS was forced to substitute its vice presidential nominee, Edmundo Jarquin, late in the campaign. The MRS still ended up capturing 6 percent of the vote, a strong showing under the circumstances, but not enough to deprive Ortega of victory.

When Daniel Ortega took the oath of office in January 2007, he therefore did not enjoy widespread popular support. A substantial 55 percent of his fellow Nicaraguans had voted for one of his two liberal opponents, and 6 percent of Sandinista voters had preferred the MRS candidate. Despite this, goodwill was cautiously extended to him. His "honeymoon" approval ratings briefly approached 60 percent, as presumably a majority of Nicaraguans were willing to give him the benefit of the doubt. However, it was no surprise when those approval ratings plummeted. If there was a surprise, it was how fast and far they dropped. Within six months of taking office, Ortega's support polled in the 20 to 30 percent range.[1] To be sure, polls are not terribly reliable in Nicaragua, where poll-rigging is a cottage industry and misleading pollsters a national sport. It is also far–fetched to believe that Ortega lost his hardcore support—the 38 percent or more who vote for him in every election. Even so, it was obvious that Ortega would not be a popular president.

Ortega took immediate steps to shore up his support. Just as he had learned to campaign in a manner that enabled him to attract as many votes as possible, he also immediately established a public relations apparatus (headed by Murillo) designed to stimulate support for his presidency. During the campaign his vice presidential choice, Jaime Morales, had not merely been a former contra but the very person who used to own his house, the one confiscated in the aftermath of the revolution and signed over to Ortega in the *piñata*. He also changed his theme song—again—this time to John Lennon's "Give Peace a Chance." Murillo saw to it that billboards and banners portraying her husband were prominently displayed throughout the country, usually with the pastel-clad president urging the poor to rise up. His speeches were broadcast on Sandinista radio and television, and even published in pamphlets. A slick presidential Web site was created, called "El Pueblo Presidente." Although this could be translated as simply "President of the Country," *pueblo* has warmer connotations—more like "people" than "country." Murillo established her own Web site too, calling it "With Love Nicaragua" ("Con Amor Nicaragua"). She even distributed CDs of popular songs praising Ortega's leadership.

Murillo's public relations efforts had the hint of propaganda about them. They persuaded next to no one who was not already a loyal Danielista, and they drew the ire of others who were not. Many of the billboards were quickly defaced by vandals, who spray-painted words like "dictator" over them, while it was the rare club that played the pro-Ortega songs. What appeared to be genuine pro-FSLN graffiti did remain in some of the poorer barrios, but elsewhere Ortega's pretensions to popularity were met with hostility and disgust. Such leading Sandinistas as Gioconda Belli, Ernesto Cardenal, Carlos Fernando Chamorro, Sergio Ramírez, and Dora María Téllez openly denounced both him and Murillo's propaganda campaign. Indeed, Dora María Téllez led a very public hunger strike in Managua during the summer of 2008 against what she called his "dictatorship," and the strike prompted several large demonstrations (and counterdemonstrations). At one demonstration in the city of León, a banner was unfurled that depicted Anastasio Somoza Debayle and Ortega together. The caption read, "Ortega and Somoza: The Same Thing." The banner was splattered with red paint and "signed" by Rigoberto López Pérez, the poet who had assassinated the elder Somoza in 1956. The implication was that someone should assassinate Ortega. Clearly Murillo's propaganda campaign was not working, and was perhaps even backfiring.

Ortega showed little concern about any of this. In particular, he did nothing to appease his critics. They were mainly concerned with his authoritarian manner, yet Ortega acted in ways that fueled these concerns. Instead of taking up residency in the presidential palace, for example, he continued to live and work in his own private compound. Since this doubled as the FSLN headquarters and was guarded by private FLSN security forces, governing from there sent the unmistakable message that person, party, and government were fused in the Ortega administration—precisely the wrong message to send to those fearful of just such an authoritarian fusion. In addition, instead of attempting to mollify his critics by holding frequent press conferences and perhaps even public forums—tactics he used with considerable success in his first presidential term during the 1980s—Ortega slammed the door on the press.[2] Although Nicaragua still enjoyed a "free press," Ortega denied it access to his administration. His only interviews were granted abroad—to Al Jazeera and to friendly leftist media in Venezuela and Cuba—while all Nicaraguan media not controlled by the FSLN (that is, by Murillo) were kept at arm's length. An Ortega "press conference" amounted to his delivering whatever speech he wanted to give, then leaving. There were no question and answer periods. In fact, even today there is not a way for the press to contact the president, or at least to do so with any assurance that the contact is received. E-mails to "El Pueblo Presidente" receive no responses, nor do the mandatory written requests left with the guards at his compound. Secrecy so shrouds Ortega that there are rumors that an illness prevents him from being able to endure more than brief exposures to sunlight. Whether or not these rumors are true is less important than the fact that he governs behind the kind of veil of secrecy that permits them to flourish. Ortega even acted with apparent vindictiveness against some of his critics. He had Ernesto Cardenal, his minister of culture during the 1980s, arrested on a long-dormant minor charge, and raided the offices of Carlos Fernando Chamorro, the previous editor of the Sandinista newspaper *Barricada*, on the basis of suspected irregularities in the finances of his independent media company (irregularities that were never found). Taken together, Ortega's actions and style stimulated the very accusations of authoritarianism that a politician concerned about his popular image would want to defuse.

The inescapable conclusion is that Ortega was not especially concerned about his popular support within Nicaragua, or at least not concerned enough about it to do more than shore it up among his base. This in turn signals a significant change in, or at least hardening of, his political style since the 1980s. Then, he was not especially concerned with popular opinion either, at least as measured by the "raffle" of elections, but he was considerably more open to the public and the press. Seventeen years later, though, he displayed a very different political persona. Perhaps the change can be explained psychologically. Ortega had to have been hurt by the defections of so many of his former friends from the FSLN, as well as by their blistering personal attacks. It is possible that he reacted in the ways that his prison years had taught him to: by hunkering down, becoming tougher and more ruthless, withdrawing. Yet there is a political explanation for the change as well. Years of "governing from below" convinced him that public support is of limited value in Nicaraguan politics. Rather it is the people and institutions he controls, on the one hand, and the policies he promotes, on the other, that are important. Insofar as public support is necessary, he may reason that it can be earned by delivering tangible results to a desperately poor population, which for the most part does not care how he achieves those results.

The Ortega presidency is thus a curious one. On the one hand it bears many marks of a dictatorship, even a family dynasty, in the making—and the comparisons to Somoza are not far-fetched. Although Humberto tired of politics and retired to Costa Rica a few years before Daniel was reelected, power is concentrated in the Ortega-Murillo family, which remains insulated from outside interference. On the other hand, unlike the classic caudillo, Ortega gives little evidence of being motivated by personal aggrandizement or even by wealth. Instead he appears driven by the promise his presidency offers to improve the lives of Nicaraguans. Toward this end he has launched one usually thoughtful and effective program after another, while there is nary a hint that he is interested in augmenting his personal wealth or tempted by financial corruption. As such, the Ortega administration is probably better compared to "authoritarians of the left"—leaders like Fidel Castro in Cuba and Hugo Chávez in Venezuela—than to the more prevalent "authoritarians of the right," like Somoza was. These "authoritarians of the left" use many of the same tactics as their counterparts on the right, but on behalf of different goals.

Whether Nicaraguans will embrace the comparison of Somoza and Ortega, only time will tell. At the moment they are coming to grips with another curiosity of the Ortega presidency. He is not merely modeling his administration after other "authoritarians of the left" but also openly joining forces with them with the aim of creating a global left axis within which Nicaragua will be situated. Unnoticed by critics who object to his dictatorial tendencies and assume they indicate a thirst for dynastic power in Nicaragua, by the time Ortega was finally reelected president, his horizons had broadened well beyond his homeland. He did not think like a Somoza or even an Alemán, who were content with wealth and power in Nicaragua, but rather like a global strategist who sees nations as pieces of a puzzle that can be fitted together differently for different results. Ortega is not indifferent to Nicaragua, but he is convinced that it will only be improved as the result of a larger leftist global program. Accordingly, he governs Nicaragua from an internationalist rather than a nationalist perspective. It is as if, after sixteen years of "governing from below," Ortega decided to bypass the messy middle where most of his fellow Nicaraguans and even most in the world expected him to be in favor of governing from above—from far above.

Governing from Above

TWO OF THE FIRST experiences that Nicaraguans had of the Ortega presidency were that their lights came on and Venezuelan president Hugo Chávez was driving Ortega's SUV. The two experiences were related. Prior to Ortega's reelection, the country did not have enough energy to allow everyone to turn their lights on at once, or at least to be able to rely upon them to continue operating if they did come on. Although Nicaragua has the potential to develop both hydroelectric and geothermal power, like most things in the country, there has been little long-term investment in developing these resources.[3] As a consequence, as recently as the first year of Ortega's term, Nicaragua endured rolling blackouts. These were an improvement over the random blackouts that had preceded them, but both were more than inconveniences. Businesses left Nicaragua, or refused to locate there, over the problem of an unreliable energy supply. Ortega solved this problem by striking a deal with Chávez to import Venezuelan oil at an attractive price and terms. Chávez even threw in the promise of building a refinery in Nicaragua. In fact, the deal helped to solve other problems in Nicaragua as well, since as a condition for supplying the oil, Chávez insisted that a certain amount of the revenues be earmarked for social welfare expenditures. Nicaragua therefore not only finally had an adequate power supply, but it also received additional funds to assist the poor. The process did not happen overnight, but within about a year the blackouts were mostly a memory and social welfare funds were being distributed. Over the same period, Hugo Chávez became a frequent visitor to the Central American state. Moreover, since Ortega was known to prefer to drive himself, Nicaraguans noticed when photographs surfaced showing Chávez driving Ortega's SUV—with Ortega in the passenger seat.

Though of symbolic importance, the issue was of course not who drove whose vehicle. While Ortega displayed considerable deference to Chávez (who is said to have bankrolled his 2006 presidential campaign too), no one needs to worry about Ortega involuntarily falling under the influence of anyone else. With the sole exception of Castro, those who have dealt with Ortega have generally been bested by him. Insofar as there is a competition between Ortega and Chávez, smart money would bet on the Nicaraguan. More to the point, as with Castro, Ortega's bond with Chávez is sincere. There is no reason for Ortega to resist Chávez's influence, because he likes and agrees with him. Out of thousands of photographs taken of Ortega over the years, the only ones that show him in a full belly laugh are a few of him and Chávez together. Ortega's association with Chávez clearly runs deeper than a political alliance, and Ortega can hold his own in those anyway.

The issue is instead the nature of the political alliance between Ortega and Chávez, and thus between Nicaragua and Venezuela. And the issue is broader than the bilateral relationship between the two countries. It extends to Nicaragua's relationship with most countries in the world and raises questions about Ortega's authoritarianism. The global ramifications evolve from both Chávez's objective for offering Nicaragua assistance and Ortega's objective for accepting it. That objective is to build a network of nations opposed to the capitalist world that can usher in what Chávez has famously called "twenty-first-century socialism." Together with Castro, Chávez created the general framework for this left-wing alliance in 2004, named the Bolivarian Alliance for the Peoples of Our America (ALBA). On Ortega's first day in office, he signed an agreement that incorporated Nicaragua into ALBA, which very quickly included Bolivia, Honduras, and the Dominican Republic as well. In one fell swoop, Nicaraguans found themselves absorbed into a global left-wing political alliance by a president who lacked popular support. Worse, as they studied—or tried to study—the oil deal, they discovered that Ortega had not even entered into it as the president of Nicaragua, but as the head of the FSLN. Neither the oil revenues nor the attendant social welfare expenditures would therefore flow through the government of Nicaragua, or be subject to public accounting or oversight. They would be handled privately by Daniel Ortega under the auspices of the FSLN. In exchange for getting their lights turned on and additional social welfare assistance, Nicaraguans found themselves absorbed into a left-wing global alliance headed by Hugo Chávez, and under the thumb of a president who personally controlled their national oil supply.

It is not clear that ALBA per se is a worrisome development, or that Nicaragua is worse off for joining it. ALBA's principal goal is to provide member countries with financial institutions that offer an alternative to having to participate in those of the wealthy Western countries that press the neoliberal agenda. Further goals of ALBA include fully funding a Bank of the South as an alternative to the World Bank and International Monetary Fund for global lending, as well as the creation of a common Latin American currency, more or less similar to the euro. There has been some discussion within ALBA of creating a common military force, that is, a standing ALBA army that is more than a military alliance, but ALBA is very much in the throes of the creation process and initiatives like these lie far in the future, should they ever be pursued. Meanwhile, critics observe that ALBA's prospects depend a lot on the global price of oil, which is ALBA's primary source of income, and naturally question ALBA's likelihood of success on other grounds. In short, it is premature to worry much about ALBA, and initial evaluations may even be cautiously optimistic. Certainly having an alternative to Western-dominated global markets is not ipso facto contrary to the interests of Nicaragua (or even to the West for that matter). Judgments about ALBA, and Nicaragua's membership in it, should therefore probably be withheld until there are concrete developments.[4]

There is more reason to be alarmed about the oil purchases bypassing the government and its oversight. This smacks of authoritarianism, and many Nicaraguans are outraged by it. Interestingly, the entire arrangement may be legal.[5] There is evidently nothing to prevent Ortega, in this capacity acting as a "businessman" and party leader, from negotiating an arrangement with the government of Venezuela to import and then sell oil in Nicaragua. Moreover, to some extent Ortega can be credited rather than faulted for negotiating the deal. In principle, there was nothing to prevent the Bolaños administration together with the legislature from negotiating a similar deal with Venezuela. Chávez may perhaps have resisted such overtures, since he wanted to help Ortega politically, but he has not made membership in ALBA a condition of accepting his attractive oil offers. Costa Rica buys low-priced oil from Chávez without having joined ALBA, for example.[6] Thus, while the ramifications of the deal are questionable, Ortega can be defended on the usual grounds—he is getting the job done when others did not. Even so, the whole arrangement suggests an ideological authoritarian entanglement among person, party, and state. This concerns many both inside and outside Nicaragua. Inside Nicaragua, though, the concerns extend beyond the political to include more nebulous issues of the nation's cultural identity.

IN 2009, NICARAGUANS SENT around one of those humorous e-mails that are distributed widely among friends and acquaintances. This purported to describe some of the distinctive features of their culture, following the structure "You know you are Nicaraguan when . . ." and then listing various Nicaraguan idioms, customs, and characteristics (most of them funny). One was "having family members in the United States, Costa Rica, or both." It was accompanied by a drawing of a family tree that branched out into the two other countries, and the humor resided in the implication that it is distinctly Nicaraguan to have ties to two other countries. Like most attempts at humor, this one contained more than a kernel of truth. It is not clear how many Nicaraguans reside in either country, but the census bureau reports that almost a quarter million Nicaraguans live in the United States, while the much sketchier figures for Costa Rica place the number of Nicaraguans living there (legally and illegally) at between two hundred thousand and a million. Given Nicaragua's small population, these figures mean that at any one time 10 to 25 percent of the population is living in one of these two countries.

Costa Rica is a special case. It is a proudly Latin country—Spanish is the official language and Roman Catholicism the official religion—and it has been known to defy the United States. However, its development model has emphasized tourism, mainly from the United States, and it has been quite successful in growing this industry. An estimated seven hundred thousand tourists from the United States visit Costa Rica annually.[7] In fact, in the opinion of some (including Daniel Ortega), Costa Rica has been too successful in promoting tourism. Vast stretches of its Pacific coastline are now dominated by condominiums and hotels, primarily owned and occupied by North Americans, while towns sometimes have signs in English as well as Spanish, attesting to the size of the English-speaking population. The permanent expatriate community of North Americans in Costa Rica is large enough to populate a medium-sized city and support an American Legion Post (despite Costa Rica being officially pacifist and having no standing army) and two English-language newspapers. In short, any Nicaraguan who lives there will be exposed to a large number of U.S. citizens.

Other connections Nicaraguans have to the United States are at least as plentiful, especially among the elites. Nicaragua's presidents exemplify them. The Somozas were all educated in the United States, as were Violeta Chamorro, Arnoldo Alemán, and Enrique Bolaños. In fact, the only presidents since the 1920s who were not were René Schick, the Somoza regime's puppet president from 1963 to 1966, and Daniel Ortega. (It is not clear where Lorenzo Guerrero Gutiérrez, who served very briefly after Schick, was educated.) Prior to the 1930s, several presidents were schooled in the United States, while others lived there for various intervals. Even Eduardo Montealegre, founder and leader of the ALN, was educated there. At less elite levels, the cultural influence of the United States is considerable. Nicaraguans have long watched television programs produced in the United States, been fans of Hollywood movies, followed North American baseball, drunk Coca-Cola, and listened to U.S. popular music—often without even understanding the English-language lyrics. When Michael Jackson died in 2009, it was same-day news in Nicaragua. A lead story about the capture of Carlos Fonseca in *La Prensa* forty years earlier was across from an equally prominent story about the Woodstock music festival on the opposite page. In ways too numerous to recount but that extend well beyond the political, Nicaragua simply has deep cultural ties to the United States.

One difficulty the Sandinistas confronted from the beginning was that they had far fewer of these cultural ties. To some extent, of course, this was a product of Sandinista ideology. Like Sandino, they viewed the United States as an imperialistic power, and they wanted it to leave Nicaragua alone. To a greater extent than is usually recognized, however, the personal backgrounds of the Sandinistas also failed to include the kinds of connections to the United States that were common in their country. The only Sandinista leader during the 1980s who had studied in the United

States, for example, was Moisés Hassan, and he was Palestinian, which provided him with a global frame of reference at some odds with the normally pro-Israel position of the United States. Many, like Henry Ruíz on the National Directorate, had studied in the Soviet Union, as had Leticia Herrera. Carlos Fonseca was a "Nicaraguan in Moscow" before he was ever a Sandinista, and he never set foot in the United States. Meanwhile, Sergio Ramírez came to the Front after living in West Germany, Jaime Wheelock after living in both Europe and Chile, Víctor Tirado (a member of the Directorate) from Mexico. Rosario Murillo was schooled in Europe, not the United States. Measured simply by their backgrounds, the Sandinistas had a different worldview than was customary in their country, especially among the elite.

Daniel Ortega's background was similar to that of his fellow Sandinistas—and similarly at odds with the majority of Nicaraguans. If anything, his diplomatic travels on behalf of the Front during the 1980s gave him more personal acquaintance with countries outside the U.S. sphere of influence than even his fellow Sandinistas. By the time of his defeat in 1990, he was probably one of the better traveled heads of state in the world. While his itineraries after 1990 are sketchier, and dominated by what for all practical purposes was a second home in Cuba, his globe-trotting continued far beyond that island state. Indeed, after he was reelected president, the habit persisted. In May 2009, opposition legislators in the National Assembly called unsuccessfully for his ouster on the grounds that he had been out of the country more than the fifteen days per month that the constitution permits a president to be abroad. When he was reelected president in 2006, Ortega was simply the most cosmopolitan president Nicaragua had ever had—although also one with the least sympathy to the United States.

Ortega's global exposure coupled with his ideological proclivities therefore put him at some odds from his fellow Nicaraguans, but it is by no means clear that his worldview is deficient or even bad for Nicaragua. He insists that the world is now multipolar, not bipolar, and sees a brighter future for Nicaragua positioned autonomously within this multipolar world rather than dependent primarily upon the United States and its allies. This is arguably smart strategic thinking. However, quite apart from any specific reservations they had over either the ideological direction he was steering Nicaragua or his authoritarian manner, Nicaraguans experienced Ortega's presidency as culturally destabilizing. He was governing not merely from far above, but not even from the international perspective of most of his predecessors or most Nicaraguans.

EVEN MEMBERSHIP IN ALBA and alliance with Chávez did not prepare Nicaraguans for the belligerence of their new president's rhetoric toward the United States and its allies. The tone was unmistakably set in a September 2007 speech that Ortega delivered to the United Nations in which he accused the United States of being a dictatorship. Whereas many in Nicaragua might have agreed with Ortega's opinion about the United States, most believed that his speech was unnecessarily confrontational.[8] Nicaragua was not, after all, at war with the United States any longer, and while reasonable people could disagree about the role that the United States continued to play in Nicaragua, the superpower's role was at least superficially supportive of the country's economic development. Nevertheless, this was only Ortega's opening salvo. In remark after remark, he accused the United States and increasingly Western European countries of being imperialist marauders and worse.[9] Indeed, warnings by Western European countries that they would be compelled to cut off aid to Nicaragua if the Ortega administration did not correct its deficiencies in political transparency were sometimes rebuffed by Ortega saying that Nicaragua cannot be bought for thirty pieces of silver and calling the European donor countries "flies that land on filth."[10] Ortega also regularly accused the United States of meddling in Nicaragua's internal politics, but then, McCarthy-like, only promised to show proof later. (The proof has rarely been produced.) Anti-U.S. rhetoric resurfaced in the speech that Ortega gave at the summit meeting of the Organization of American States in April 2009.[11] About the same time, Ortega abruptly withdrew Nicaragua's delegates from trade negotiations between the European Union and Central America because the Europeans refused to discuss Nicaragua's demands for what would in effect be reparations for past exploitation. Nicaragua's withdrawal threatened the entire negotiation process for all the countries. Although Ortega's hard-line position was eventually agreed to as a topic for discussion and the talks resumed, the stridency of the Nicaraguan position did not go unnoticed.[12] Neither did Ortega's dismissive attitude toward Costa Rica's president, Oscar Arias, who was reelected around the same time as Ortega. His disdain for Arias (who he accused of being a lackey for the United States) was palpable. In these instances and others, President Ortega displayed an abrasive belligerence toward foreign countries and foreign leaders that even many of his supporters found excessive.

He was obviously a man on a mission, though, and a global mission. Upon closer inspection, his alliance with Chávez was only its economic and ideological centerpiece. Ortega quickly took to canvassing the globe with an eye toward forging alliances with any enemy of the West that would befriend Nicaragua. One of these enemies, or rather former enemies, was Russia. Immediately after the Russian-backed republics of South Ossetia and Abkhazia attempted to break away from the former Soviet client state of Georgia in 2008, and as Russia sent troops in to oppose Georgia, Ortega publicly declared Nicaragua's support for the breakaway republics.[13] Nicaragua and Russia stood bizarrely alone in the world in taking this position. (A year later Chávez added Venezuela's support.)

But this was of minor significance compared to the alliance that Ortega forged with Iran's President Mahmoud Ahmadinejad. Iran offered to build a $230 million hydroelectric plant on Nicaraguan's Caribbean coast, and Ortega accepted.[14] However, the deal went somewhat deeper for both countries. Ever since President George W. Bush fingered Iran as one of three countries comprising an "axis of evil" in his 2002 State of the Union speech, among Iran's principal strategies has been to forge alliances with Latin American countries. The idea, grossly simplified, is that if the United States attacks Iran, Iran can counterattack from Latin America, or better yet prevent an attack by threatening retaliation from Latin America and otherwise having good relationships with countries there. Ortega gave Iran the friendly relationship it sought (plans include building a large Iranian embassy in Nicaragua), and in exchange made an ally out of another enemy of the United States. Indeed, there followed some loose talk about the similarity between the Iranian and Nicaraguan revolutions, although it seems to be limited to the facts that the revolutions were both directed more or less against the United States and occurred about the same time.

Ortega's global maneuverings sometimes took even more inexplicable turns. The weirdest may have been his naming Thailand's ousted prime minister, Thaksin Shinawatra, a "special ambassador" to Nicaragua in 2009 and giving him a diplomatic passport.[15] It is possible that Ortega followed Thailand's troubled politics with sufficient studiousness to have decided that Shinawatra's faction was the one he preferred, but if he had it was news to Nicaraguans. He also never explained why he took the initiative to forge this relationship. It appeared that Ortega just picked up global friends wherever he could find them.

Yet for the most part Ortega's international involvements betrayed a clearer underlying rationale, and a rationale consistent with his affiliation with Chávez. His actions toward Colombia are a case in point. When the opportunity presented itself, Ortega immediately extended Nicaraguan asylum to captured members of the Revolutionary Armed Forces of Colombia (FARC). In addition to striking many as a brazen intrusion into Colombia's internal affairs, this was a slap in the face to Colombia's President Álvaro Uribe. He had made valiant efforts to counter what had frankly become more of a criminal organization of drug traffickers and kidnappers than a revolutionary force, and enjoyed considerable popular support within his country for doing so. When Ortega followed his granting of asylum to FARC members with an offer to help negotiate a truce between the FARC and the government of Colombia, his offer was understandably quickly rebuffed. Meanwhile, Ortega briefly withdrew Nicaragua's ambassador to Colombia in a gesture of support for Venezuela when the two countries had a border dispute, although he soon sent the ambassador back when the tensions subsided. Beneath these seemingly erratic and ineffectual moves lurks more than the frantic acts of a nostalgic revolutionary. Not only do Uribe's generally friendly relations with the United States place him in the camp of Ortega's enemies, but leftist strategy in Latin America also sees Colombia as a plum waiting to be picked by a leftist alliance. Both the presence of the FARC in Colombia and the fact that the country has one of the most unequal distributions of wealth in Latin America make it a prime candidate for a leftward move, runs the strategic thinking. Although they have yet to succeed, Ortega's actions vis-à-vis Colombia have fit with his broader notion of the global challenge.[16]

The list of Ortega's attempts to position himself, and therefore Nicaragua, into a global leftist alliance in which he enjoys substantial influence can and probably will grow longer. During the summer of 2009, for example, deposed Honduran president and Chávez sympathizer Manuel Zelaya found both haven in and rhetorical support from Ortega's neighboring Nicaragua. Ortega even heightened the crisis by implying that the CIA had been behind the coup that ousted Zelaya. He is clearly alert to any opportunity to bolster his global agenda and quick to pursue it. Taken together, Ortega's international involvements thus appear to reveal a global orientation that goes beyond his association with Chávez. Whereas Chávez and ALBA remain the lynchpins, Ortega's goal of constructing an anti-U.S. global alliance with Nicaragua in a pivotal position includes plenty of other international initiatives.

It is as if he were attempting to carve out a semi-autonomous position for himself and Nicaragua beyond that which his association with Chávez provides. Indeed, while Chávez remains Ortega's biggest financial backer, Ortega usually gets something out of all his global deals. Just as he got oil and social welfare dollars out of Chávez and a power plant out of Iran, he convinced Russia to donate a fleet of buses. Deal by deal, Ortega is slowly positioning himself as a global power broker, more or less the same way he clawed his way back into the presidency.

Of course, Ortega requires power within his home country from which to pursue his global ambitions. Accordingly, maintaining his power in Nicaragua remains a priority. Nicaraguans may notice this more than they do his global maneuverings, even though his global initiatives are probably more important in the long run.

The 2008 Elections

Amid growing concerns over Ortega's authoritarian leanings, Nicaragua held its 2008 municipal elections. These provided Ortega's critics with what they considered to be the most egregious evidence of his dictatorial ambitions. The problem was not merely that the elections were riddled with irregularities that suggested fraud, but also that the elections were of minor importance to the consolidation of Ortega's power. FSLN victories in these elections, mostly mayoral offices, would make it easier for Ortega to control events at the local level and provide him with local officials loyal to him. He had insisted that FSLN candidates for municipal offices sign a pledge agreeing to work with his Councils of Citizen Power. This in effect provided Murillo and Ortega with leverage over the officials elected on the FSLN ticket. It was not a lot of leverage, however, in part because membership on the Councils of Citizen Power was not limited to party members or even party loyalists. Although the Councils were creations of the FSLN and ultimately reported to Murillo, they were also to some extent nonpartisan, genuinely democratic bodies. Thus, the fact that Ortega would interfere in these relatively unimportant municipal elections showed the lengths to which he was willing to go to fortify his power. By then he already effectively controlled both the courts and the Supreme Electoral Council, via the appointees that his pact with Alemán had permitted him to make. Together with his own office of the presidency, this gave him influence if not control over three of the four branches of Nicaragua's national government. Only the National Assembly, the legislature, remained partially independent.

There is also little doubt but that Nicaragua's 2008 elections were replete with "irregularities" that on the whole swung the outcomes more solidly in the FSLN's favor than would have otherwise been the case. Unfortunately, there is no way of knowing how much fraud occurred during the elections, because Nicaragua's Supreme Electoral Council refused either to certify most impartial international observers prior to the elections or to undertake a thorough post-election investigation of the irregularities. Ortega's influence over the Supreme Electoral Council probably led to these decisions. Since he did not want transparent elections, the Supreme Electoral Council did not want them either—and so much for the autonomy of this supposedly independent fourth branch of government. Anecdotal evidence of electoral fraud is substantial. This includes opposition ballots discovered in garbage cans, vote tallies being "reported" from selected precincts before the votes were counted, mysterious precinct closings, selected challenges to voter registrations, and so on. Perhaps the fairest assessment of the extent of the irregularities comes from Ethics and Transparency, the Nicaraguan branch of the global elections-monitoring group Transparency International. Although they were not allowed privileged access to polling sites, they did post thousands of observers outside polling places throughout the country. Their estimate is that roughly a third of the 146 races were suspicious enough to have warranted investigation.[17]

The reaction to Ortega's election rigging was accordingly swift and strident. In his 2008 year-end "news analysis," for instance, *Nica Times* editor Tim Rogers opined that the elections that year were of "transcendental" importance to Nicaragua's history, a "game-changer" and a "watershed," because they signaled more clearly than anything else had the rise of an Ortega "dictatorship."[18] Others were not much less hyperbolic. Immediately after the elections, the *Washington Post* editorialized against Ortega's "emerging dictatorship" and complained that he was "seeking autocratic power."[19] About the same time, Roger Noriega wrote in the *Miami Herald* that the "shameless attempt by Sandinista dictator Daniel Ortega to steal last Sunday's municipal elections" attested to his "iron grip on Nicaraguan politics" and the dangers of "authoritarian populism."[20] In Nicaragua's Spanish-language press, the director of *El Nuevo Diario*, Francisco Chamorro, decisively departed from his paper's historic support for the FSLN by accusing the Sandinismo of Ortega of having become merely the "family project" for him, Murillo, and their children, while comparing it to Hitler's National Socialism.[21]

Of course, many Nicaraguans did not wait for the elections to denounce Ortega as "another Somoza." Five months earlier former FSLN leader Dora María Téllez had launched her well-publicized hunger strike against Ortega's government, and between then and the elections various demonstrations and counterdemonstrations wracked Nicaragua's major cities of Managua and León. Even so, the elections were the watershed event for critical reactions to Ortega's presidency. Summarizing the global reaction to them, Rory Carroll wrote in Britain's *Observer* that Ortega's "authoritarianism and accusations of election rigging have led to fears that he is becoming just another Latin American dictator." Carroll added that most Western governments were not merely criticizing. Within two months of the elections, European countries had already suspended ninety million dollars in aid to Nicaragua, while the U.S. government had suspended sixty-four million more.[22] Eventually the United States cancelled its aid altogether.

While Ortega's interference in the 2008 elections certainly signaled his growing authoritarianism, a broader view of Nicaragua's political culture once again suggests a more forgiving, or at least more nuanced, evaluation. To start, it is widely believed that election tampering is commonplace in Nicaragua on all sides, even when foreign observers are present. In particular, it is generally conceded that considerable fraud was perpetrated against Ortega and the FSLN in the 1996 elections. The Carter Center, which helped to monitor the 1996 elections, attested to this in its final report. The electoral irregularities in 2008 do not appear to have been any more egregious than those in 1996. Nor do they appear to have determined the outcomes of many races. At the very most, even if every one of the races that Ethics and Transparency reported as questionable had gone against Ortega's FSLN candidate, the FSLN still would have won over a third of the races. As it was, the Front won two-thirds of them. Since it is doubtful that all or maybe even most of the victorious FSLN candidates in questionable races would have lost in cleaner elections, it appears that FSLN candidates would have won most of the races anyway. There is a widespread misconception among elites, born perhaps of the fact that FSLN supporters tend to be poorer and less articulate than the Front's opponents, that the party of Daniel Ortega is weak. It is not. If it has trouble amassing a majority, it easily comes within striking distance.

The election for mayor of Managua, the most hotly contested race, illustrates this problem of underemphasizing FSLN strength and then crying "fraud" when the FSLN candidate wins in an atmosphere of mutual mistrust. The most reliable poll on the eve of the vote, conducted by CID-GALLUP, showed the FLSN candidate, popular ex-boxer Alexis Argüello, five points ahead of his chief rival, Eduardo Montealegre, who had rebounded from his defeat in the 2006 presidential election to attempt to capture the mayor's office in Managua.[23] Granted, there were reasons to believe that Montealegre would win that race. He had negotiated his own pact with Alemán, for one, which allowed the liberal forces to be rejoined for the election.[24] Other polls, meanwhile, showed a slight advantage for Montealegre, and he naturally claimed to have commissioned polls that showed him ahead and gaining. However, Agüello was popular too, polls in Nicaragua are notoriously unreliable, and the most reliable one forecast an FSLN victory of almost the exact magnitude of the final vote tally. It is simply not clear that irregularities in selected Managua precincts determined the outcome of that contest, and it frankly appears that Argüello was the preferred candidate in that city of mostly poor barrios. Yet Montealegre wasted no time in crying fraud. After claiming victory shortly after midnight on the day of the vote, he led a demonstration against the alleged fraud the very next day, when only 30 percent of the votes had been counted.[25] Rosario Murillo anticipated that he would do this, and had earlier accused him of releasing rigged poll results prior to the election to prepare his case for fraud in advance.[26] The high level of distrust and animosity that permeates Nicaragua's political culture is such that even a clean electoral victory would likely have been tainted by accusations of fraud. One is hard pressed to fault Ortega for playing rough in the 2008 elections—especially when the field of FSLN candidates was strong to begin with.

Perhaps Ortega should have permitted more impartial international observers to monitor the elections, acquiesced to demands for a recount, and so forth. Actions like these would have gone a long way to quiet his critics. It is likely that he refused to take these actions because he frankly did want to tweak the results of any important races that did not fairly go to the FSLN, and then proceeded to do just that. The rationale he provided was that Nicaragua is a sovereign country, not dependent upon any foreign government, and it was time for Nicaraguans to trust their own democratic institutions. Coupled with this, in rhetoric directed mostly to the faithful, Ortega as usual railed against foreign intervention and imperialism, which he equated with welcoming foreign elections observers. If Ortega seemingly exaggerated this threat—surely election observers are not imperialist invaders—his defiant words contained kernels of truth. Dora María Téllez's hunger strike and the demonstrations that followed it were indirectly financed by the United States, although the links are circuitous. The United States did not directly finance Ortega's opponents in 2008, but it did provide funds that were intended to foster democracy to organizations that included Ortega's opponents. Ortega and the FSLN have never received these funds from the United States themselves, so it is not unreasonable for them to suspect that foreign involvement in Nicaragua, even under the innocuous guise of elections monitoring, is tantamount to welcoming the fox to tea in the henhouse.

And what was the objective of Téllez's hunger strike and the ensuing demonstrations? No one produced any set of demands that Ortega could negotiate, much less meet. Instead, they protested his "dictatorship." Short of falling on his own sword, which is a rather undemocratic thing to expect a constitutionally elected president to do, this did not leave anything that Ortega could do to placate the protesters. The one specific grievance that the protesters aired was their objection to the Supreme Electoral Council having prohibited the MRS and another minority party from participating in the 2008 elections on the basis of "technicalities." Téllez and others considered the exclusion of her party to be an assault on democracy itself. However, according to the head of the Supreme Electoral Council, Roberto Rivas, the fault was wholly with the MRS, who had revised its slate of party representatives throughout Nicaragua and was obligated to provide the names of the new representatives to the council. It did not do this, even after the council sent the MRS a letter reminding the party of this obligation. Reading a little between the lines, although drawing also from Rivas's comments, the basic problem was that the MRS was too small and disorganized a party to field the required representatives throughout the country. The party had in fact never garnered more than 6 percent of the vote in a national election, and almost all of its votes came from Managua. The merits of laws that exclude minority parties from participating in elections can be debated, but every democracy has to establish a minimum threshold that minority parties must reach to earn a position on the ballot. The MRS simply failed to meet what appears to be a reasonable threshold according to Nicaraguan law. To consider this an assault on democracy and to complain that the MRS was excluded based upon "technicalities" is all rather far-fetched. Even more far-fetched is a protest against Ortega's "dictatorship" over this issue. Whatever informal influences Ortega had over it, the Supreme Electoral Council is formally an independent branch of Nicaragua's government. Ortega did not have the constitutional authority to override its decision, and, as Rivas said, the law stipulates that the courts must be used to appeal its decisions. Téllez and other demonstrators were on one hand complaining that Ortega was a dictator, but on the other demanding that he behave like one by overriding the constitutional authority of an independent branch of government.[27]

Another observation that might be made about the hoopla that swirled around the exclusion of the MRS was that, if anything, it was probably in the FSLN's interest to have MRS candidates on the ballot. In reality, although the MRS is a rival Sandinista party, acrimony between the members of the two parties had reached such a pitch that few affiliated with the MRS would consider voting for the FSLN instead. After their exclusion, not a single MRS leader urged a vote for the FSLN candidates—although many encouraged voting against the FSLN. Had the MRS been on the ballot, it is likely that it would have divided the anti-FSLN vote, and thus advantaged the FSLN. If Ortega had engineered the exclusion of the MRS in the hope that doing so would augment the FSLN's vote, he probably miscalculated—or at least took a huge political risk. Since by 2008 Ortega was hardly politically naïve, or given to taking unnecessary political risks, it is frankly doubtful that the exclusion of the MRS had anything to do with his attempt to rig the outcome of the elections. The whole affair might have simply been a matter of the Supreme Electoral Council following the law, or at worst an instance of Ortega's tendency to act vindictively against former friends who turned against him.

Other accusations made against Ortega for election tampering do not hold up much better. One involved the charge that a smattering of pre-election raids made by authorities on a few NGOs was part of a package of intimidation intended to tweak the elections in favor of the FSLN. No one knows for sure, but it does appear that these raids were attempts to intimidate opponents. The state maintained that it had the right to investigate the records of these organizations, and it did, but the investigations had the whiff of selective harassment about them, and in fact no irregularities were discovered in the records. If Ortega's objective was to intimidate his opponents, he failed. Instead of quieting the opposition, the investigations became an issue around which they galvanized. Similarly, Ortega postponed elections on the Atlantic coast because, as he explained, the devastation from Hurricane Felix in 2007 had left the region with an inadequate infrastructure to hold November 2008 elections. His critics accused him of engineering even more fraud via this delay. If there was anything underhanded about this postponement, nobody was able to find it. The elections were held in February, as Ortega promised.

There is little question that Ortega's opponents were predisposed to see the worst in him—and were not always as civic-minded or democratically disposed as they pretended to be. Indeed, even when broader issues like Ortega's unwillingness to talk to the Nicaraguan press are considered, they raise questions about the civic- and democratic-mindedness of the media almost as much as they do of the president. For all the talk about an Ortega-Murillo political dynasty, most of the major independent media in Nicaragua are owned and operated by the Chamorro family, which is in effect a journalistic dynasty. More practically, journalists who write articles critical of a political figure in Nicaragua rarely bother to ask the politician or his or her supporters for a reaction prior to publishing their stories. Anyone who tried to practice journalism this way in the United States would have serious run-ins with responsible editors, who consider at least attempting to balance criticisms with reactions to them a core principle of ethical journalism. But such principles are rarely practiced in Nicaragua, where one-sided stories are routinely run as news accounts. Perhaps, if the press were more attentive to its civic responsibilities, Ortega would be more forthcoming. There is little indication, after all, that reporters critical of Ortega even try to ask him or his supporters for their side of whatever story they run. This culture of press irresponsibility seems to infect the English-language press in Nicaragua too. When Ortega announced that his administration would help to fund a revival of a then-defunct Nicaraguan baseball league, the *Nica Times* turned to his critics, who denounced it as a "bread and circuses" strategy of a dictator.[28] When popular initiatives like reviving a baseball league are spun into additional "evidence" of dictatorial tendencies in a news story, it is obvious that a free press is not necessarily a fair press.

The stridency of Ortega's opponents, coupled with their unwillingness to abide by the rules of democratic fair play themselves, finally reached a bizarre apex in the aftermath of the 2008 elections when a majority of the National Assembly boycotted the legislative sessions in protest over the elections. This prevented the National Assembly from achieving a quorum, which in turn prevented it from conducting business, and thus compelled Ortega to govern temporarily by decree. Pressing matters needed to be addressed, including a budget authorization for teachers' salaries and granting permission to a Russian naval fleet to enter Nicaraguan waters. Predictably, Ortega's critics cried foul and insisted that his willingness to govern by decree was even more evidence of his authoritarianism.[29] Ortega, however, was left with no other choice—not if teachers wanted to be paid. Then, as had become his practice, Ortega negotiated a behind-the-scenes deal with his opponents that persuaded the National Assembly to reconvene. Specifically, he called in a final favor from Arnoldo Alemán, who convinced his liberal legislators to take their seats—and even convinced them to give the FSLN control over the legislature's executive committee and thus de facto control over the National Assembly. That same day the Nicaraguan Supreme Court mysteriously cleared Alemán of all charges and made him a free man.[30] The exchange was obvious to all, and the deal was cited as even more evidence of Ortega's unsavory and manipulative political style. He did get the legislature back to work. Meanwhile, few seemed to notice that after having formed the ALN in part in opposition to the Alemán-Ortega pact, Montealegre negotiated his own pact with Alemán in his attempt to win the 2008 mayoral race. Everybody in Nicaragua played by the same rules. The difference was that Daniel Ortega was winning. Call this "authoritarian populism" if you must, but Ortega had simply mastered a process in which others remained amateurs.

Ideologies and Actions

WHILE ORTEGA WAS WINNING elections for the FSLN within a firestorm of controversy, he also won prizes for the Nicaraguan people in an atmosphere of equally strident criticisms. Interestingly, while Ortega is often regarded as being wildly ideological, closer inspection suggests that his critics may be more beholden to ideology themselves. The perception that Ortega is driven by ideology while his critics are not may be more a function of his leftist views than of their ideological underpinnings. Leftist opinions tend to appear ideological to a degree that conventional moderate ones do not, mainly because conventional opinions are assumed to be true while leftist opinions are assumed to be false. Yet it may be that the conventional moderate opinions draw from even deeper, albeit less well noticed wellsprings of ideology. This appears to be the case with respect to the Ortega administration's initiatives in three broad areas: democracy, economic development, and the rights of women. While his critics battle against ideological windmills in each of these areas, Ortega quietly achieves results.

Democracy is of course the reigning political creed in the world today, and Ortega's critics insist that he violates its tenets. Few champions of democracy, however, give as much evidence as Ortega does of having thought through what democracy really requires, or of being more practical in their attempts to implement it. Whether or not the United States can be characterized as a dictatorship, as Ortega alleged in his United Nations speech, it does not take much cynicism to suspect that many who believe that the United States is a democracy hold that belief as an article of ideological conviction more than on the basis of evidence. Surely it is difficult to maintain that a country in which contested races for even the House of Representatives (the people's chamber) can carry a price tag in the tens of millions of dollars and require over a hundred thousand votes for victory is a satisfactorily functioning democracy. It appears to be more of a plutocracy by any less ideological evaluation. It takes even less cynicism to question whether the United States ever really favored democracy in Nicaragua. The record of U.S. involvement in Nicaragua has been one of promoting the interests of elites in the United States, not the interests of a democratic Nicaragua or even those of the majority in the United States. The United States fought a war against Ortega that was not supported by the majority of its citizens or even approved by Congress. Beginning in 1984, every one of the five elections in which he was a candidate found the United States backing his opponent. The very fact that the Nicaraguan constitution allows foreign governments to finance political campaigns inside Nicaragua is an anathema to democracy, yet the United States lobbied to have this provision included. Then, when the avarice and hubris of some of the candidates who have been "democratically" elected in recent Nicaraguan elections is recalled, it is very difficult to defend the "democracy" that is practiced there. To continue to champion democracy in the face of so little evidence that it is practiced successfully by those who promote it would therefore seem to require wearing a large set of ideological blinders.

In contrast, Ortega has actively promoted quite democratic initiatives in his current administration. Immediately upon assuming the presidency in 2007, for example, he launched yet another literacy crusade. The campaign had fifty-four thousand volunteers and as of 2009 had already provided lessons in reading and writing to over four hundred thousand illiterate Nicaraguans. The goal was to eradicate illiteracy in the country immediately, while eventually bringing every citizen up to at least the educational attainment of a primary school graduate (which fewer than half currently are).[31] He eliminated fees for public school education. In terms of any full understanding of democracy, these are thoroughly democratic initiatives. Ortega is trying to create the very kind of "educated and enlightened citizenry" necessary for a viable democracy, rather than have the mere "oxen" that Somoza—and to judge from the fall off in literacy rates and educational achievement 1990–2007, Nicaragua's supposedly more democratic presidents—preferred. In a more measured way, since their control by the party does create reasons for reservations, Ortega's creation of the Councils of Citizen Power is an attempt to advance the practice of participatory democracy.[32] As controversial as they properly are, the Councils of Citizen Power are democratic institutions. They encourage average citizens to join together and act in concert for their mutual well-being. Though answering to the party, they do not require participants to be party members or even party sympathizers. Surely no one would argue that these are the ideal institutional forms that democracy should take. Nevertheless, they are one institutional form that democracy can take. Moreover, they should be juxtaposed against the alternatives. Nicaragua has never experienced a democracy in a form that Ortega's critics would welcome—and when the critics have celebrated democratic achievements in Nicaragua, they have usually been mistaken. Against this reality, Ortega's concrete efforts to promote democracy shine fairly brightly.

The assessment is similar with respect to Nicaragua's poor. Most of Ortega's critics (and all of his major electoral opponents) favor neoliberal policies to help the poor, and what is neoliberalism except an ideology?[33] Its proponents keep saying that it should work, because the ideology says it will, but sixteen years of neoliberal policies in Nicaragua did not work. In fact, by many measures Nicaraguans were worse off economically when Ortega took office in 2007 than they were when he left office in 1990. One such measure is simply poverty. A 2005 study showed that poverty rates rose during the neoliberal Bolaños administration, leaving over 48 percent of the population living on less than the official poverty level of $427 per year.[34] Another measure involves the number of Nicaraguans who leave the country. During the 1980s, an average of thirty thousand Nicaraguans left the country each year. The annual average during the 2002–2006 Bolaños administration was 140,000.[35] These were also comparatively flush years for the global economy, a period when, if neoliberal policies could have proved their effectiveness in Nicaragua, they would have. But instead they were a period of economic desperation. Meanwhile, the population simply became more dependent upon foreign aid. When protests over the delivery of foreign aid occurred on the Caribbean coast during the summer of 2008, aid workers explained that for many of the recipients, living on foreign aid was the only economic life they have ever known, so they naturally protest when the aid is tardy or not to their liking.[36] Surely sixteen years of neoliberal policies failed in Nicaragua.

By contrast, as soon as he took office, Ortega immediately provided subsidies to lower food staple prices for the poor, provided free access to medical care, and embarked upon programs to assist the poor with housing. Then he launched two eminently practical antipoverty programs. One, called Zero Usury, is a microcredit program that in its first year provided small business loans to approximately thirteen thousand mostly urban merchants. The other, Zero Hunger, distributes a package of farm goods (typically including chickens, a cow or pig, worms to keep the soil rich, seeds, etc.) to rural families with the intention of enabling the families to become self-sufficient at farming. Within its first year

the program reached twelve thousand rural poor. Critics p
problems with the programs' implementation: some rural fa
lies simply slaughter and eat the donated animals rather that us
them as a basis for ongoing self-sufficient farming, and the microcredit loans are not always repaid. Since nearly half of the programs' budgets are eaten up by administrative costs, many also
suspect that a good deal of corruption or at least inefficiencies
dog them. There are even complaints over the manner in which
political ideology infiltrates the programs. Although many participants are not supporters of the FSLN, the Councils of Citizen
Power do play a role in selecting participants, and these Councils
are controlled by the party. Similarly, while some of the funding
for the programs comes from elsewhere, the bulk of it is supplied by ALBA. One of the stated objectives of Zero Hunger is
even to encourage collectivized farming, a socialist-style goal that
gives some people pause. Even so, no one is forced into collective
farming, just as no participant on either program is compelled to
support the FSLN. Meanwhile, the participants in both programs
receive tangible assistance designed not merely to help them at
the moment but also to help them build a future for themselves
that does not require ongoing assistance. Moreover, Ortega strives
to avoid allowing these programs to become politicized. He purposely chose an out-of-the-way rural village to announce Zero
Hunger, for example, in order to avoid wrangling over ideology
with critics, which would probably have followed his announcing
the program in a more cosmopolitan setting. His goal with these
programs is to help the poor, not to win ideological debates, and
the speed with which the programs were enacted coupled with
their ambitious scope suggests that he is genuinely committed to
this goal.[37]

One of the domestic crises that Ortega was called upon to
solve early in his second administration helps to underscore his
pragmatic rather than ideological approach to the problems of
poverty. It involved protests by scavengers in Managua's largest
trash dump, La Chureca. The scavengers were angry over a new

nitted only city garbage trucks access to the
considered unfair since their only livelihood
ng there (where many of them also live). Yes,
re reduced to battling over access to garbage,
d lived that way—in the garbage dump—
_tega finally settled the dispute by bringing
the various parties together and hammering out a compromise.
In the process he ordered the police, who by law should have
evicted the scavengers, not to interfere until a compromise could
be negotiated. Some human rights groups chided him for issuing
an "illegal order" to the police not to interfere. Ortega shook his
head and marveled, "This is the only country in the world where
human rights groups request police intervention to remove poor,
humble people."[38]

A third line of ideological criticism against Ortega comes from
some feminists. While they level fair criticisms—chiefly against
his avoiding trial over the accusation that he sexually molested his
stepdaughter and his support for Nicaragua's ban on therapeutic
abortions—their voices tend to drift toward a global feminist ideological agenda and away from the concerns of real Nicaraguan
women. Indeed, the global dimensions of the feminists' criticisms
are grand. Ortega was publicly asked not to visit Paraguay, for
instance, since that country's minister-elect for women's affairs,
Gloria Rubin, considered him a "rapist," while feminist protests
have been organized in connection with his arrival in countries
that he has visited.[39] The chief problem Nicaraguan women face
is poverty, intensified by their even more limited opportunities to
escape it than men have. There are no accurate numbers, but many
are sold into prostitution by an impoverished mother (about half
of Nicaragua's households do not have an adult male present) and
others sell themselves to the sex industry as a consequence of poverty. Then, for every victim of the ban on therapeutic abortions,
there are at least a hundred who die of poverty—whether from
malnutrition, a disease that medical attention could have cured,
or other afflictions. Indeed, the ban on therapeutic abortion is a

problem only for poor women, since those with the wherewithal can have the abortion performed in another country. Feminism driven less by ideology and more by the needs of real women might have somewhat different priorities.

Ortega has demonstrated just such different priorities. In fact, both Zero Usury and Zero Hunger are programs for which only women are eligible. Every dollar that has been distributed has gone to women (twenty-five thousand of them in the first year), and in the case of Zero Hunger a woman's eligibility depended upon her having at least one child. Zero Hunger establishes female-headed family farms. Meanwhile, since the literacy rates and educational achievements of women are lower than they are for men in Nicaragua, the literacy campaign disproportionately helps women. While some feminists rail against Daniel Ortega, his key anti-poverty programs—the domestic policy pillars of his administration—have been designed with the needs of women uppermost in mind.

Ortega quietly enacts surprisingly pragmatic policies that undercut much of this ideological criticism. Indeed, this leftist has consistently submitted balanced budgets to the National Assembly, budgets that meet the approval of the International Monetary Fund and other international auditors. Inflation remains in check, Nicaragua weathered the 2008–2009 global recession better than many countries, and most indicators point to growth in Nicaragua's economy coupled with an increasing standard of living. At the same time, partly with the assistance of Chávez, Ortega is improving the highway on the Pacific coast that is used primarily by tourists. He insists that Nicaraguan tourism be distinctly Nicaraguan, ideally Nicaraguan-owned and -operated. He does not want to develop this industry the way Costa Rica has, namely as a foreign-owned and -operated industry catering to foreigners where the local population must content itself with being bellhops, bartenders, cab drivers, and maids. He actively promotes a vibrant tourism industry and has so far succeeded at this. He is even welcoming gringos.[40] In fact, his right-hand man—the ɔ drafts his budgets, for example—is Paul O'Quist, a Sandinista supporter from the United States. In Wash-Ɔ., of all places, he is reported to have forged strong personal relationships and to have developed the reputation of being a "man of his word."[41] Beneath the shrill ideological rhetoric, Ortega is a surprisingly pragmatic and effective president.

The Challenge to Daniel Ortega's Nicaragua

DANIEL ORTEGA'S GRIP ON power in Nicaragua is now so tight that little short of a premature death or coup d'état could foreseeably loosen it. Death is a distinct possibility. No one knows whether rumors of his ill health should be believed or not, and he points to his mother's longevity as evidence that they should not be, but his father died at sixty-nine or seventy and his sister passed away in her forties. If Ortega runs for reelection in 2011, as he hopes to, the election will coincide with his sixty-sixth birthday. The banner at the 2008 MRS rally calling for his assassination suggests that this is also a possibility. A coup d'état, however, is unlikely. As it has matured, the Nicaraguan military has emerged as an oasis of professionalism, independent of partisanship. This is not to say that there are not forces that want to depose Daniel Ortega—there are rumors of the usual guerrilla groups in the jungles plotting an overthrow of his regime—but his influence over the institutional apparatus of Nicaragua makes it unlikely that a successful revolt could be launched from within. Prior to the 2008 municipal elections, he already had influence over the courts and Supreme Electoral Council via his pact with Alemán, as well as of course the presidency. The 2008 elections increased his influence over local officials throughout the country, while negotiations with Alemán in the aftermath of those elections gave him effective control over the National Assembly. There are not many—or really any—gaps in his power.

It will be interesting to watch how he goes about maintaining power. In October 2009 he succeeded in persuading a panel of

Sandinista justices on the Supreme Court to remove the restriction on his right to seek reelection to the presidency in 2011, but he still has to win that election. While he is not above manipulating elections, there is a limit to how much he could interfere in his reelection and still claim legitimacy. No one knows how rough he is willing to play, but if there were evidence that he had anything to do with Lewites's death in 2006, for instance, that would probably be too much for Nicaraguans or the international community to tolerate. A few months after being elected Managua's mayor in the hotly contested 2008 election, Argüello was found dead by a gunshot wound to the chest. The death was ruled a suicide, and it probably was, but it stimulated rumors that Ortega had ordered him assassinated. Since a rationale for Ortega eliminating the FSLN candidate he wanted remains elusive, the rumors probably only highlight the atmosphere of suspicion that surrounds his governance rather than pointing to a believable criminal act. Even so, that atmosphere of suspicion is a liability for Ortega, and campaigning for reelection within it limits the shenanigans that he might otherwise use to win. Moreover, since either a coordinated liberal opposition rallying behind a popular candidate or a strong MRS candidate dividing the Sandinista vote could deprive Ortega of reelection, victory in 2011 is not a foregone conclusion. At the moment, his principal reelection strategy is the old-fashioned democratic one of trying to merit the voters' support by means of practical accomplishments. Early signs suggest that this strategy may be effective. For the first time since his "honeymoon," summer 2009 polls showed him with majority support in the rural regions. Zero Poverty is a very popular program there, as are the elimination of fees for public school attendances and medical care.[42] Ortega reasons, probably correctly, that if he can achieve results for the people, they will reward him with their votes.

And it is not clear that this would be so awful for Nicaragua. Almost everyone would prefer to see a popular but more principled political figure emerge and deprive Ortega of his dynastic ambitions. Although political opinions obviously vary, a candidate from the center-left and perhaps from the MRS—someone like Herty Lewites—would seem ideal. Yet history suggests that this may be a pipe dream. Rivals to Ortega from the center-left have thus far shown themselves to be long on principle but short on practicality. They simply cannot win elections, or seemingly even organize a party that can legally compete in them. Ortega's serious rivals thus come from the right. With the primary exception of the ineffectual Bolaños, few of these have displayed ethical principles any loftier than Ortega's, and some have behaved more scandalously. Even Eduardo Montealgre is tainted. Although his indictment on charges of financial corruption is scarcely worth mentioning, since unless proven that indictment may be a baseless attempt by the Ortega forces to weaken him politically, he did end up negotiating a pact with Alemán in connection with his 2008 mayoral campaign after having formed the ALN party in opposition to Alemán and his pact-making.[43] There is simply little reason to trust the liberals to adhere to a more principled form of politics than Ortega's FSLN. There is even less of a reason to trust them with the reins of government. Again, sixteen years of liberal rule left Nicaraguans poorer, sicker, and less well educated than they were when Ortega left the presidency in 1990. Since early indicators point to improvements in each of these areas under the Ortega administration, it is difficult to conclude that Nicaragua would be better off replacing him with a liberal opponent.

Neither is there good reason to wish success for a candidate who would pull Nicaragua back into the orbit of the United States and its allies. To be sure, Nicaragua's long-term interests may not be well served by becoming too entangled in the webs spun by Chávez and other "authoritarians of the left," and excessively friendly relations with countries like Iran give pause. So does referring to Western powers that have provided Nicaragua with aid over the years as "flies that land on filth" and comparing them to Judas Iscariot. Even so, it probably is in Nicaragua's interest to reduce its dependency upon the West, especially the United

States. The problem is not merely that the United States cannot be trusted. As Ortega correctly points out, the United States has time and again invaded Nicaragua, and between invasions has openly regarded the sovereign Central American country as its own "backyard." Thus, even if the United States is helpful at the moment, which in recent years it generally has been, it is not a country into which it would be prudent for Nicaragua to place much trust. The other problem is the aid that the United States provides with one hand is taken away by the other. Since 1990, the United States has given $1.4 billion to Nicaragua in foreign aid. However, owing to a provision inserted into the Foreign Assistance Act in 1994 by Senator Jesse Helms and Representative Henry Gonzalez, the United States must cancel aid to any country that confiscates the property of U.S. citizens, even if the property owners were not U.S. citizens at the time the property was confiscated. The result of this retroactive provision has been that the Nicaraguan government has been forced to pay $1.2 billion to former National Guardsmen and business people who divested from Nicaragua and became U.S. citizens. After doing the arithmetic, real U.S. aid to Nicaragua has amounted to about $180 million over seventeen years—about two dollars per person per year—and more than this was spent on influencing elections.[44] Add that the aid fuels corruption among elites and dependency among the people and it is surely not worth it. No one knows exactly how Nicaragua can break the stranglehold of its dependence upon foreign aid, but stirring up the pot of global alliances would seem to be a good start. It is a multipolar world, and it is probably wise for Nicaragua to reposition itself in that world.

Nicaragua confronts a deeper problem than that posed by an Ortega dynasty—enfeebled traditions of civic responsibility coupled with a quixotic penchant for political hyperbole. If political bosses like Ortega can be faulted for strong-arming institutions like the courts and the legislature, even for stealing elections, this is only possible because judges, lawmakers, poll workers, and others permit themselves to be used in this manner, presumably for whatever small increments of power or affluence they receive in compensation. Corruption, whether political or financial, is rarely the responsibility of a few. Its success depends upon the willing participation of others. Indeed, Transparency International's annual ranking of 180 countries on the extent to which they are perceived by business leaders and others to be corrupt put Nicaragua at 123 in 2006, the year before Ortega assumed the presidency. (For comparison purposes, Mexico ranked 72, Costa Rica 46, and the United States 20.)[45] To single Ortega out for special criticism overlooks a far more systemic problem. Then, to participate in systems of corruption only to turn around and object to "dictators" who acquire power in them suggests a civic disconnect of the first order. It is not the leaders or the followers alone who are responsible for the rise of caudillos like Ortega, but rather both together. The challenge confronting Nicaragua is not merely ridding itself of the caudillos but of transforming a culture that has only known power imposed by above with one in which power is responsibly exercised throughout the society.

Since the revolution, and to some extent before it, Nicaragua has made great strides in creating a democratic political culture where none had existed before. The beginnings were probably in the popular church, where ordinary Nicaraguans came together to discuss their common concerns in light of their shared religious values. Further steps were taken in the insurrection itself, when tens of thousands of *muchachos* took violent control of their own destiny, then exercised surprising restraint after their victory. The Sandinista Defense Committees as well as the literacy crusade furthered these experiences of self-rule, as ordinary citizens left their private homes to work together for the common good. Later, Nicaraguans formed and joined so many civic associations that it sometimes it seems like there are more acronym organizations in Nicaragua than there are people. Indeed, an estimated four thousand NGOs alone operate there—about one for every seven hundred citizens age sixteen or older—while the number of other clubs, parties, unions, and interest groups is surely larger. Given where they started, it can fairly be concluded that Nicaraguans have come a long way in "learning democracy."[46]

These experiences, however, have obviously not been enough for Nicaraguans to develop the sturdy civic culture they require, and trumpeting them too enthusiastically overlooks a more important underlying problem. Though plentiful, Nicaragua's civic associations tend to operate in the same kind of ephemeral elite realm that its politics do. They are invariably established and operated by elites, and always financed by them (often the financing does not even originate in Nicaragua). While average Nicaraguans may be nominal members of one or more of these associations, it is difficult to imagine many participating in them in a manner that inculcates many habits of civic responsibility. The associations are not really grassroots, but external impositions on the grassroots. At the grassroots, life for most Nicaraguans is dominated by the near-constant struggle for survival, and its civic horizons rarely extend beyond the networks of kinship and neighborhood in which the lives of the poor are always embedded. Basically, overlooked in the hoopla about "civil society" (of which there is a lot in Nicaragua) is that Nicaraguans as a whole are too poor, too uneducated, and too desperate to benefit from participation in civic associations to the degree that the champions of these associations might wish. Indeed, while full equality is surely not a prerequisite for cultivating the habits of civic responsibility that accrue from membership in civic associations, a semblance of equality is. An illiterate or semiliterate population worried about obtaining enough to eat is better suited to participation in mob actions than in a deliberative civic association that might inculcate a sense of democratic responsibility—and there are a lot of moblike actions in Nicaragua.

The more fundamental challenge to Nicaragua is therefore the one that Daniel Ortega is most adamant about addressing: to alleviate the wrenching poverty that saps the citizenry of the opportunity to focus on issues beyond survival, and to develop a strong middle class in its place. To be sure, this is not a goal to be pursued in isolation from other ones. Fortifying civic associations, improving education, raising literacy levels, empowering women, and so on are goals that are wisely pursued in tandem with economic development. Yet to pretend that accomplishment in these areas can substitute for eliminating poverty and creating a middle class is to ignore the proverbial elephant in the room. Not since before Aristotle has any persuasive political thinker imagined that a good society is possible in one as grossly poor and unequal as Nicaragua. Alleviating poverty is simply Nicaragua's most urgent challenge.

While the approaches that Nicaragua could take to combating poverty and building a middle class are debatable, the evidence suggests that three broad approaches are mostly dead ends. One of these approaches is the socialized chaos of the 1980s. It is only fair to concede that the Sandinistas' initiatives during this period were hamstrung by the debt they inherited from the Somoza dictatorship coupled with the daunting tasks of rebuilding a tattered economy while constructing a functioning government. It is also only fair to emphasize that their efforts met with the colossal force of the United States, which aimed at forcing the new government's economy to fail. Nevertheless, next to no one credits the first Sandinista government with more than bumbling good intentions. Whatever path Nicaragua follows, it must resist heavy-handed state attempts to micromanage the economy. However, the opposite approach, that of neoliberalism, proved to be even more disastrous for Nicaragua. The best defense for its failures argues that it might have worked better if the country's elites had not stolen so much of the money that was supposed to spark economic development. This is an awfully big "if." Worse, once it is appreciated that even successful neoliberal policies might only lead to a replication of the "banana republic" type of economy in which the bulk of the population labors for exporting elites, it is not clear that this approach would be effective in building a middle class anyway. The third approach that must be rejected is undue reliance upon foreign aid. No doubt some foreign aid is helpful, and not all donors give it with one hand to take it away with the other the way the United States has done. Nevertheless, for the thirty years following the revolution, the billions of foreign aid dollars that poured into Nicaragua had no aggregate beneficial effect on the country's economy. In fact, the overall effect heightened the corruption of the elites while instilling an entitlement mentality into others. The spigot of foreign aid can probably not be turned off immediately without disastrous consequences, but the Nicaraguans who drink the sweet water do so at their long-term peril.

Since these three approaches to tackling Nicaragua's economic challenges must be rejected, the solution that begins to take shape is the unexciting but obvious one of stimulating private business development within an overall framework of state management. This is, after all, how almost every other modern state has managed to combat poverty and grow a middle class. Granted, Ortega and others on the Latin American left are correct to insist that the wealth of the West was generated in large part by its exploitation of other countries—including Nicaragua. However, right next door to Nicaragua stands the glaring example of Costa Rica. It too has a "banana republic" heritage—if fact, the offshoots of the United Fruit Company continue to operate there—but by the time of Ortega's reelection it enjoyed a GDP five times larger than Nicaragua's and comfortable status as a middle-income country.[47] It is simply not true that a legacy of dependency destines a country to a future of poverty. Neither is it true that natural resources, like Venezuela's oil reserves, are necessary for economic advancement. Costa Rica has no more natural resources than Nicaragua has, and maybe even fewer given Nicaragua's arguably superior agricultural potential. States like Costa Rica do not succeed without carefully balancing state direction of the economy with a more or less autonomous private sector. This is not what Ortega sometimes calls the "savage capitalism" of the United States, which probably would be unworkable in a small state like Nicaragua were it even desirable, but rather a tempered capitalism akin to the small state that the Sandinistas once took as one of their models, Sweden. Allowing for plenty of national differences, it is also the form of capitalism practiced by other successful emerging economies, like the Asian Tigers (which include Singapore and Taiwan). It appears to be the middle path that Nicaragua must follow to achieve its most urgent goals of economic development.

One gets the sense that Ortega is well aware of all this, and is in fact trying to steer Nicaragua down this path. Although his rhetoric sometimes suggests otherwise, his actions reveal a fairly encouraging attitude toward private business development, at least within an overall framework of what he believes is in the long-term interest of Nicaragua. Economists like Francisco J. Mayorgia, who was chief economist in the Chamorro administration, openly discourage fellow free-market advocates from worrying about Ortega's economic policies, since in Mayorgia's opinion Ortega's policies are smart for free markets.[48] Ortega's willingness to promote the development of a tourism sector coupled with his efforts to ensure that Nicaraguans rather than foreigners own and manage the industry is a quintessential example of his pragmatic attempt to balance state involvement with private industry. Surely tourism is a fast way to generate cash, but just as surely it must be carefully managed so as not to leave the host country with only a fraction of the profits. Since Ortega's economic initiatives appear to be on the right track—and his administration followed three previous decidedly pro-business administrations—the question is why Nicaragua has not been any more successful in stimulating private business development than it has been.

More specifically, the question is why Nicaragua has attracted so little foreign investment. There is no mystery why there is limited business development in Nicaragua. As most Nicaraguans will quickly point out, there is limited business development in Nicaragua because there is limited capital investment there. Without capital, there can be no capitalism—and Nicaragua still lacks capital. A comparison between Nicaragua and Costa Rica

illustrates this problem. Costa Rica attracts more thaɪ
the foreign investment dollars that Nicaragua does, and
try that is six times wealthier it also has more investmeɪ
available within the country.[49] At the narrowest level, Nicä
problems are rooted in the simple lack of investment capitɪ .

Nicaragua's inability to attract investment capital is not easily explained, either. Since approximately 20 percent of the Costa
Rican work force is Nicaraguan and many Nicaraguans in Costa
Rica start and run businesses, it is not a deficiency in any "work
ethic" or "entrepreneurial spirit" that deprives Nicaraguans of
investment capital at home and sends it to Costa Rica instead.
Neither are the frequently mentioned excuses like the political
stability and corruption or inadequate infrastructure of Nicaragua convincing explanations for the flow of foreign investments
into Costa Rica but not into Nicaragua. Costa Rica was attract-
ing investments within a generation of its civil war in 1948, and
recent presidents Rafael Angel Calderón (1990–1994) and Miguel
Angel Rodríguez (1998–2002) both became embroiled in corruption scandals that rival the scope of Arnoldo Alemán's in Nicaragua. Whereas Costa Rica is perceived to be less corrupt and
more stable than Nicaragua, the differences are in degree and of
fairly recent vintage. An explanation for the discrepancy in foreign investments in terms of infrastructure is also far-fetched.
Costa Rica did not offer business an elaborate and reliable infrastructure initially either; rather, that infrastructure was steadily
improved with business growth. Then, too, since investors seek
profits and there are more to be made in an economy with greater
potential for growth, savvy investors would be predicted to prefer
Nicaragua to Costa Rica, not the reverse.

The explanation for Nicaragua's insufficient investment capital—which in turn is the problem that underlies its limited capacity for economic growth, thus the problem of poverty, and thus
the problem of enfeebled civic traditions—unfortunately appears
to lie in its relationship with the United States. Nicaragua's main
problem is not its failure to attract foreign investments, but its not

having its own investor class. Without a local investor class, there is no seed money to jump-start business development, which foreign investors can then build upon, and neither are there local partners who could guide foreign investors through Nicaragua's business sector. There is next to no local business sector in Nicaragua, minus the market women and small farmers. U.S. census data show why not. During the 1980s, 44,100 Nicaraguans became legal residents of the United States, fully 5,590 of them qualifying as refugees. During the 1990s, the number who became U.S. residents rose to 60,300, while the number whose residency was granted on the basis of their refugee status increased to 22,234 (a number equivalent to the number of Iranians receiving refugee status during the same period, despite Iran being a much more populous country and seemingly having a much more authoritarian ruler). Given the delays in processing residency applications, most of those who were granted legal residency during the 1990s can be assumed to have arrived in the United States and applied for it earlier. While these numbers may not appear extreme, they are high relative to the population of Nicaragua. One in about every 150 Nicaraguans ended up being granted residency as a refugee in the United States during the two decades following the revolution, while one in every fifty Nicaraguans acquired residency in the United States in one or another category. Census data also reveal that the Nicaraguan immigrants to the United States were better educated and more affluent than those who remained in Nicaragua. For comparison purposes, imagine that the roughly similar-size population of metropolitan Atlanta, Georgia, lost 104,400 of its most affluent and best educated residents over the same two decades—and add that those remaining had an average per capita income of around $1,000 a year, elementary school educations, and limited access to outside investments. It is obvious that U.S. immigration policy helped to deplete Nicaragua of the human and financial capital that it needed to develop its private sector. Indeed, out of all of Latin America, only Cuba contributed more "refugees" to the United States during this period, and presumably for the same reason: an ideological fear of "communism." Illogically, though, this immigration policy deprived Nicaragua of the very capitalist class that could have prevented Nicaragua from taking a leftward turn. It is probably beside the point, in any event, to ask why foreigners do not invest in Nicaragua when Nicaraguans do not invest there either.[50]

There is therefore something deeply troubling about the rhetoric of civil society and civic responsibility in reference to Nicaragua when it is appreciated that these lectures are delivered to the mostly poor people who remain there, while many of those who had the resources to contribute responsibly to their society simply left it. They may not perhaps be blamed, especially when the United States welcomed them with open arms, and who is to cast judgment on any particular person's desire to emigrate? However, Anastasio Somoza, who confessed that he knew the United States better than the country he ruled and whose family settled in Miami long before he was deposed, set a bad precedent by describing Nicaragua as "my farm" and admitting that he wanted Nicaraguans to be his "oxen."[51] Insofar as they follow his example, the able and affluent Nicaraguans who have abandoned their homeland have ensured that their country remains a farm with oxen—though oxen who sometimes become outraged enough to stampede.

Sometimes it is said that people do not get the leaders they want but rather the leaders they deserve. This is obviously not true for the people in Nicaragua, who must endure authoritarian rulers like Daniel Ortega and others. They deserve better. However, it may well be true for Nicaraguans as a whole, including those in the United States. When they abandoned their country and left primarily the poor behind, they might as well have placed a welcome mat out for an "authoritarian of the left." The good news is that they can always come home, where even Daniel Ortega will welcome them. For all his faults, Ortega is foremost a patriot committed to improving the lives of the poor, and in this endeavor he is surprisingly supportive of private businesses.

Indeed, while routinely accused of being a former Marxist guerilla who lacks understanding of or sympathy for business, the truth is Ortega grew up the son of a struggling entrepreneur, working in his family's store. In order for him to succeed, though—that is, to succeed, not to conquer—he needs the help of an absent investor class. If he can get that help, both can succeed together. When they do, they will achieve a serendipitous victory: to turn Nicaragua into a country that no longer needs leaders like Daniel Ortega. When this happens, the liberation that the revolution promised will finally be realized.

NOTES

Acknowledgments

1. I mention only the first surname of Latinos in what I hope is an unnecessary attempt to protect their privacy. El Toro has never told me his, although his first name is Marco.

Chapter 1: The Making of a Revolutionary

1. Unless otherwise noted, these and other facts about Nicaragua's history are drawn from Thomas W. Walker, ed. *Nicaragua: Living in the Shadow of the Eagle*, 4th ed. (Cambridge, MA: Westview, 2003).
2. Quoted in Salman Rushdie, *The Jaguar Smile: A Nicaraguan Journey* (New York: Henry Holt, 1987), p. 23.
3. Peter Davis, *Where Is Nicaragua?* (New York: Simon and Schuster, 1987), pp. 242–262.
4. Claudia Dreifus, "Playboy Interview: Daniel Ortega," *Playboy* (November 1987).
5. See, e.g., Hector Perez-Brignoli, trans. Ricardo B. Sawrey A. and Susana Stettri de Sawrey, *A Brief History of Central America* (Berkeley: University of California Press, 1989).
6. See, e.g., Stephen Kinzer, *Overthrow: America's Century of Regime Change from Hawaii to Iraq* (New York: Henry Holt, 2006), pp. 58–59.
7. José Luis Rocha, "The Chronicle of Coffee: History, Responsibility, and Questions," *Envío* (August 2001).

8. Tomás Borge, trans. Russell Bartley, Darwin Flakoll, and Sylvia Yoneda, *The Patient Impatience: From Boyhood to Guerilla: A Personal Narrative of Nicaragua's Liberation* (Willimantic, CT: Curbstone Press, 1992), p. 62.

9. Quoted in Donald C. Hodges, *Intellectual Foundations of the Nicaraguan Revolution* (Austin: University of Texas Press, 1986), pp. 8–9.

10. Robert A. Pastor, *Not Condemned to Repetition: The United States and Nicaragua*, 2nd ed. (Boulder, CO: Westview Press, 2002), pp. 3–4.

11. Walker, *Nicaragua*, p. 11.

12. Walter LaFeber, *Inevitable Revolutions: The United States in Central America*, 2nd ed. (New York: Norton, 1993), pp. 225–226.

13. Cited in Matilde Zimmermann, *Sandinista: Carlos Fonseca and the Nicaraguan Revolution* (Durham, NC: Duke University Press, 2000), p. 149.

14. This is of course the master explanatory concept in Paul Kennedy's *The Rise and Fall of the Great Powers: Economic Change and Military Conflict from 1500 to 2000* (New York: Random House, 1987).

15. Anna Husarska, "One Step Forward: Nicaragua's Revolution in Evolution," *The New Leader* 71 (8 February 1988).

16. "Ortega Lauds Obama's Campaign as 'Revolutionary,'" *Nica Times* (22 February 2008).

17. General Humberto Ortega Saavedra, *La Epopeya de la insurrección* (Managua: Lea Grupo, 2004), p. 35. The specific barrio in which the Ortega family lived is today called San Antonio, and it frankly appears that it was named San Antonio then too. The word Humberto Ortega uses, though, is "colonia," not barrio. The larger neighborhood was evidently called Colonia Somoza and the smaller one San Antonio.

18. In an interview, "Lydia Saavedra de Ortega," pp. 243–251 in Denis Lynn Daly Heyck, ed., *Life Stories of the Nicaraguan Revolution* (New York: Routledge, 1990), Lydia Saavedra said that her son Daniel was born in 1946 rather than 1945. There are other sources (perhaps drawing on this interview) that express uncertainty about the year. However, it is almost certain that 1946 was just a misprint in the published interview. Among other reasons to suspect this is that in *La Epopeya de la insurrección*, p. 41, Humberto Ortega lists his birth date as January 10, 1947. He could not have been born only two months after his brother.

19. Ortega, *La Epopeya de la insurrección*, p. 41.

20. See, e.g., Roger N. Lancaster, *Life Is Hard: Machismo, Danger, and the Intimacy of Power in Nicaragua* (Berkeley: University of California Press, 1992).

21. This narrative of the Ortega family is largely drawn from Ortega's *La Epopeya de la insurrección*. However, Ortega conveniently neglects to

mention that his uncle held a prominent position in the Somoza government. It is generally known, and other sources mention it.

22. "Lydia Saavedra de Ortega."

23. Walker, *Nicaragua*, p. 116. Of course, it merits emphasis that the 20 percent were hardly elites, but rather closer to a middle class, which otherwise did not exist in Nicaragua.

24. In "Lydia Saavedra de Ortega," she indicates that the cause was malaria, although she simply calls it "the fever."

25. Ortega, *La Epopeya de la insurrección*, p. 41.

26. Quoted in Holly Sklar, *Washington's War on Nicaragua* (Boston: South End Press, 1988), p. 36.

27. James D. Cockcroft, *Daniel Ortega* (New York: Chelsea House, 1991).

28. Clifford Krauss, *Inside Central America: Its People, Politics, and History* (New York: Summit Books, 1991), p. 126, writes that the elder Ortega went bankrupt during the middle 1950s. He provides no citation indicating the source of this information, though, and includes it in a passage that, while generally accurate, may not have all the details exactly correct.

29. Rushdie, *The Jaguar Smile*, pp. 125–126.

30. Ortega, *La Epopeya de la insurrección*, p. 37.

31. Quoted in Ibid., p. 38 (author's translation).

32. Ibid., p 38.

33. Ibid., p. 154.

34. "Lydia Saavedra de Ortega."

35. Borge, *The Patient Impatience*, p. 89.

36. In Ibid., p. 91, Borge admits to having been vaguely informed.

37. Zimmermann, *Sandinista*, p. 50.

38. Ibid., p. 105.

39. Ibid., p. 77.

40. Quoted in Pilar Arias, *Nicaragua: Revolución, relatos de combatientes del frente sandinista* (Mexico: Siglo XXI, 1980), p. 15 (author's translation).

41. Borge, *The Patient Impatience*, p. 138.

42. Zimmermann, *Sandinista*, provides a full account of Fonseca's communism as well as other aspects of his life and thought.

43. Borge, *The Patient Impatience*, p. 81. Though a few years older than Fonseca, Borge was raised in Matagalpa too, and the two knew each other from childhood.

44. Zimmermann, *Sandinista*, p. 61.

45. In addition to Hodges, *Intellectual Foundations of the Nicaraguan Revolution*, see David Nolan, *The Ideology of the Sandinistas and the Nicaraguan*

Revolution (Coral Gables, FL: Institute of Interamerican Studies, University of Miami, 1984), for an account of Sandinista ideology.

46. The "Statutes" of the FSLN, which include these and other rules, are reprinted in Borge, *The Patient Impatience*, pp. 247–256. They appear to have been drawn up collaboratively during the Pancasán campaign of 1967 and "published" later in Cuba.

47. Zimmermann, *Sandinista*, p. 35.

48. Ortega, *La Epopeya de la insurrección*, pp. 121, 144.

49. Arias, *Nicaragua: Revolución*.

50. Zimmermann, *Sandinista*, p. 71.

51. Ortega, *La Epopeya de la insurrección*, p. 120.

52. Ibid., p. 123.

53. "Lydia Saavedra de Ortega."

54. Luís Hernández Bustamante, "Jacinto Suárez Espinoza: La derecha quiere un gabinete," *7 Dias* (September 3–9, 2007).

55. "Prisión a rebeldes Rivenses," *La Prensa* (January 8, 1964).

56. "Lydia Saavedra de Ortega."

57. Ibid.

58. Borge, *The Patient Impatience*.

59. "Seguridad Pone Sitio a Instituto," *La Prensa* (February 13, 1966).

60. Pastor, *Not Condemned to Repetition*, p. xvii.

Chapter 2: A Few More Murderers Among Murderers

1. In Dreifus, "Playboy Interview: Daniel Ortega," Ortega describes the assassination, although he curiously misremembers the date and says it took place in August (or perhaps the interviewer or interpreter got the date wrong). Borge, *The Patient Impatience*, p. 246, supplies the date. Ortega's remarks about not knowing whether he killed in guerrilla combat were made to David Frost in a 2009 interview. http://english.aljazeera.net/programmes/frostovertheworld/2009/03/2009378501399631.html (accessed June 10, 2009).

2. Dreifus, "Playboy Interview: Daniel Ortega."

3. Ortega describes the experience in Ibid.

4. "600 Mil en 10 Asaltos Del Frente Sandinista," *La Prensa* (September 21, 1968).

5. Zimmermann, *Sandinista*, p. 120.

6. Borge, *The Patient Impatience*, p. 227.

7. Ibid., p. 185.

8. Ortega, *La Epopeya de la insurrección*, p. 169.

9. Ibid., p. 437.

10. Ibid., pp. 183–184.

11. Borge, *The Patient Impatience*, p. 237, 178.

12. Ibid., p. 244.

13. "Jacinto Suárez: Decisión es irreversible, Daniel será el candidato," *Radio La Primerísima* (November 1, 2005).

14. "600 Mil en 10 Asaltos Del Frente Sandinista," *La Prensa*.

15. Borge, *The Patient Impatience*, p. 228.

16. "En 20 Minutos Condenaron a Dos Del FSLN," *La Prensa* (March 16, 1969).

17. Dreifus, "Playboy Interview: Daniel Ortega."

18. Another one killed in the November 4 raid was the person with whom Ortega worked organizing students at the University of Central America the year before, Casimiro Sotelo. See Luis Hernández Bustamante, "Jacinto Suárez Espinoza: 'La derecha quiere gabinete con apellidotes,'" *7 Días* Edición 526 del 3 (September 9, 2007).

19. Zimmermann, *Sandinista*, p. 84.

20. Descriptions of the trial, including remarks made during it, are drawn from "En 20 Minutos Condenaron a Dos Del FSLN," *La Prensa*.

21. Descriptions of prison life are drawn from Dreifus, "Playboy Interview: Daniel Ortega," and "Jacinto Suárez, decisión es irreversible, Daniel será el candidato."

22. See, e.g., "Otra huelga de hambre de reos del FSLN," *La Prensa* (January 25, 1972).

23. Ortega, *La Epopeya de la insurrección*, pp. 199, 203.

24. Gioconda Belli, translated by Kristina Cordero and Gioconda Belli, *The Country Under My Skin: A Memoir of Love and War.* (New York: Knopf, 2002). p. 37, briefly describes Murillo at about this time.

25. Ortega, *La Epopeya de la insurrección*, p. 248.

26. Francisco de Asís Fernández, *Poesía Política de Nicaragua* (Managua: Ministerio de Cultura, 1986), pp. 227–232.

27. Quoted in Ed Vulliamy, "In the Lion's Den," *Observer of London* (September 2, 2001).

28. See, e.g., Jerry D. Rose, *Outbreaks: The Sociology of Collective Behavior* (New York: Free Press, 1982).

29. Quoted in Sklar, *Washington's War on Nicaragua*, p. 29.

30. Walter LaFeber, *Inevitable Revolutions*, pp. 147, 164.

31. Ibid., p. 163.

32. Ibid., p. 164.

33. Borge, *The Patient Impatience*, pp. 170–171.
34. Pastor, *Not Condemned to Repetition*, p. 37.
35. Quoted in LaFeber, *Inevitable Revolutions*, p. 161.
36. Quoted in Ibid., pp. 161–162.
37. Ibid., p. 150.
38. Ibid., p. 164.
39. Quoted in Ibid., p. 154.
40. Ibid., p. 153.
41. Ibid., p. 165.
42. Ibid., p. 165.
43. A main theme in Pastor, *Not Condemned to Repetition*, is how much of U.S. policy toward Nicaragua was directed by Washington's fears that it would become "another Cuba." Perhaps because he served in the State Department during the Carter administration, Pastor seems to sympathize with this comparison. Many experts on Nicaragua, however, believe that the equating of the Nicaraguan and Cuban revolutions was a tragic mistake made by U.S. policymakers. To this day, it does not appear that the State Department is an especially reliable source of unbiased information about Nicaragua. Its September 2008 "Background Note: Nicaragua," available at www.state.gov/r/pa/ei/bgn/1850.htm (accessed June 15, 2009), for instance, claims that the FSLN "established an authoritarian dictatorship soon after taking power" and that it "maintained links to international terrorists." It omits any mention of the 1984 elections, which the FSLN won handily, and conveniently refers to the Washington-orchestrated war against Nicaragua during the 1980s as "the Nicaraguan resistance." These interpretations of Nicaragua's recent history are within range of those extant, but they veer decidedly to the right of where most scholars of Nicaragua would place the truth. Given this continuing bias, it may be no wonder that the United States repeatedly and against evidence saw Nicaragua as "another Cuba."
44. Central Intelligence Agency, "The Political Prospects in Nicaragua over the Next Year or So," Special National Intelligence Estimate, Number 83.3-67, October 12, 1967, LBJ Library, Case Number 93-87, Document Number 126.
45. Zimmermann, *Sandinista*, pp. 91–92.
46. See Ibid., p. 105.
47. John A. Booth, *The End and the Beginning: The Nicaraguan Revolution*, 2nd ed. (Boulder, CO: Westview Press, 1985), p. 141. See also Omar Cabezas, *Fire from the Mountain: The Making of a Sandinista*, foreword by Carlos Fuentes, afterword by Walter LaFeber (New York: Plume, 1985).

48. Krauss, *Inside Central America*, p. 127.

49. LaFeber, *Inevitable Revolutions*, p. 227.

50. Krauss, *Inside Central America*, p. 127.

51. Quoted in Davis, *Where Is Nicaragua?* p. 244.

52. LaFeber, *Inevitable Revolutions*, p. 227.

53. Krauss, *Inside Central America*, p. 127.

54. Belli, *The Country Under My Skin*, p. 92.

55. Ibid., p. 99.

56. Ibid., p. 100.

57. Ibid.

Chapter 3: The Battle Within and Without

1. Dreifus, "Playboy Interview: Daniel Ortega."

2. Quoted in Vulliamy, "In the Lion's Den."

3. Rushdie, *The Jaguar Smile*, pp. 92–93.

4. "Leticia Herrera" (interview), pp. 87–105, in Heyck, ed., *Life Stories of the Nicaraguan Revolution.*

5. Dreifus, "Playboy Interview: Daniel Ortega."

6. Ortega, *La Epopeya de la insurrección*, p. 291.

7. Dreifus, "Playboy Interview: Daniel Ortega."

8. Ibid.

9. Quoted in John A. Booth, *The End and the Beginning*, p. 134.

10. Ortega, *La Epopeya de la insurrección*, p. 260.

11. Shirley Christian, *Nicaragua: Revolution in the Family* (New York: Random House, 1985), p. 34.

12. Ibid., p. 82.

13. In *La Epopeya de la insurrección*, p. 315, Humberto Ortega writes that after the death of Eduardo Contreras the Terceristas were directed by the Ortega brothers alone.

14. Belli, *The Country Under My Skin*. Omar Cabezas, *Fire from the Mountain*, also describes the recruitment process, though in León.

15. Christian, *Nicaragua*, pp. 319–322.

16. Belli, *The Country Under My Skin*, pp. 150, 169.

17. Humberto Ortega Saavedra, *50 años de lucha sandinista* (Habana: Ciencias Sociales, 1980).

18. Ortega, *La Epopeya de la insurrección*, p. 315.

19. Pastor, *Not Condemned to Repetition*, p. 50.

20. In *La Epopeya de la insurrección*, p. 317, Ortega describes the recruitment of Sergio Ramírez into the Group of Twelve as the result of his and

Daniel's personal efforts. In Arias, *Nicaragua*, p. 129, Ramírez verifies that this was true. He mentions Humberto and Daniel Ortega as the "principal" members of the Front with whom he spoke, but in fact mentions no other member.

21. Ortega, *La Epopeya de la insurrección*, p. 317; and Arias, *Nicaragua*, p. 129.

22. The Group of Twelve included Felipe Mántica, a businessman and physician; Joaquín Cuadra Chamorro, a lawyer; Emilio Baltodano, a coffee exporter; Ricardo Coronel Kautz; Miguel D'Escoto, a priest; Ernesto Castillo, a lawyer and bookseller; Sergio Ramírez Mercado, a writer; Fernando Cardenal, a priest; Carlos Tünnermann Bernheim, a teacher; Arturo Cruz Porras, an economist; Casimiro Sotelo, an architect living in the United States; and Carlos Gutiérrez, a dentist.

23. Walker, *Nicaragua*, p. 34, quotes a statement issued by the Group of Twelve in October 1977 that outlines their position.

24. Initially the group had a slightly different name and the acronym was COSIP, although by the late 1970s COSEP was used.

25. "Nicaragua—The Strategy of Victory" (interview with Humberto Ortega), pp. 53–84, in Bruce Marcus, ed., *Sandinistas Speak: Speeches, Writings, and Interviews with Leaders of Nicaragua's Revolution* (New York: Pathfinder Press, 1982), p. 69.

26. Ibid., p. 59.

27. Ibid., p. 58.

28. In *La Epopeya de la insurrección*, pp. 315–331, Ortega provides a thorough account and assessment of the plan.

29. Belli, *The Country Under My Skin*, pp. 168–169.

30. Pedro Miranda, translated by Stephen M. Gorman, "Interview with Daniel Ortega," *Latin American Perspectives* VI (Winter 1979), pp. 114–118.

31. Ortega, *La Epopeya de la insurrección*, p. 331; Pastor, *Not Condemned to Repetition*, p. 49.

32. Ortega, *La Epopeya de la insurrección*, p. 391.

33. Belli, *The Country Under My Skin*, pp. 220–224.

34. Ibid., p. 193.

35. Ortega, *La Epopeya de la insurrección*, p. 340.

36. "Leticia Herrera" (interview).

37. In Ibid., the editor's introduction describes Herrera as Ortega's "former wife."

38. Ibid.

39. Belli, *The Country Under My Skin*, p. 170.

40. "Leticia Herrera" (interview).

41. Belli, *The Country Under My Skin*, p. 170.
42. "Testimonio de Zoilamérica Narváez contra de su padre adoptivo Daniel Ortega Saavedra." www.sandino.org.zoila.htm (accessed September 12, 2008).
43. Belli, *The Country Under My Skin*, pp. 270, 272.
44. In personal communication with sources who ask to remain anonymous, I have been informed of several affairs that Ortega has had with other women. The sources appear to be reliable, although the evidence is hearsay.
45. Belli, *The Country Under My Skin*, p. 113.
46. Quoted in Roger Miranda and William Ratliff, *The Civil War in Nicaragua: Inside the Sandinistas* (New Brunswick, NJ: Transaction, 1993), pp. 53–54.
47. Ibid., p. 54.
48. Ibid., p. 55.
49. Ibid., p. 54.
50. Quoted in Stephen Kinzer, "Ortega's Last Straw in Nicaragua," *Los Angeles Times* (September 3, 2008).
51. "Case 12,220: Zoilamérica Narváez vs. the Nicaraguan State," *Envío* 248 (March 2002).
52. Karen Kampwirth, *Feminism and the Legacy of Revolution: Nicaragua, El Salvador, Chiapas* (Athens: Ohio University Press, 2004), pp. 118–120.
53. "Desaire a Ortega," *El Nuevo Diario* (August 14, 2008).
54. "Testimonio de Zoilamérica Narváez."
55. Ibid. (author's translation).
56. The working assumption of many family therapists in incest or incest-like situations is that mother and daughter have reversed roles. The daughter becomes something of a surrogate wife while the mother becomes the pampered child. Although there is no reason to impose a general textbook interpretation onto this specific situation, a remark made in passing by Belli in *The Country Under My Skin*, p. 170, is suggestive. She writes that she "watched, amazed, at the maternal devotion with which Zoilamérica looked after her little brother, Tino, who was only a few months old." Since there is no reason for Belli to have included this memory in her memoir—it furthers no point she ultimately makes—it has to be taken as a strong but random memory of the Murillo family a few months before Ortega was included in it. As such, it suggests that a kind of mother/daughter role reversal was already underway before Ortega became a participant in the family drama.

57. Pastor, *Not Condemned to Repetition*, p. 49, suggests that in fact Somoza had not ordered the assassination. However, most Nicaraguans believed that he had.

58. Christian, *Nicaragua*, pp. 45–48.

59. Walker, *Nicaragua*, pp. 35–36.

60. Ortega, *La Epopeya de la insurrección*, p. 338.

61. See Michael Dodson and Laura Nuzzy O'Shaughnessy, *Nicaragua's Other Revolution: Religious Faith and the Political Struggle* (Chapel Hill: University of North Carolina Press, 1990), for a discussion of the role of the churches.

62. Pastor, *Not Condemned to Repetition*, pp. 68, 77, writes that the number of Guardsmen grew from 6,000 to 15,000 during 1978.

63. Ibid., p. 80.

64. The letter is published in Christian, *Nicaragua*, p. 57.

65. Ibid., p. 59.

66. Larry Rohter, "Nicaraguan Archrivals Are Just Hometown Boys," *New York Times* (February 21, 1985).

67. "Nicaragua—The Strategy of Victory" (interview with Humberto Ortega).

68. Ortega, *La Epopeya de la insurrección*, p. 395.

69. Pastor, *Not Condemned to Repetition*, p. 311, n. 2, discusses Pastora's claim to have been an original founder of the FSLN and the evidence for it.

70. Christian, *Nicaragua*, p. 104.

71. Ibid., p. 105.

72. Swedish journalist Peter Torbiornsson claims that a bomb intended to kill Pastora in 1984 was planted on orders from Tomás Borge, who as a member of the National Directorate would not likely have made that decision without the Directorate's consent. See Tim Rogers, "Bombing Survivor Seeks Truth, Closure," *Nica Times* (January 30–February 6, 2009).

73. Ortega, *La Epopeya de la insurrección*, p. 362.

74. Belli, *The Country Under My Skin*, pp. 179, 268–269.

75. "Introduction," pp. 1–20 in Heyck, ed., *Life Stories of the Nicaraguan Revolution*, p. 14.

76. Pastor, *Not Condemned to Repetition*, p. 137.

77. Anastasio Somoza, as told to Jack Cox, *Nicaragua Betrayed* (Belmont, MA: Western Islands Publishers, 1980).

78. Pastor, *Not Condemned to Repetition*, pp. 56–57.

79. Quoted in Christian, *Nicaragua*, p. 86.

80. Ortega, *La Epopeya de la insurrección*, p. 380.

81. Christian, *Nicaragua*, p. 117; and Pastor, *Not Condemned to Repetition*, p. 161.

82. Walker, *Nicaragua*, p. 92.

83. Christian, *Nicaragua*, pp. 116–117. See also Christopher Dickey, *With the Contras: A Reporter in the Wilds of Nicaragua* (New York: Simon & Schuster, 1987).

84. Cockcroft, *Daniel Ortega*, p. 73.

85. Belli, *The Country Under My Skin*, p. 245.

Chapter 4: Governing an Embattled Republic

1. Quoted in Pastor, *Not Condemned to Repetition*, p. 163.

2. Quoted in Christian, *Nicaragua*, p. 122.

3. Quoted in Ibid., p. 120.

4. Pastor, *Not Condemned to Repetition*, p. 161.

5. John A. Booth, *The End and the Beginning*, p. 254.

6. Christian, *Nicaragua*, p. 141.

7. Ibid., pp. 126, 141; and "Nicaragua—Prologue," *The Multinational Monitor* 6 (April 1985).

8. Holly Sklar, *Washington's War on Nicaragua*, p. 219.

9. Quoted in Ibid., p. 171.

10. Ibid., p. 141.

11. Quoted in Peter Davis, *Where Is Nicaragua?*, p. 244.

12. Miranda and Ratliff, *The Civil War in Nicaragua*, p. 48.

13. Walker, *Nicaragua*, p. 53.

14. Sweden in turn was among Nicaragua's staunchest supporters, not merely contributing aid that amounted to $160 million between 1979 and 1989 but also organizing conferences with other donor countries and otherwise standing ready to assist in any way that it could. See Anne-Sofie Nillson, "Swedish Social Democracy in Central America: The Politics of Small State Solidarity," *Journal of Inter-American Studies and World Affairs* 33 (Fall 1991), pp. 169–200.

15. Miranda and Ratliff, *The Civil War in Nicaragua*, may provide the most candid portrait of the inner workings of the National Directorate, albeit from the perspective of a defector. Miranda was a top aid to Humberto Ortega and evidently attended most meetings of the Directorate prior to his defection to the United States.

16. Quoted in David Nolan, *The Ideology of the Sandinistas and the Nicaraguan Revolution*, p. 56.

17. Jaime Wheelock, "Nicaragua's Economy and the Fight Against Imperialism," pp. 113–126, in Marcus, ed., *Sandinistas Speak*, p. 120.

18. Quoted in Christian, *Nicaragua*, p. 131.

19. Krauss, *Inside Central America*, p. 137; and LaFeber, *Inevitable Revolutions*, p. 237.

20. See Dodson and O'Shaughnessy, *Nicaragua's Other Revolution*, for a detailed discussion of the debate over priests serving in the government.

21. Gary Ruchwarger, *People in Power: Forging a Grassroots Democracy in Nicaragua* (South Hadley, MA: Bergin & Garvey, 1987), develops the contrast between British and French traditions of democratic thinking as a way of describing Sandinista Nicaragua's democratic philosophy. As will be shown below, Ortega draws a similar contrast between United States–Protestant and Spanish-Catholic traditions.

22. "Vidaluz Meneses" (interview), pp. 227–241, in Heyck, ed., *Life Stories of the Nicaraguan Revolution*, p. 236.

23. Daniel Ortega, "Nicaragua's View of Nicaragua," pp. 5–9, in Peter Rosset and John Vandermeer, eds., *Nicaragua: Unfinished Revolution, The New Nicaragua Reader* (New York: Grove, 1986).

24. Quoted in Davis, *Where Is Nicaragua?* pp. 242–262.

25. Quoted in Stephen Kinzer, *Blood of Brothers: Life and War in Nicaragua* (Cambridge, MA: Harvard University Press, David Rockefeller Center Series on Latin American Studies, Harvard University, 2007), p. 246.

26. Krauss, *Inside Central America*, p. 137.

27. Tomás Borge, "On Human Rights in Nicaragua," pp. 85–104, in Marcus, ed., *Sandinistas Speak*, p. 90.

28. Sklar, *Washington's War on Nicaragua*, pp. 39–40.

29. See, e.g., Walker, *Nicaragua*, pp. 128–129; and Ruchwarger, *People in Power*, pp. 108–115.

30. "Nubia Gómez" (interview), pp. 299–307, in Heyck, ed., *Life Stories of the Nicaraguan Revolution*, p. 302.

31. Krauss, *Inside Central America*, p. 138.

32. Ibid., p. 137.

33. Quoted in Sklar, *Washington's War on Nicaragua*, p. 10.

34. See, e.g., Christian, *Nicaragua*, pp. 129–130.

35. Ruchwarger, *People in Power*, offers this interpretation for the expansion of the Council of State.

36. John Vinocur, "Nicaragua: A Correspondent's Portrait," *New York Times* (August 16, 1983).

37. See, e.g., Pastor, *Not Condemned to Repetition*, p. 174.

38. Miranda and Ratliff, *The Civil War in Nicaragua*, pp. 59–60.

39. "Central America: Why the Crisis Will Deepen," *Business Week* (May 23, 1983), pp. 62–70.
40. Booth, *The End and the Beginning*, pp. 245–246.
41. Ruchwarger, *People in Power*, p. 219; and Walker, *Nicaragua*, p. 91.
42. Booth, *The End and the Beginning*, p. 244.
43. Ibid.
44. Walker, *Nicaragua*, p. 91.
45. Sklar, *Washington's War on Nicaragua*, p. 172.
46. Quoted in LaFeber, *Inevitable Revolutions*, p. 350.
47. Krauss, *Inside Central America*, p. 166.
48. LaFeber, *Inevitable Revolutions*, p, 306.
49. Quoted in Ruchwarger, *People in Power*, p. 71.
50. Quoted in Krauss, *Inside Central America*, p. 144.
51. Pastor, *Not Condemned to Repetition*, pp. 192–195.
52. Dreifus, "Playboy Interview: Daniel Ortega."
53. In *La Epopeya de la insurrección*, Humberto Ortega emphasizes the Cold War context of Reagan's motivations.
54. See, e.g., Craig Allen Smith, "Leadership, Orientation, and Rhetorical Vision: Jimmy Carter, the 'New Right,' and the Panama Canal," *Presidential Studies Quarterly* 16 (Spring 1986).
55. Pastor, *Not Condemned to Repetition*, p. 189.
56. Dreifus, "Playboy Interview: Daniel Ortega."
57. Sklar, *Washington's War on Nicaragua*, p. 100.
58. Quoted in LaFeber, *Inevitable Revolutions*, p, 334.
59. Sklar, *Washington's War on Nicaragua*, pp. 232–233.
60. Quoted in Ibid., p. 231.
61. Ibid., pp. 231–232.
62. Dreifus, "Playboy Interview: Daniel Ortega."
63. Sklar, *Washington's War on Nicaragua*, p. 99. See also Bob Woodward, *Veil: The Secret Wars of the CIA 1981–1987* (New York: Simon & Schuster, 1987).
64. George Bush, *All the Best: My Life in Letters and Other Writings* (New York: Simon & Schuster, 1999), p. 447.
65. Sklar, *Washington's War on Nicaragua*, p. 347.
66. Ibid., p. 339.
67. "Address by Nicaraguan President Daniel Ortega to the United Nations," October 8, 1987, pp. 79–88 in Rod Holt, ed., *Assault on Nicaragua: The Untold Story of the US "Secret War"* (San Francisco: Walnut Publishing Co., 1987).
68. Sklar, *Washington's War on Nicaragua*, p. 137

69. Pastor, *Not Condemned to Repetition*, p. 196.

70. Quoted in Sklar, *Washington's War on Nicaragua*, p. 367.

71. Ibid., p. 281.

72. Quoted in Ibid., p, 275.

73. Quoted in Ibid., p. 327.

74. Lawrence E. Walsh, *Firewall: The Iran-Contra Conspiracy and Cover-Up* (New York: Norton, 1997), p. 17.

75. Sklar, *Washington's War on Nicaragua*, p. 77.

76. Ibid., p. 220.

77. Quoted in Ibid., p. 117.

78. Ibid., p. 126.

79. Quoted in LaFeber, *Inevitable Revolutions*, p. 337.

80. Quoted in Sklar, *Washington's War on Nicaragua*, p. 288.

81. Quoted in LaFeber, *Inevitable Revolutions*, p. 339.

82. Sklar, *Washington's War on Nicaragua*, p. 221.

83. Ibid., p. 279.

84. Ibid., p. 145.

85. Vinocur, "Nicaragua: A Correspondent's Portrait."

86. Rushdie, *The Jaguar Smile*, p. 131.

87. Sklar, *Washington's War on Nicaragua*, pp. 41, 266, 368.

88. Ibid., p. 135.

89. Krauss, *Inside Central America*, p. 150.

90. Quoted in Sklar, *Washington's War on Nicaragua*, p. 210.

91. Ibid., pp. 132–133, 195, 219, 385.

92. Quoted in Pastor, *Not Condemned to Repetition*, p. 204.

93. Kinzer, *Blood of Brothers*, p. 176.

94. Stephen Kinzer, "Man in the News: A Sandinista on the Move," *New York Times* (November 6, 1984); and Stephen Kinzer, "Will Ortega, Now 1 of 9, Be Undisputed No.1?" *New York Times* (March 19, 1986).

95. Stephen Kinzer, "Sandinista Denies Leaders Are Split," *New York Times* (February 9, 1988).

96. Quoted in Kinzer, "Will Ortega, Now 1 of 9, Be Undisputed No.1?"

97. Rushdie, *The Jaguar Smile*, p. 36.

98. Miranda and Ratliff, *The Civil War in Nicaragua*, p. 23.

99. Notes from an interview of Edén Pastora conducted by William Ratliff, 19 March 1992, Edén Pastora Gomez Collection, Box 1, Interviews, Hoover Institution Archives, Stanford University.

100. Quoted in Pastor, *Not Condemned to Repetition*, pp. 204–205.

101. Ibid., p. 205.

102. Sklar, *Washington's War on Nicaragua*, pp. 192, 194.

103. These figures are estimated by R. Pardo-Maurer in *The Contras, 1980–1989: A Special Kind of Politics* (New York: Praeger and the Center for Strategic and International Studies, 1990), p. 137. The estimates are almost certainly exaggerated, since as a former contra affiliated with the conservative American Enterprise Institute, Pardo-Mauer would seemingly have had an incentive to exaggerate the amount of Soviet aid. That he compares the amount of Soviet aid to the much smaller amount of official U.S. aid to the contras—ignoring the hundreds of millions of dollars that were unofficially funneled to the contras by the Reagan administration—suggests a bias. Pardo-Maurer's estimates of the amount of Soviet military aid to Nicaragua are also considerably higher than those reported by Sklar, who could be accused of the opposite bias, in *Washington's War on Nicaragua*. Given that the numbers are uncertain and in dispute, it seems preferable to cite the probably exaggerated estimates of Soviet military aid in order to avoid accusations of a pro-FSLN bias. Since no one disputes the primary reliance of the Sandinistas on Soviet military aid or that Ortega personally solicited much of it, quibbling over the absolute amounts would seem to be pointless.

104. Larry Rohter, "Sandinista Unveils New Initiative," *New York Times* (February 27, 1985).

105. Edward Schumacher, "Nicaragua's President Praises Moscow as a Friend," *New York Times* (May 12, 1985).

106. Maureen Dowd, "The U.N.'s Anniversary: Reporter's Notebook: Ortega Chic," *New York Times* (October 25, 1988).

107. Leslie Maitland Werner, "Two in US Charged in Plot to Kill Nicaragua's Chief," *New York Times* (May 8, 1987).

108. Roberto Suro, "Pope Reinforcing Clerics in Dispute with Sandinistas," *New York Times* (September 4, 1986). For a fuller discussion, see Dodson and O'Shaughnessy, *Nicaragua's Other Revolution*, where on p. 86 Ortega is quoted.

109. Quoted in Kinzer, *Blood of Brothers*, p. 329.

110. Quoted in Ibid., p. 342. Kinzer attributes the remark to Bayardo Arce. However, it would appear to have been made by other members of the National Directorate too. LaFeber, *Inevitable Revolutions*, p. 342, attributes it to the Sandinistas in general.

111. Quoted in Ibid., p. 345.

112. Arias describes some of his views about the process in Oscar Arias Sanchez, *Horizons of Peace: The Costa Rican Contribution to the Peace Process in Central America* (San José: Fundación Arias para la Paz, 1994).

113. Kinzer, *Blood of Brothers*, p. 348.

114. Quoted in Ibid., p. 356.

115. Ibid., p. 351.

116. Ibid., p. 359.

117. Ibid., p. 372.

118. Quoted in Ibid., p. 373.

119. Sklar, *Washington's War on Nicaragua*, p. 386.

120. "Olliemania Breaks Out All Over," *Time* (July 20, 1987).

121. LaFeber, *Inevitable Revolutions*, p. 336.

122. Walker, *Nicaragua*, p. 57. Walker does not opine that the resources of the FSLN were superior, but others do.

123. Quoted in Belli, *The Country Under My Skin*, p. 354.

124. Some of the details presented here are drawn from Anna Husarska, "One Step Forward: Nicaragua's Revolution in Evolution," *The New Leader* 71 (August 8, 1988).

125. Walker, *Nicaragua*, p. 57.

126. Belli, *The Country Under My Skin*, p. 317.

127. Walker, *Nicaragua*, p. 56.

128. Vinocur, "Nicaragua: A Correspondent's Portrait."

129. Pastor, *Not Condemned to Repetition*, p. 260.

130. Ibid., p. 157.

131. Ibid., p. 262.

132. The text of the speech, in English translation, can be found at the Web site of *Envió*. www.envio.org.ni/articulo/2594 (accessed January 29, 2009).

Chapter 5: Governing from Below

1. Pastor, *Not Condemned to Repetition*, p. 279.

2. Roger Cohen, "Sandinista Salon: Ortega Woos Publishers," *New York Times* (September 1, 1990).

3. Personal communication with a person who asks to remain anonymous.

4. "Preface to the 1997 Edition," pp. xv–xvii in Rushdie, *The Jaguar Smile*.

5. Tim Rogers, "President Calls for New Model," *Nica Times* (October 24–31, 2008); and Tim Rogers, "Food Crisis Punishes Poor Households," *Nica Times* (May 2, 2008).

6. Richard Stahler-Sholk, "Structural Adjustment and Resistance: The Political Economy of Nicaragua Under Chamorro," pp. 74–113, in Gary Prevost and Harry E. Vanden, eds., *The Undermining of the Sandinista Revolution* (New York: St. Martin's, 1997). See also Mario Arana, "General Economic Policy," pp. 81–96, in Thomas W. Walker, ed., *Nicaragua Without Illusions: Regime Transition and Structural Adjustment in the 1990s* (Wilmington, DE: Scholarly Resources, 1997).

7. See, e.g., Blake Schmidt, "IMF Team Evaluates Nica Economy," *Nica Times* (March 7, 2008).

8. Stahler-Sholk, "Structural Adjustment and Resistance"; and Arana, "General Economic Policy."

9. Ibid.

10. Rushdie, *The Jaguar Smile*, pp. 116–123.

11. Sworn statement and deposition of former Nicaraguan vice minister of the presidency, Antonio Jose Maria Ybarra-Rojas, voluntarily made to Garrett Grigsby, representing the Republican staff of the United States Senate Committee on Foreign Relations. Done in Cochabamba, Bolivia, from February 18, 1993, to March 9, 1993. Antonio Ybarra Rojas collection, Folder ID 2004C57-10V, Hoover Institution Archives, Stanford, CA.

12. Ibid.

13. Ibid. See also Hannah Strange, "Nicaragua Accused of Helping Colombian Drug Lords to Establish Trafficking Routes," *Times* London (May 1, 2010).

14. Pastor, *Not Condemned to Repetition*, p. 272.

15. Deposition of Antonio Ybarra-Rojas.

16. Ibid.

17. Ibid.

18. Ibid. Regarding Cerna, see, e.g., J. Michael Waller, "Will Sandinistas Face Justice?" *Insight on the News* (July 26, 1999).

19. Deposition of Antonio Ybarra-Rojas.

20. Dionisio Marenco, "I Know the FSLN's History Well, But Can't Envision Its Future," *Envío* 326 (September 2008).

21. See Gary Prevost, "The FSLN," pp. 149–164, in Walker, ed., *Nicaragua Without Illusions*.

22. There are numerous descriptions and interpretations of Alemán. One succinct synopsis is found in Walker, *Nicaragua*, pp. 63–67.

23. "Democracy Prevails in Nicaragua's 1996 Presidential Election," The Carter Center (December 2, 1997). www.cartercenter.com/news/documents/doc206.html (accessed May 11, 2009).

24. "Epilogue: The 1996 National Elections," pp. 305–311, in Walker, ed., *Nicaragua Without Illusions*.

25. In "I Know the FSLN's History Well, But Can't Envision Its Future," Marenco, who was present at some of the early negotiating sessions, describes this process of pact formation. Regarding the pact itself, there are hundreds of sources that attempt to describe and explain it. One typical one is Tim Rogers, "Nicaragua Strongmen's Pact Under Strain," *Time* (January 27, 2009). Rogers makes the usual assumption that because the initial results of the pact were not apparent to the public until 1999, the

pact was not negotiated until then. Marenco tells us that basic outlines of the pact were negotiated and agreed upon two years earlier.

26. Tim Rogers, "Why Nicaragua's Caged Bird Sings," *Time* (May 2, 2007).

27. Quoted in Walker, *Nicaragua*, p. 69.

28. Ibid., p. 66.

29. "Nicaragua," World Policy Institute (October 25, 2001). www.world-policy.org/projects/globalrights/nicaragua/2001-Nicaragua-election-background.html (accessed May 13, 2009).

30. Data drawn from "Background Notes: Nicaragua," U.S. Department of State (September 2008). www.state.gov/r/pa/ei/bgn/1850.htm (accessed May 4, 2009); "Nicaragua at a Glance," World Bank (September 24, 2008). http:77devdata.worldbank.org/AAG/nic—aag.pdf (accessed May 4, 2009); Brenda Walker, "Remittances Becoming More Entrenched: The Worldwide Cash Flow Continues to Grow." www.limitstogrowth.org/WEB-text/remittances.html (accessed May 4, 2009); and "Nicaragua: Incidence and Nature of Child Labor," U.S. Department of Labor (May 13, 2009). http:77www.dol.gov/ilab/media/reports/iclp/tda2004/Nicaragua.htm (accessed May 13, 2009).

31. Deisy Francis Mexidor, "US Blockage on Cuba Must Be Lifted Unconditionally: Speech of Comrade Daniel Ortega, President of Nicaragua, at the Round Table TV Show," *Granma Daily*. www.periodico26.cu/english/features/mar2009/daniel-roundtable042309.html (accessed May 13, 2009).

32. In "Superficially Democratic Regimes," *Internationalist Viewpoint* (February 2009), Dianne Freeley goes so far as to suggest that the inclusion of the Church made the Alemán-Ortega pact "three-way." This would seem to overstate Alemán's involvement, however. Regarding the Church's reaction, see "Pope Praises Nicaragua's Recent Ban on Therapeutic Abortions," Catholic News Service (September 25, 2007).

Chapter 6: Toward a Dynasty of the Left

1. Tim Rogers, "Ortega Drops in Polls, Brief Honeymoon Ends," *Nica Times* (June 29, 2007).

2. See, e.g, Tim Rogers, "Gov't–Media Relations Hit New Low," *Nica Times* (April 25, 2008).

3. Tim Rogers, "Country Looks Beyond Oil Dependency," *Nica Times* (June 6, 2008).

4. See, e.g., Jodie Neary, "Venezuela's ALBA in the Face of the Global Economic Crisis," *Upside Down World* (December 29, 2008).

5. See Tortilla con Sal, "ALBA: Hope for the Impoverished," *Scoop* (August 4, 2008). www.scoop.co.nz/stories/HL0808/500035.htm (accessed May 16, 2009).

6. Vanessa I. Garnica, "Skids Are Greased for Venezuelan Oil Deal," *Tico Times* (January 9, 2009).

7. The estimate is the State Department's. See www.state.gov/r/pa/ei/bgn/2019.htm (accessed August 23, 2009).

8. Tim Rogers, "U.N. Speech Gets Chilly Response," *Nica Times* (October 5, 2007).

9. Tim Rogers, whose growing anti-Ortega opinions became increasingly apparent in his news coverage of the administration over time, at one point interviewed psychiatrists to help explain Ortega's anti-U.S. rhetoric. See his "Ortega's Diatribe Against Plotters Called Paranoid," *Nica Times* (May 9, 2008).

10. See, e.g., "Defining Moments in Ortega's Foreign Relations," *Nica Times* (September 5, 2008); and Matikde Córdoba, "EmbUSA amenazada," *El Nuevo Diario* (April 23, 2009).

11. Howard LaFranchi, "Chummy Obama, Chávez Mark 'Spirit of Cooperation' at Summit," *Christian Science Monitor* (April 19, 2009).

12. Vanessa L. Garnica, "Nicaragua Pulls Out of EU Talks," *Tico Times* (April 2, 2009).

13. See, e.g., "Nicaragua Recognizes South Ossetia, Abkhazia," Reuters (September 3, 2008). http://uk.reuters.com/article/gc07/idUKN0330338620080903 (accessed May 15, 2009).

14. See, e.g., Todd Bensman, "Iranians Plant Their Flag in the Wilds of Nicaragua," *New York Sun* (February 7, 2008); and Blake Schmidt, "Iranian Hydro Project Stirs Concerns," *Nica Times* (June 6, 2008).

15. "Nicaragua en oscuros manejos internacionales," *El Nuevo Diario* (April 16, 2009).

16. See, e.g., "Ortega Offers Asylum to FARC Camp Survivor," *Nica Times* (April 25, 2008); Tim Rogers and Blake Schmidt, "Ortega's FARC Involvement Questioned," *Nica Times* (May 23, 2008); and Blake Schmidt, "Ortega Takes Heat for FARC Support," *Nica Times* (August 8, 2008).

17. "How to Steal an Election," *Economist* (November 13, 2008).

18. Tim Rogers, "Municipal Elections: 'Nicaragua's 9-11'," *Nica Times* (December 24, 2008).

19. "Nicaragua's Spoiled Ballot," *Washington Post* (November 16, 2008).

20. Roger Noriega, "U.S. Shouldn't Ignore Ortega's Power Grab," *Miami Herald* (November 14, 2008).

21. "Ortega repite los errores," *El Nuevo Diario* (November 22, 2008).

22. Rory Carroll, "Second Coming of the Sandinistas Turns Sour," *Observer* (January 11, 2009).

23. Eric Sabo, "Ex-Boxer Runs for Mayor in Nicaragua Capitol," *San Francisco Chronicle* (November 9, 2008).

24. Tim Rogers, "Liberals Form Big Alliance vs. Sandinistas," *Nica Times* (March 7, 2008).

25. Ramón H. Potosme, "Montealegre rechaza resultados preliminares del CSE," *El Nuevo Diario* (November 10, 2008); and Nery García, "Eduardo Montealegre llega a las instalaciones del CSE," *El Nuevo Diaria* (November 10, 2008).

26. Ary Pantoja, "Rosario Murillo descalifica encuesta," *El Nuevo Diario* (October 23, 2008).

27. Tortilla con Sal IV with Roberto Rivas, "Interview with the President of the Supreme Electoral Council in Nicaragua, Roberto Rivas," *Scoop* (October 14, 2008. www.scoop.co.nz/stories/HL0810/500207.htm (accessed October 20, 2008).

28. Tim Rogers, "Gov't Aims to Revive Old Ball League," *Nica Times* (November 7–14, 2008).

29. See, e.g., Tim Rogers, "Presidential Decree Worsens Crisis," *Nica Times* (January 9–16, 2009).

30. Tim Rogers, "Alemán Freed, 'El Pacto' Strikes Again," *Nica Times* (January 23–30, 2009).

31. José Adán Silva, "Nicaragua: Literacy Campaign Changing Women's Lives," *IPS* (April 27, 2009); and Blake Schmidt, "Education Revolution Underway," *Nica Times* (February 1, 2008).

32. See, e.g., Tim Rogers, "Gov't Implements 'Direct Democracy,'" *Nica Times* (December 7, 2007).

33. This is of course a central theme in Joseph E. Stiglitz's *Globalization and Its Discontents* (New York: Norton, 2003).

34. Blake Schmidt, "Study: Extreme Poverty Still on the Rise," *Nica Times* (October 24–31, 2008).

35. Tim Rogers, "Study Finds 40% of Nicas Receive Remittance Money," *Nica Times* (February 8, 2008).

36. Blake Schmidt, "Hunger, Fires Threaten Post-Felix RAAN," *Nica Times* (August 8–15, 2008).

37. Blake Schmidt, "Hambre Cero Changing Lives in Campo," *Nica Times* (February 13–19, 2009); "Zero Hunger," *Envío* (May 2007); and José Adán Silva, "Development—Nicaragua: Despite Efforts, MDGs Still Distant Goals," *IPS* (February 7, 2008).

38. Blake Schmidt, "Ortega Trashes Rights Groups over Dump War," *Nica Times* (April 4, 2008).

39. Tim Rogers, "Latin American Feminists Unite Against Ortega," *Nica Times* (October 24–31, 2008).

40. Tim Rogers, "Tourism Showing Slow Signs of Recovery," *Nica Times* (May 9, 2008); and Tim Rogers, "Tourism Still a Bright Spot, Up 7% in 2008," *Nica Times* (January 16, 2009).

41. Tim Rogers, "Ortega's Friendships Help U.S. Relations," *Nica Times* (March 14, 2008).

42. Nicaragua Network Hotline, 21 July 2009. www.nicanet.org/?p=739 (accessed August 23, 2009).

43. Regarding allegations of Montealegre's financial wrongdoing, see, e.g., "Montealegre Implicated in Banking Certificate Scandal," *Nica Times* (September 21, 2007); and "Montealegre, 38 Others Accused in Cenis Case," *Nica Times* (July 11, 2008).

44. "State Department Grants 'Waiver' on Property Issues," Nicaragua Network Hotline, 21 July 2009. www.nicanet.org/?p=739 (accessed August 23, 2009).

45. "The 2006 Transparency International Corruption Perceptions Index." www.infoplease.com/ipa/A0781359.html (accessed August 26, 2009).

46. The phrase and the thesis are drawn from Leslie E. Anderson and Lawrence C. Dodd, *Learning Democracy: Citizen Engagement and Electoral Choice in Nicaragua, 1990–2001* (Chicago: University of Chicago Press, 2005). See Ruchwarger, *People in Power,* for an account of the growth of civic associations following the Revolution.

47. See www.state.gov/r/pa/ei/bgn/1850.htm and www.state.gov/r/pa/ei/bgn/2019.htm for the State Department's figures on Nicaraguan and Costa Rican GDP, respectively (accessed August 25, 2009). Since the populations of the two countries are similar in size, there is no reason to include figures on per capita GDP.

48. Blake Schmidt, "Economist Doesn't Sweat Socialist Plans," *Nica Times* (April 18, 2008).

49. According to State Department figures, in 2007 Nicaragua attracted $335 million in foreign investment dollars compared to Costa Rica's $1.896 million. See www.state.gov/e/eeb/ifd/2008/101855.htm for Nicaragua and www.state.gov/e/eeb/othr/ics/2009/117428.htm for Costa Rica (accessed August 25, 2009).

50. See www.census.gov/prod/2003pubs/02statab/pop.pdf (accessed August 25, 2009).

51. Sklar, *Washington's War on Nicaragua,* pp. 8, 10; and LaFeber, *Inevitable Revolutions,* p. 162.

SELECTED BIBLIOGRAPHY

Pilar Arias. *Nicaragua: Revolución, relatos de combatientes del frente sandinista.* Mexico: Siglo XXI, 1980.

Francisco de Asís Fernández, editor. *Poesía política de nicaragua.* Nicaragua: Ministerio de Cultura, 1986.

Gioconda Belli. Translated by Kristina Cordero and Gioconda Belli. *The Country Under My Skin: A Memoir of Love and War.* New York: Knopf, 2002.

John A. Booth. *The End and the Beginning: The Nicaraguan Revolution,* second edition. Boulder, CO: Westview Press, 1985.

Tomás Borge. Translated by Russell Bartley, Darwin Flakoll, and Sylvia Yoneda. *The Patient Impatience: From Boyhood to Guerilla: A Personal Narrative of Nicaragua's Struggle for Liberation.* Willimantic, CT: Curbstone Press, 1992.

Omar Cabezas. Foreword by Carlos Fuentes; afterword by Walter LaFeber; translated by Kathleen Weaver. *Fire from the Mountain: The Making of a Sandinista.* New York: Plume, 1985.

Shirley Christian. *Nicaragua: Revolution in the Family.* New York: Random House, 1985.

Peter Davis. *Where Is Nicaragua?* New York: Simon and Schuster, 1987.

Christopher Dickey. *With the Contras: A Reporter in the Wilds of Nicaragua.* New York: Simon and Schuster, 1987.

Michael Dodson and Laura Nuzzi O'Shaughnessy. *Nicaragua's Other Revolution: Religious Faith and Political Struggle.* Chapel Hill: University of North Carolina Press, 1990.

Claudia Dreifus. "Playboy Interview: Daniel Ortega." *Playboy,* November 1987, 59–78, 130.

Denis Lynn Daly Heyck, editor. *Life Stories of the Nicaraguan Revolution.* New York: Routledge, 1990.

Donald C. Hodges. *Intellectual Foundations of the Nicaraguan Revolution.* Austin: University of Texas Press, 1986.

Katherine Hoyt. *The Many Faces of Sandinista Democracy.* Athens, OH: Center for International Studies, Ohio University, 1997.

Stephen Kinzer. *Blood of Brothers: Life and War in Nicaragua.* Cambridge, MA: David Rockefeller Center for Latin American Studies, Harvard University, 2007.

Clifford Krauss. *Inside Central America: Its People, Politics, and History.* New York: Summit Books, 1991.

Walter LaFeber. *Inevitable Revolutions: The United States in Central America,* second edition. New York: Norton, 1993.

Roger N. Lancaster. *Life Is Hard: Machismo, Danger, and the Intimacy of Power in Nicaragua.* Berkeley: University of California Press, 1992.

Bruce Marcus, editor. *Nicaragua: The Sandinista People's Revolution.* New York: Pathfinder Press, 1985.

Bruce Marcus, editor. *Sandinistas Speak: Speeches, Writings, and Interviews with Leaders of Nicaragua's Revolution.* New York: Pathfinder Press, 1982.

Roger Miranda and William Ratliff. *The Civil War in Nicaragua: Inside the Sandinistas.* New Brunswick, NJ: Transaction Publishers, 1993.

David Nolan. *The Ideology of the Sandinistas and the Nicaraguan Revolution.* Coral Gables, FL: Institute of Interamerican Studies, Graduate School of International Studies, University of Miami, 1984.

Daniel Ortega Saavedra. Prologue by Carlos Fuentes. *Combatiendo por la paz.* Mexico: Siglo XXI, 1988.

General Humberto Ortega Saavedra. *La Epopeya de la insurrección.* Managua: Lea Grupo, 2004.

Robert A. Pastor. *Not Condemned to Repetition: The United States and Nicaragua,* second edition. Boulder, CO: Westview Press, 2002.

Hector Perez-Brignoli. Translated by Ricardo B. Sawrey A. and Susana Stettri de Sawrey. *A Brief History of Central America.* Berkeley: University of California Press, 1989.

Gary Prevost and Harry E. Vanden, editors. *The Undermining of the Sandinista Revolution.* New York: St. Martin's Press, 1997.

Margaret Randall. *Sandino's Daughters: Testimonies of Nicaraguan Women in Struggle.* New Brunswick, NJ: Rutgers University Press, 1995.

Peter Rosset and John Vandermeer, editors. *The Nicaragua Reader: Documents of a Revolution Under Fire.* New York: Grove Press, 1983.

Peter Rosset and John Vandermeer, editors. *Nicaragua: Unfinished Revolution, The New Nicaragua Reader.* New York: Grove Press, 1986.

Gary Ruchwarger. *People in Power: Forging a Grassroots Democracy in Nicaragua.* South Hadley, MA: Bergin and Garvey Publishers, 1987.

Salman Rushdie. *The Jaguar Smile: A Nicaraguan Journey.* New York: Henry Holt, 1987.

Holly Sklar. *Washington's War on Nicaragua.* Boston: South End Press, 1988.

Thomas W. Walker. *Nicaragua: Living in the Shadow of the Eagle,* fourth edition. Boulder, CO: Westview Press, 2003.

Thomas W. Walker, editor. *Nicaragua Without Illusions: Regime Transition and Structural Adjustment in the 1990s.* Wilmington, DE: Scholarly Resources, 1997.

Matilde Zimmermann. *Sandinista: Carlos Fonseca and the Nicaraguan Revolution.* Durham, NC: Duke University Press, 2000.

Philip Zwerling and Connie Martin. *Nicaragua: A New Kind of Revolution.* Westport, CT: Lawrence Hill, 1985.

INDEX